A History of Modern Experimental Psychology

Other books by George Mandler

The language of psychology (with William Kessen)

Thinking: From association to Gestalt (with Jean Matter Mandler)

Mind and emotion

Mind and body: Psychology of emotion and stress

Cognitive psychology: An essay in cognitive science

Human nature explored

Interesting times: An encounter with the 20th century

Consciousness recovered: Psychological functions and origins of conscious thought

A History of Modern Experimental Psychology

From James and Wundt to Cognitive Science

George Mandler

A Bradford Book
The MIT Press
Cambridge, Massachusetts
London, England

MIT Press books may be purchased at special quantity discounts for business or sales promotional use. For information, please e-mail ⟨special_sales@mitpress.mit.edu⟩ or write to Special Sales Department, The MIT Press, 55 Hayward Street, Cambridge, MA 02142.

This book was set in Stone Serif and Stone Sans on 3B2 by Asco Typesetters, Hong Kong. Printed and bound in the United States of America.

Library of Congress Cataloging-in-Publication Data

Mandler, George.
A history of modern experimental psychology : from James and Wundt to cognitive science / by George Mandler.
    p. cm.
"A Bradford book."
Includes biliographical references and index.
ISBN 978-0-262-13475-0 (alk. paper)
1. Psychology, Experimental. 2. Cognitive psychology. I. Title.

BF181.M27   2007
150.9—dc22   2006046226

10 9 8 7 6 5 4 3 2 1

In memory of Alan Isaacs, William Kessen, Hans Matzka—
Friends

Contents

Preface

Following my retirement in 1994, I wrote the books and papers that I had left undone or postponed in previous years. With those projects out of the way, I could plan a new task. My increasing discomfort with the relative neglect of the history of our field—in particular, the history of the new cognitive psychology—proved to be an adequate motivation. So I started this little book, which has kept me occupied and increasingly involved.

This volume has many antecedents. One of them is my European background, which seems to have fostered in me an interest in historical roots that in part I have expressed in my autobiography and in an examination of personal histories.[1] Another source is my research in the history of my field, which for some forty years has gone hand in hand with my empirical and theoretical interests. A major source is the book that Jean Mandler and I published over forty years ago that presented original early works (including translations) on human thinking, and I am most grateful to Jean for her work on that volume,

1. Mandler (2001) deals almost exclusively with my life and loves, not with psychology.

which made the present book possible. Then, in 1996, I published a paper on the history of psychology that was intended as an outline for a book, and portions of that paper form part of the scaffolding of this volume. I have used edited selections from the thinking book and have rewritten, rearranged, and edited my publications from the past several decades. The acknowledgments show the various publications from which materials have been selected, usually by being updated and rearranged.

The intent of this book is not to present the history of psychology; that task requires a larger and more comprehensive volume. Instead, here I outline the advent of the modern psychology of thought and memory. I write history with a "point of view" rather than attempt to "just tell what happened." I do not believe the latter is possible and at best hides the writer's prejudices.[2] My own viewpoints will be fairly obvious. Two main orientations inform the book: a general attempt to place recent psychological history in the context of the general social and political culture in which it occurs and a preference for organizational over associationist accounts of psychological processes. The initial chapters summarize the history of the psychology of thought and memory from antiquity to the middle of the twentieth century. The last four chapters deal with a neglected part of the history of psychology—the emergence of a new and robust cognitive psychology.

2. In the course of a correspondence in the 1960s, Edwin G. (Garry) Boring, then the dominant American historian of psychology, responded to a review of mine in which I had wondered why nobody was writing histories of psychology from a consistent point of view. Boring asked what I might have meant: what would a point of view be for a historian? According to him, "Either you tell the facts, or you give a functional account of how things got to be what they are."

To the extent that this volume is a culmination of a long involvement with research and teaching of psychology, I am indebted to all my friends and students over the past fifty-plus years—Jean Mandler and my departed friend William Kessen in particular—as well as my colleagues and the students who participated in my courses and seminars on the history of psychology. Over the years, Peter Mandler has tried to keep me aware of what it means to be a historian, and Michael Mandler has helped by arguing points of method.

Acknowledgments

Selections from the following publications were used in the text, with the acquiescence of the original publishers.

Mandler, J. M., & Mandler, G. (1964). *Thinking: From association to Gestalt*. New York: Wiley. Reprint edition: Westport, CT: Greenwood Press, 1982. Copyright Jean and George Mandler.

Mandler, J. M., & Mandler, G. (1968). The diaspora of experimental psychology: The Gestaltists and others. In D. Fleming & B. Bailyn (Eds.), *The intellectual migration: Europe and America, 1930–1960* (pp. 371–419). Cambridge, MA: Harvard University Press. Copyright Harvard University Press.

Mandler, G. (1979a). A man for all seasons? Retrospective review of William James's *Principles of psychology*. *Contemporary Psychology, 24*, 742–744. Copyright American Psychological Association.

Mandler, G. (1985a). From association to structure. *Journal of Experimental Psychology, 11*, 464–468. Copyright American Psychological Association.

Mandler, G. (1996). The situation of psychology: Landmarks and choice-points. *American Journal of Psychology, 109*, 1–35. Copyright George Mandler.

Mandler, G. (2002d). Psychologists and the National Socialist access to power. *History of Psychology, 5*, 190–200. Copyright Educational Publishing Foundation.

Mandler, G. (2002c). Origins of the cognitive (r)evolution. *Journal of the History of the Behavioral Sciences, 38*, 339–353. Copyright John Wiley and Sons.

Mandler, G. (2002b). Organization: What levels of organization are levels of. *Memory, 10*, 333–338. Copyright Psychology Press.

Mandler, G. (2006). Mind: Ghosts, machines, and concepts. In K. Pawlik & G. d'Ydewalle (Eds.), *Psychological concepts: An international historical perspective*. Hove, UK: Psychology Press. Copyright George Mandler.

Introduction

Modernity comes in many flavors and arrives at various times. In the world of art, it is usually dated to around 1860, whereas in literature the date is more often the beginning of the twentieth century, sometimes as late as the beginning of the Great War. In general, *modernity* refers to new ways of thought, more openness to different influences, and often radical departures. For psychology, modernity came with the adoption of experimental methods and the symbolic end of its ties to philosophical speculations, though it still clung to many of its historical presuppositions. It is probably appropriate to date the coming of a modern experimental and theoretical psychology at around 1880 to 1890 with the establishment of the first formal laboratory in 1879 by Wilhelm Wundt (1832–1920), the creation of independent chairs in psychology, and the publication in 1890 of *The Principles of Psychology* by William James (1842–1910). I present some excursions into the history of the period from those beginnings to the late twentieth century, with an emphasis on the psychology of thought and memory. I do not explore the important and earlier development of sensory psychology, also known as *psychophysics*, as developed and practiced by Gustav Fechner (1801–1887), Johannes Müller (1801–1858), and Hermann von Helmholtz (1821–1894).

I also do not dwell on aspects of this history that are best called *metaphysical*. Particularly during its first two thousand or so years, psychological speculation went hand in hand with philosophical and theological concerns. Most of the great thinkers before the twentieth century had important things to say about material bodies, immaterial or material minds, souls, and origins. To some degree, these thoughts have influenced psychological concerns. I cover some of these issues, but I steer clear of metapsychological disputes. They tend to muddle the scientific and quasi-scientific concerns and contribute primarily historical antecedents rather than to testable hypotheses.

Different parts of psychology differ in the degree to which they are scientific—that is, they produce temporary approximations toward a satisfactory explanation of some empirical phenomena but acknowledge that our current state is temporary and destined to be replaced by a better model or theory. Experimental psychology and its theories (mainly of memory and thought) are among the more disciplined fields with a definable historical past. Histories of science tend to be whiggish, seeing the past as prologue to the current state. I share that inclination, though I also discuss the political and cultural influences that shape psychology—and the other sciences.[1]

1. I need to declare this bias because one of my excursions into the history of the psychology of emotion has been labeled as "tacitly teleological" and ignorant of influences from outside of psychology (Dixon, 2003). I do intend to be focused on the precursors of our current state, but I also am not insensitive to outside influences.

I discuss aspects of the history of psychology to show how various psychologies reflect the characteristics and values of the society in which they are embedded. I am neither competent nor prepared to answer the big question: how does the structure of a society—its development, technology, economy, and social relations—favor one or the other set of values? I can only try to begin asking similar questions about psychology in particular. Specifically, what social forces are likely to have influenced the course of psychological science and the values that inform it? In what follows, I present some sketches of the influence of larger social forces on the psychological enterprise. In the process, I argue not only that psychology is not value-free but that the values that motivate psychologists can be found in the culture that surrounds them and of which they are a part. And psychology is shaped not just by the general culture but also by specific influences from other sciences. Its practitioners' desire for psychology to be experimental is, in part, influenced by their intention for it to be a hard, natural science. And in the recent past, the emergence of the information sciences and the development of the computer have influenced psychological thinking. Conversely, it is not just a one-way street of culture shaping sciences: changes in the sciences and their institutions also affect the social fabric of society.

The discussion of social influences on scientific labors—the situating of science as culture—has become of interest to philosophers, sociologists, and historians of science. The movement started in a serious way in the 1930s—for example, in Ludwig Fleck's tour de force (1935, English in 1979) on the treatment of syphilis and in Marxist analyses initially marked by rather extravagant treatments, such as that of Isaac Newton by Boris M.

Hessen (1971, originally published in 1931). It has now become a general enterprise, and for a refreshing antidote to some of its excesses see the balanced view of Philip Kitcher (1993). In psychology, this kind of approach has been relatively rare.

The general themes of the culture are to be found in the contemporary social sciences, not in a one-to-one correspondence in time but rather in the sense that similar themes will be distributed over a particular time period. In brief, I want to treat social science as much as part of the contemporary culture as its clothes, rituals, foods, music, art, ethnic prejudices, and so forth. Social science—like many other social activities—is a symptom of the embedding culture and society. I also believe that the human (social) sciences are more subject to the demands of the embedding culture than are the "natural" sciences—if for no other reason than that the phenomena they address are themselves embedded in the culture. There are two possible sources of social and historical influences on the structure and content of psychological research. One is the influence of the social context on the possible topics and theories that a researcher or theorist may think about and act on. The other is a function of the fact that practically all our research on human psychology is conducted with products of our culture and that therefore the behavior of our research subjects is to some (unknown) extent a social product.

If we accept that the sciences, and the social sciences in particular, are to some extent culture-driven, is it possible that we may still discern some progress or advancement in our understanding of human thought and action? Depending on one's orientation, one might see laudable advancements in the history of psychology, as in the institutionalization of the experimental method by Wundt and his peers or in the displacement of the associationism of the nineteenth century by labeled associations and organizational structures. Changes, however, are clothed in the contemporary culture's values. Wilhelm Wundt reflects the ambivalences of his and Germany's history, Gestalt psychology mirrors the changes in visual and intellectual culture of the turn of the century, behaviorism embodies the parochial and puritanical concerns of early twentieth-century America, and current cognitive psychology is a product of the information and communication revolutions that have taken place since World War II. Finally, noticeable developments are symptomatic of the influence of the general culture.[2] I illustrate this phenomenon by showing a few instances where the same notions and approaches were developed independently but contemporaneously by different groups of people. These cooccurrences are good examples of how the pervasive culture influences new developments.

In the balance between empirical details and theoretical developments, I favor the latter. Theories and their waxing and waning speak to the bigger and major themes of a period. And in the process of discussing the past fifty years, I introduce some of my own contributions to the field.

My major thematic stress is on the themes of the five quarter centuries of our history. Except for a few major figures, I stress what men and women did and wrote and do not attempt to uncover their motivations and interests. I leave that to a more extensive monograph still to be written by some other psychologist. This is a history of the emergence of cognitive psychology, not a monograph on its detailed constructions and motivations.

2. The notion that particular trends exhibit some general influences has in the past been called the *Zeitgeist* ("the spirit of the times") without specifying exactly how that spirit comes about or influences events.

The book starts with a chapter on the meaning and history of the concept of mind. This seemed appropriate and necessary since the period I cover starts in the late nineteenth century with a commitment to a substantial or insubstantial but real and often mystical notion about the existence of a mind but ends with *mind* simply being used as a summary term for human (and sometimes animal) thinking competencies. The book then covers the early beginning of a psychology of memory and thought, eventually in a Germany preoccupied with science and development. There follows the "discovery" of the unconscious—that is, that problem solutions can be found without any conscious presence of the intervening steps between problem and solution. I continue with the development of Gestalt psychology and the need for both lawful construction and useful structure. I briefly attend to the behaviorist interlude in America, primarily to understand the cognitive revolution that formed one of the antecedents of the present. I then examine the upheaval in Western thought produced by the anticivilization events of the Hitler period and its effect on psychology and the subsequent move of its center of gravity to the United States. There follows an examination of the cognitive revolution and its various sources and symptoms and the development of contemporary cognitive psychology and the umbrella of cognitive science. I end with apparently important events of the second half of the twentieth century, including some instances in which similar developments occurred independently. I stress trends that might still be called historically important some decades hence, though at this short remove these are probably in many instances reflections of temporary as well as personal influences.

A History of Modern Experimental Psychology

1 The Modern Mind: Its History and Current Use

Cultural influences have set up the assumptions about the mind, the body, and the universe with which we begin; pose the questions we ask; influence the facts we seek; determine the interpretation we give these facts; and direct our reaction to these interpretations and conclusions.

—Gunnar Myrdal

I start with a discussion of the concept of mind because it occurs frequently in the literature to be discussed later. It occurs not only in its clothing as mind but also as soul, psyche, and so forth. In writing about the history of thought and memory, we cannot carry with us old baggage in mystical language but need to agree on a reasonable definition.

Mind—at least in one of its versions—is one of those things in the world that everybody is willing to talk about but nobody has ever seen or touched. In that respect, it is even more intangible than consciousness (discussed later), which at least most people are willing to say that they have in some sense experienced. In 1949, Gilbert Ryle coined the apposite expression about mind being "the ghost in the machine," which I take as my starting point in exploring the concept of mind.

A number of different meanings have been assigned to the notion of mind, which seems to apply exclusively to humans, though some would also apply it to nonhuman animals. I start with its various meanings, a short lexical excursion, and a review of the historical landmarks for the concept. I then discuss the ways that psychologists have used the idea of a mind and characterize the contemporary philosophy of mind, which often intrudes into psychology, and end with some thoughts about the mind-body problem.

The Various Uses of Mind

Much of modern psychology (and some philosophy) has been concerned with the struggle to remove mystical and metaphysical implications from the use of the concept of mind. In the process, we have generally banned the ghost from the machine but are not quite clear about the kind of a machine we wish to put in its place. I define various uses of mind, starting with the original postulation of its ghostly characteristic and moving toward functional and even empirical definitions:

Mind as soul: *Mind* has often been used as a synonym for the ancient sense of "spirit" or "soul." In some versions, its use harks back to theological origins as a god-given elevation of humans over other animals. The version that became a less mystical mainstay up through the Middle Ages was Aristotle's exposition in *De Anima* (*Peri psuchés*). For Aristotle, the soul (*psuché*, derived from the original meaning of *breath*, the vital breath of life) was the actualization of the body's potential. The meaning of *mind* as "soul" still exists in everyday speech, in philosophy, and even in some psychological writings. In this sense, mind still distinguishes humans from other animals and has many ties to the theological uses of soul.

Mind as faculty: The use of *mind* without the supernatural sense but still as some extramaterial manifestation of human thought and action is frequently found in contemporary thought. Mind is considered in a sense as a faculty or as an organ of the body that somehow is removed from a basic materialist view.

Mind as a brain function: Under this view, mind is seen as the summary manifestation of human brain functions, as in a functionalist description that "the mind is what the brain does."

Mind as a summary term for complex human thought and action: Here *mind* is used as a summary but vaguely defined concept that brings under a single notion human cogitation, cognition, conation, and so on. It is similar to the previous definition but lacks any necessary allusion to brain functions.

Mind as consciousness: The confusion between consciousness and mind, which equates mind with human consciousness, creates serious problems for any general concept of mind. Since the contents of consciousness are limited in time and restricted to a subset of possible human thoughts and actions, this error makes mind a less powerful concept and also confuses the functions of consciousness.[1]

1. For example, Mandler (2002a). There are occasional uses of mind to conform to particular theoretical stances. For example, Baars (1988) equates mind with information, and Humphrey (1992) uses it as a vehicle for speculations about human cognitive functions and his interpretation of consciousness.

Mind and Its Meanings

When we examine the meaning of the word *mind* as put forth in various dictionaries and also in its translation and use in various Western languages, we find confusions similar to those described in the previous section. The following definitions attempt to distill various dictionary definitions.

The origin of the expression *mind* is partly Germanic (as in *minna*), but it also has solid Old English ancestry in *gemynd*, and most early meanings were tied in part to the notion of memory. When it comes to defining *mind*, most dictionaries tend to agree to some version that sees it as "a human faculty representing understanding and the intellect" but also as "the soul in distinction from the body." However, one also comes across definitions such as mind representing "human consciousness manifested in thought, perception, emotion, will, memory, and imagination." Here we are faced with a concatenation of mind as consciousness on the one hand and as a summary term on the other. Finally, mind is sometimes seen as the depository and locus of human thought, so that thought may be defined as the content of mind.

I turn briefly to the notion of mind as a repository of the classic functions of cognition, conation, and cogitation. *Cognition* (from the Latin *cognoscere*, "to become acquainted with") refers to knowing, knowledge, and perception; *conation* (from the Latin *conatio*, refers to mental processes or behavior directed toward action or change); and *cogitation* (from the Latin *cogitatio*, "think or reflect") refers to meditation.[2]

2. The currently popular terms *cognitive psychology* and *cognitive science* sometimes are used refer to thinking organisms, when they actually denote an information-processing psychology.

The concept of mind in Western languages is often confusing and confused by different language habits. Whereas I noted earlier that the English *mind* is derived from Germanic and Old English roots, much of Western usage derives from the Latin *mens,* a less metaphysical reference than the apparently older *anima.* The Romance languages in general have benefited from this derivation (*mente* in both Italian and Spanish), but surprisingly no equivalent exists in French, which uses *esprit* but has adopted the adjective *mentale.* German, despite the extensive history of exploration of the mind in German lands, has no true equivalent in modern usage but relies on *Geist* and *Psyche*, and both terms have metaphysical overtones. Because there is no objective referent to mind, it is not surprising that different though intimately related language cultures fail to agree on terminology. Notwithstanding these ambiguities, the notion of mind—however defined or used—is vastly popular. During the past twenty years, the scientific literature has used the term in some five hundred to one thousand titles per year.[3]

Landmarks in the History of Mind

I have already noted some of the philosophical and theological origins of mind, although in Western intellectual history the major role is undoubtedly played by Aristotle. Apart from the notion that the mind or psyche actualizes the body's potential, Aristotle also ascribed to the psyche the potential for rational thought and moral action. These were basically philosophical or psychological approaches, in contrast to Plato's concern with psyche as the vehicle for his political structures.

3. Courtesy of WebofScience.

The next major changes in the Western view of mind came with the Renaissance, and they started with a fatal step—René Descartes's bifurcation of body and mind. Some such notions had been implicit before, but never before had anybody made the distinction with such force and such success. Descartes made the proposal initially in his *De homine* which was suppressed and not published until some twelve years after Descartes's death; his 1642 *Meditationes* became the banner book for the mind-body distinction.[4] The so-called mind-body problem—how the material body interacts with an immaterial mind or, more rationally, how a material body can generate such things as thoughts and consciousness—has been with us ever since. We may have given up the notions of a rational soul interacting with animal spirits, but the distinction has bedeviled philosophers to this day. I return to this issue later. Also in Descartes's century, Thomas Hobbes published his *Leviathan*, which influenced our notions of mind in part by adjusting to and sometimes incorporating Hobbes's view on human nature in the raw.[5]

The three major eighteenth-century figures in the history of the mind were David Hume, Immanuel Kant, and Franz Brentano. Though Hume's major contributions at the time were his analyses of causal phenomena and his questioning of deistic notions, his philosophizing about mind were more psychological than philosophical, with his insistence that the human constructs the world from its imperfect impressions.[6] Kant followed

4. Descartes (1662, 1642).

5. Hobbes (1651).

6. Hume (1739–1740).

up Hume's skepticism by developing his ideas about the structure of the human mind and its a priori dependence on space and time as initially givens.[7] And Brentano convinced the philosophical community about the importance of *intentionality*— that human thought is always *about* some object.[8] The ideas had been known for some time, and Aristotle suggested similar notions about intentionality and directedness, but Brentano came at the right time and place to make them central.

With the end of the nineteenth century came the detachment of psychology from philosophy. The foundations for the separation had been laid earlier in the century,[9] but a new psychology with less of the philosophical baggage (and without mind?) was created by the empiricist-experimentalist Wilhelm Wundt and the philosopher-encyclopedist William James (more about both in later chapters). Both Wundt and James, in the end, described the wide-ranging functions and structures of the mind without paying more than lip service to its existence.

Psychology's next step in the functional definition of *mind* came in its abandonment of consciousness as the be-all and end-all of psychological observation. Though earlier writers had considered problems of unconsciousness[10] and Sigmund Freud made it his foundation stone, as far as the psychologies of cognition were concerned the major insight into the importance of nonconscious processes came early in the twentieth century in

7. Kant (1929, originally published in 1781).

8. Brentano (1874).

9. E.g., Herbart (1816).

10. E.g., Hartmann (1869). I return to the history of the unconscious in chapters 5 and 13.

the work of the Würzburg school and the discovery of "image-less thought" (see chapter 5).

Philosophies of Mind

In the twentieth century, psychologists generally gave up any systematic investigation of a mind entity and used the term primarily as a *façon de parler*. In part, this created a vacuum of interest, and in the twentieth century the philosophy of mind developed as a separate field and took over the topic as its principal domain. That development turned into a storm of contributions in the last quarter of the century as philosophy awakened from a place-holding slumber and abounded with conjectures and speculations about mind and consciousness. I cannot do justice to the full range of opinions expressed, but I sketch here a few positions that are relevant to a psychology of consciousness and mind. The sheer number and variety of labels for different and contradictory positions in philosophy— eliminative materialism, analytic functionalism, analytic behaviorism, homuncular functionalism, direct realism, commonsense relationism, and many more—are enough to deter one from trying to summarize contemporary philosophy.

Anyone who attempts to delimit a philosophy of mind confronts two major problems: first, some philosophers are not sure that it is possible to arrive at any understanding of mind, whatever it is, and second, there is no agreement about whether *mind* refers to the contents of consciousness or whether it implies something else or more.

Thomas Nagel is an excellent example of a philosopher who, though implicitly claiming otherwise, denies the possibility of understanding the mind without quite telling us what this mind might be. He describes it as a general feature of the world (like matter)[11] that cannot be understood by any physical reduction and that also is beyond any evolutionary explanation. Nagel assures us that something else must be going on, and he is sure that whatever it may be, it is taking us to a truer and more detached understanding of the world (p. 79). It is difficult to follow his refusal to examine current psychological knowledge and his insistence that the methods needed to understand ourselves do not yet exist (p. 10). Nagel contends that the world may be inconceivable to *our* minds. Humans are by no means omniscient, but they cannot claim to know or to prejudge what knowledge is or is not attainable. There surely are aspects of the world that are currently inconceivable, and others that were so centuries ago, but many of the latter are not inconceivable now, and the former may not be so in the future. It may be characteristic of basic scientific optimism that psychologists refuse to concede such impossibilities.

As I have shown, there is no public agreement about the referent for the ubiquitous term *mind*. To return briefly to the lexical problem, Webster's dictionaries are quite catholic in admitting (1) the complex of elements in an individual who feels, perceives, thinks, wills, and reasons; (2) the conscious mental events and capabilities in an organism; and (3) the organized conscious and unconscious adaptive mental activity of an organism. Philosophers rarely tell us which of these minds they have in mind. Apart from the public display of disunity, it is likely that most philosophers would agree to a use of *mind* as a quasi-theoretical entity that is causally involved in mental events, including consciousness. I return to the conflict between

11. Nagel (1986, p. 19).

mind as representing the contents (and sometimes functions) of consciousness and *mind* as summarizing the various mechanisms that we assign to conscious and unconscious processes.

Having happily accepted one or another form of Cartesian dualism for nearly three hundred years, Anglophone philosophy briefly partook of behaviorist escapades in the first half of the twentieth century while wrestling with the purified attitudes of logical positivism. Things changed radically around 1960 with the advent of the currently favored way of dealing with the mind—*functionalism*.[12] At its simplest, philosophical functionalism depends on sensory inputs and observable behaviors that are linked by a set of causal relations to describe (in various ways) the "how" of consciousness and mind. Among the many different uses of the term *functionalism* in science, linguistics, and philosophy, the latter has used it extensively and sometimes variously.

Partly a reaction against the identity theory of mind and brain, philosophical functionalism was part of the general change in the cognitive and social sciences that took place in the late 1950s and early 1960s. William Lycan, in defending a strong version of functionalism as honest-to-goodness natural teleology, is interested in the various components as they serve the supervening current operation or function of a system.[13] He invokes a hierarchical system for all complex phenomena, with any level of the hierarchy being unpacked into many lower levels of lesser complexity, thus avoiding the problem of a simple homuncular regression.[14] The general concern, here and

12. See Putnam (1960).

13. Lycan (1987, p. 44).

14. See also Dennett (1978).

elsewhere, is with mechanisms: how does the system, mind, or organism manage relations between inputs and outputs, and how does it achieve a particular state? Robert Van Gulick[15] similarly uses functionalism to define psychological (conscious) states within a network of perceptual conditions and organism behaviors. He concludes that such a functional approach permits us to think about content in a naturalistic way and to discern continuities that fit the facts about content. I stress this approach because it focuses on the distinction between philosophical and psychological functionalisms. Approaching that difference, Elliot Sober[16] made a distinction between the dominant machine functionalism and teleological functionalism. In contrast to the "how" questions of machine functionalism, the teleological variety also asks what the functions of particular systems, organs, or processes are. This sense of functionalism asks the kinds of questions that psychologists prefer and treats various positions as ostensibly fallible theories about the mind.[17]

Psychology: Mind as Mechanism

I have already expressed my skepticism about the point of view that mind and consciousness are coextensive. I now wish to consider another position that sees mind as the sum total of mechanisms that we ascribe to people (or even to nonhuman animals) to make their behavior understandable and coherent. Such a position sees mind and consciousness as independent,

15. Van Gulick (1980).

16. Sober (1985).

17. Note that this kind of functionalism does not fall under the rubric of functional analyses and their problems (see Cummins, 1975).

though related, concepts. It is implicitly present in many psychological discussions of mind and at times has been explicitly defined. For example, over fifty years ago, in the waning years of American behaviorism, Karl Deutsch suggested that *mind* might be provisionally defined as any self-sustaining physical process that includes the seven operations of abstracting, communicating, storing, subdividing, recalling, recombining, and reapplying items of information.[18]

Recently, the psychological concept of mind has been used in the theory-of-mind approach, originally introduced by David Premack and Guy Woodruff to refer to an ape's ability to understand the goals, thought processes, and motives of another (including a human).[19] Theory of mind has received wide application in discussions of young children's mental development. Theory of mind uses mind as a collective expression for a variety of mental processes.

An approach to mind as a collection of mechanisms is also implied by some philosophers, even though they are preoccupied with the mental functions of consciousness. For example, John Searle notes (in keeping with contemporary attitudes) that "most of the mental phenomena in [a] person's existence are not present to consciousness" and "most of our mental life at any given point is unconscious."[20] He then, however, maintains that our access to unconscious mental states is derived solely from conscious mental states. Such a view signals a return to an initial *tabula rasa* that becomes populated by the individual's conscious experiences and also denies any kind of acquisition

18. Deutsch (1951, p. 216).
19. Premack and Woodruff (1978).
20. Searle (1992, p. 18).

of skills or knowledge without conscious participation or any kind of preexperientially given structures.

A view of mind as mere mechanism may seem like some sort of Rylean behaviorism. Ryle noted, for example, that "to find that most people have minds...is simply to find that they are able and prone to do certain sorts of things."[21] Ryle then rejects any "occult" agency behind these acts, but he is unwilling to consider a *theoretical* set of mechanisms (a mind?) by which we try to understand the observed working of the individual.

Psychologists frequently equate the mind with thought. To the extent that thinking involves the manipulation of conscious symbols, it covers only a part of the umbrella notion of mind, since much of human problem solving takes place unconsciously, and some nonmanipulative processes such as sensory perception would probably also fall under a general sense of mind.

Finally, if mind is the repository of perceptual, cognitive, and behavioral mechanisms, then it can also be argued to be the function that is performed by the brain. If "mind is what the brain does," then similar relations can be seen in the form and function of other human organs.

Is There a Mind-Body Problem?

There is, strictly speaking, no mind-body *problem*; dealing with so-called minds is not incompatible with a modern materialism. Mind is what the brain does, just as energy conservation is what a liver does. Specific functions are associated with large operational units such as organs, organisms, and machines, and these

21. Ryle (1949, p. 61).

functions (and their associated concepts) cannot without loss of meaning be reduced to the constituent processes of the larger units. The speed of a car, the conserving function of the liver, and the notion of a noun phrase are not reducible to internal-combustion engines, liver cells, or neurons.[22] Mind may be viewed as an emergent function. The notion of emergence is a label that has often been applied to these new properties of larger assemblies. A sentiment related to my position is echoed in Lycan's statement that "the mystery of the mental is no more a mystery than the heart, the kidney, the carburetor, or the pocket calculator."[23]

Just as philosophers have advanced a multitude of interpretations of mind, so have neurophysiologists and neuropsychologists proposed many different suggestions for the physical location or realization of consciousness—and, by implication, of mind.[24] The argument about mind as an emergent function of the brain needs also to be placed in the context of reductionist arguments. Most current commentators are materialists, and as materialists they subscribe to the first part of what Steven Weinberg has called *grand reductionism*—"the view that all of nature is the way it is . . . because of simple universal laws, to which in some sense all other scientific laws may in some sense be reduced."[25] The claim of reduction contained in the second

22. Mandler (1985b).

23. Lycan (1987, p. 44).

24. Kinsbourne (1996) has summarized some of the various localizations of consciousness that have been proposed. That discussion is beyond the scope of this chapter since as far as I know nobody has proposed any localization of mind—other than the whole brain—or organism.

25. Weinberg (1995, p. 39).

half does not follow, and it actually refers only to a subset of materialist dogma—physicalism. In any case, complex emergent functions need their own laws and principles, which cannot without loss of meaning be reduced to the "universal laws."[26]

I have tried to show the multifaceted aspects of the concept of mind. It varies with cultures, with disciplines, and with ontological presuppositions. Today, psychologists use *mind* primarily as a summary term to bundle all the various characteristics, abilities, and functions that we use to understand and characterize complex human thought and action. Attempts to understand what mind may "really" be are confined mainly to philosophical speculations. Psychologists have also generally accepted the notion that the mind is what the brain does and thus have adopted a basic materialist stance. Having exorcised the ghost in the machine, we still are willing to think about the machine and its function.

26. See, for example, Putnam (1980).

2   Aristotle to Alexander Bain: Prolegomena of Modern Psychology

I start with an overview of the early history of the study of thought. Such an exploration is essential because the views of our forebears over the past twenty-five hundred years set the framework within which practically all subsequent work has been done.

Explorations of the nature of thought, like the rest of psychology, began life in the philosopher's armchair. The study of thought processes, however, took longer than many other areas of psychology to pull loose from philosophy. Because of the elusive, private, intensely personal nature of thought, on the one hand, and because of its relation to "truth," "knowledge," and "judgment," on the other, philosophers have been reluctant to part with this province of the study, and they have not entirely given it up today. Nevertheless, the study of thinking has moved out of the philosopher's library and into the laboratory—out of the philosopher's head and into the scientist's. Thought was introduced to the laboratory at the beginning of the twentieth century. Before that time, the psychology of thinking was strictly the philosopher's province, and so its history is studded with names of the great and near great, especially in the centuries during which empirical philosophy flourished in Great

Britain. The British empiricists are often called the British associationists because their work is based on a fundamental principle of mental life—the association of ideas. The phrase was
apparently invented by John Locke late in the seventeenth
century, but he did not originate the principles it subsumes.
Thomas Hobbes, a half century earlier, was the first writer of
modern times to describe the way in which one idea follows another, whether the process occurs in memory, thought, or imagination.[1] And his formulation, in turn, can be traced to that of
Aristotle, writing two thousand years earlier. Aristotle's priority
cannot be gainsaid; indeed, some of his most ardent defenders
denied any subsequent accretion to his fundamental ideas. The
following passage by Sir William Hamilton shows that as late as
the middle of the nineteenth century, a heated (if not altogether
enlightening) defense of Aristotle proceeded to deny the British
philosophical tradition any success with or even any contribution to the doctrine of association:

[In] truth, it might be broadly asserted, that every statement in regard
to the history of this doctrine [of the association of ideas] hazarded
by British philosophers, to say nothing of others, is more or less errone-
ous. Priestley, for example, assigns to Locke the honor of having first
observed the fact of association . . . ; and Hume, . . . arrogates to himself
the glory of first generalizing its laws. . . . Mr. Stewart . . . says that something like an attempt to enumerate the laws of Association is to be found
in Aristotle. Sir James Mackintosh, again, . . . affirms that Aristotle and his
disciples . . . confine the application of the law of association *exclusively
to the phaenomena of recollection*, without any glimpse of a more general

1. I hasten to make a distinction to be observed here and later. *Association* can be either a description of the way that mental events follow one
another or a theoretical assertion that claims that the cooccurrence of
two mental events establishes, by some theoretical fashion, their future
linkage.

operation, extending to all the connections of *thought and feeling*; while the enouncement of a general theory of Association thus denied to the genius of Aristotle is all, and more than all, accorded to the sagacity of *Hobbes*. The truth, however, is that in his whole doctrine upon this subject, name and thing, Hobbes is simply a silent follower of the Stagirite; inferior to his master in the comprehension and accuracy of his general views; and not superior, even on the special points selected, either to Aristotle or to Vives.[2]

In his *De Anima*, Aristotle postulates the mind (in its world of images) as being constituted of images as elements.[3] How this notion persisted to the present is examined in later discussions. The doctrine of association appears in its most forceful form in the section entitled *De Memoria* in the *Parva Naturalia*. In this section, Aristotle postulates the orderly sequence of experience and the three laws of association—those of similarity, contrast, and contiguity. In his discussion of recollection, he notes that memory requires the prior acquisition of some knowledge, which is most frequently laid down by habituation. He stresses what he calls the method of sequences, which channels recollection without making any effort to recall the sequence that produces it or even without recalling the sequence. Mental "movements" follow one another by habituation.

A thin line of scholarship connects Aristotle with the work of the British associationists many centuries later. Aristotle's formulations of the laws of thought were essentially unimproved upon for two millennia, and they are still in use in recognizable form today. The essence of his thought can be found in all the British philosophers' works, although it has been much

2. Hamilton (1880, originally published in 1846). The quote is from Sir William Hamilton's appendix D**, p. 890.

3. Hammond (1902).

elaborated and expanded in the last two centuries. The association theory of thought can be said to have been founded by Aristotle, but the mantle might be more reasonably placed, if placed it must be, on the shoulders of Hobbes in the seventeenth century (*pace* Sir William Hamilton). Although Hobbes worked no great elaboration or improvement on Aristotle's notions, nonetheless he started British psychology on the road it was to follow for many years. In the first place, his work led psychology away from the doctrine of innate ideas that René Descartes was propounding at that time, thus beginning a tradition of his own that was to dog the footsteps of the British associationists and to exert a powerful influence on German psychology. Hobbes, however, turned his back on the rationalist position and stressed instead the empirical basis of mental life, which insists that our ideas come from the senses and in fact are but the decaying remains of sensations. Hobbes was fascinated by the physical problem of how the world comes to be represented inside our heads. His attempts to solve this problem led to another important influence on psychology—namely, the interest in the psychophysical basis of sensation and thought. Following a trip to the continent to visit Galileo Galilei, he became intrigued with the concept of motion as a powerful explanatory principle of the workings of both the physical world and the mind. Motion was to be the "cause of all things," since if everything were at rest or moved at the same rate, discrimination would be impossible.

Rarely would it be possible during the next two centuries for a philosopher to disengage himself from this preoccupation and to write about thought without also adding some speculations about its physical basis. *Human Nature*, written in 1640 but not published until ten years later, presented Hobbes's major notions about thinking and the train of thought. It includes a discussion of the senses and the way in which ideas or conceptions are built up from sensations. Hobbes also describes contiguity as the basic principle of association or (as he calls it) coherence of the original experiences. Hobbes recognizes in passing (as does Aristotle) that imagination, thinking, and even memory do not exactly recreate past experience. He also recognizes that an experience may be paired with more than one other and yet sometimes one and sometimes the other is brought to mind. However, no solutions to these problems are offered. In the *Leviathan*, published in 1651, some hints for such further developments are presented in the discussions of motivated (directed) thinking and the influence of "desire" on the succession of thought. This topic did not receive its full appreciation until the late nineteenth and early twentieth centuries and was generally underplayed by the early associationists, who found it difficult to fit such notions into a scheme of mental life reduced to the associations of elementary sensations and ideas. The basic notion of the elementary character of experience is reflected in the following passage from the *Leviathan*:

There is no...act of man's mind [other than experience], naturally planted in him, so as to need no other thing, to the exercise of it, but to be born a man, and live with the use of his five senses. Those other faculties which seem proper to man only, are acquired and increased by study and industry.[4]

One of the problems left untreated by Hobbes—the way in which complex ideas are compounded from simple sensations—

4. Molesworth (1839, 1840).

was taken up fifty years later, in 1690, by Locke in *An Essay Concerning Human Understanding*.[5] It is difficult to place Locke in his own school ("his" because many writers have placed him as the founder of associationism). Although he did coin the phrase, he contributed little to the doctrine. In fact, as J. D. Greenwood as pointed out,[6] Locke noted that the association of ideas based on contiguity, similarity, and the like does not provide a general explanation of the processes of human reasoning. According to Locke, most of our reasoning is based on semantic connections between ideas grounded in our empirical knowledge of the world:

Some of our ideas have a natural Correspondence and Connection one with another: It is the Office and Excellency of our Reason to trace these, and hold them together in that Union and Correspondence which is founded in their particular beings.[7]

Locke's interests were threefold—epistemological, psychological, and pedagogical—and his work on the association of ideas served primarily the last of these. He recognized, for example, the effects of habit on our thinking—that various associations of ideas can be firmly ingrained in the mind, whether or not they are "true," and thus hinder the acquisition of new ideas. But he did not contribute in detail to the elaboration of an associationist theory of thinking. Locke's main purpose in the *Essay* is to develop a theory of knowledge, and the psychological aspects of the work subserve this epistemological purpose. Like the other philosophers of his time, Locke's interest in psychology was secondary to his interest in philosophical problems. He

5. Locke (1690, originally published in 1689).

6. Greenwood (1999).

7. Locke (1690, originally published in 1689).

explored the nature of the mind as a necessary step in the quest for the limits of human knowledge. The ultimate goals were the ontological and epistemological problems of what is in the world and to what degree of certainty we can know it. It was to aid this quest for validity of belief that Locke attempted to follow the development of "understanding" from its simplest beginnings in sensation to the most complex operations of reasoning.

Like Hobbes, Locke takes pains to refute the notion of innate or intuitively known ideas and stresses that all the stuff that our minds have to work with comes from experience. He goes about this empiricism in a slightly different way, however. Our ideas come from two sources—sensation and reflection (or "internal sense"), which consists of the mind's perception of its own operations. The nature of reflection is not entirely clear. It seems to contain elements of the modern term *introspection* but is primarily related to the active powers of the mind. The distinction is made, for example, between the passive reception of simple ideas of sense and the perception of more complex ideas. He mentions in a discussion that reverberates into the present that judgment, which involves reflection, influences much of our perception of the world. Reflection is not developed as a psychological term; it too serves Locke's theory of knowledge, which he considers to consist of the perception of the connection and agreement, or disagreement, of our ideas. Although the role of reflection remains psychologically vague, Locke moves a step away from the simple sensationism of Hobbes and raises the problem of how the mind takes the simple ideas that are passively received and combines and compares them to form the more complex ideas with which it customarily deals. The identification of Locke with the *tabula rasa*, which carries overtones of the passive reception of input, has overshadowed his notions about the active processing character of the mind. In that direction, Locke's use of *reflection* was an important step toward a more sophisticated theory of thinking.

For Locke, the term *idea* is a general one. It is his unit of analysis: perception, thinking, doubting, reasoning, willing, pleasure, and pain are all different sets of ideas. Using idea as a basic unit paves the way for the development of associationism: ideas can be compounded, compared, and strung together. Here lies probably the origin of the atomistic flavor of later association theory. There is nothing experiential about this concept. Psychologically different processes are built up from these neutral units, deriving their distinctive character from the way in which they are combined. In Locke's *An Essay Concerning Human Understanding*, we can follow the system from these simple building stones of his psychology—the ideas—through a discussion of perception and memory to the statements of the associative doctrine. Book IV discusses reasoning and clearly illustrates the distinction between a modern psychology of thinking and the early philosophical attempts. The early discussions are permeated by a preoccupation with content—the ideas and their associations. The process of thought—reasoning, for example—is circumnavigated in most instances by simply calling it a property of the human organism; it just happens. Note that Locke parts company with the leftover Aristotelian notion that all reasoning requires syllogistic skills and that he is willing to speculate about what the reasoning processes might be. It is also useful to keep in mind what the method of the empirical philosophers was. Locke describes and defends it himself in the following passage from one of the chapters concerned primarily with epistemological problems:

And thus I have given a short and, I think, true history of the first beginnings of human knowledge; whence the mind has its first objects, and
by what steps it makes its progress to the laying in and storing up those
ideas out of which is to he framed all the knowledge it is capable of;
wherein I must appeal to experience and observation whether I am in
the right. This is the only way that I can discover whereby the ideas of
things are brought into the understanding. If other men have either innate ideas or infused principles, they have reason to enjoy them; and if
they are sure of it, it is impossible for others to deny them the privilege
that they have above their neighbours. I can speak but of what I find in
myself.[8]

It would take another two hundred years before psychologists
would be able to speak of processes found "in others."

The use of the idea as a basic unit did not find an easy niche
in psychology, and fifty years later we find David Hume declaim-
ing that Locke's usage perverted the notion. Hume, like Locke,
was interested in epistemological questions. In his search for
what we can know with certainty, he thought it necessary to
trace the history of any idea back to its foundation to discover
how it arose in the human mind in the first place. Conse-
quently, a good deal of his main work, *A Treatise of Human
Nature*, published in 1739, looks into psychological problems,
especially the nature of thought.[9] His philosophical conclusions
are primarily negative; his treatise develops into a radical skepticism about what we can know with certainty. In fact, his conclusion is that we can know so little that we had really better give
up the philosophy game and stick to psychology: "We may well
ask, What causes us to believe in the existence of the body? but
it is in vain to ask, Whether there be body or not? That is a point

8. Pringle-Pattison (1924, p. 91).

9. Hume (1739–1740).

we must take for granted in all our reasonings." In spite of this conclusion, it is well to remember when reading the *Treatise* that Hume was first of all a philosopher and only secondarily interested in the problems that today are called psychological. Hume uses the term *idea* in a more commonsense form than did Locke. Hume divides all the "perceptions" of the human mind into two classes—impressions, which correspond to sensations and emotions, and ideas, which are faint images of these and occur during thinking and reasoning. His differentiation between these two on the basis of force, liveliness, or vividness is not a satisfactory distinction, but it is probably not central to his psychology. What is important is that every simple idea is preceded by a simple impression, of which the idea is an exact copy. Thus he has the source of the mind's ideas solidly located (perhaps a little too solidly) in the empirical world. He went to great pains to stress this isomorphic relationship, but it reinforced the atomistic conception of the mind that was continually to plague the association school. The complexities of thought are built up out of elementary sensations, and for us to know the certainty of any idea requires that we find the sensations from which it was derived. It is from this basis that Hume ultimately deduces his famous argument that we cannot prove a causal relationship. The most we can derive from our sensations are such relationships as contiguity, priority in time, and constant conjunction, but nowhere can we find a sensation (and therefore the idea) of necessary connection or power or influence of one object on another, which was held to be the crucial element in a causal relationship. The ideas we have of such a relation must stem from our habitual associations: the repetition of an association between two events arouses an expectation in the mind. But the conclusion of causal connection is an inference, not a direct perception. The failure to find an immediate perception of causality was irrefutable, and Hume could find no way to prove the validity of a causal inference. Hume's argument moves the problem of causality solidly into psychology. The perception of causality (within the framework of modern psychology)[10] is an empirical problem of human thought. Hume's *Treatise* teaches us not to confuse it with physical causality. As far as the elements of his psychology are concerned, Hume himself notes at least one apparent exception to his statement that for every simple idea there is a corresponding previous impression—the example of a person having a clear idea of a certain shade of blue he has never seen—but he thought that this was such a minor exception that it was not worth bothering with, and he proceeded apace. Other conclusions follow from this conception of the mind, and Hume, unlike his predecessor Locke, was not afraid to draw them. One such conclusion is that the mind can hold no abstract or general ideas, in the sense that it is impossible to imagine "any quantity or quality without forming a precise notion of its degrees." The inability to admit to his system any vague or blurred images stems from his premise that every simple idea is a copy of the original sense impression. Locke had been willing to say that we can form the general idea of a triangle that is neither oblique nor equilateral but more or less both at the same time. The gauntlet was taken up by Bishop George Berkeley and in turn by Hume, who swore they could imagine no such thing, and this strange and wondrous controversy continued into the twentieth century, when we find Edward Bradford Titchener still wrestling with the problem. As is noted later in the discussion of Oswald Külpe, the problem

10. See, for example, Michotte (1954).

of how the mind forms and uses abstract ideas is insoluble within the image theory of ideas, a framework of psychology that ties thinking solely to images and conscious processes.

Locke and Hume were the giants among the British philosophers in their influence on later psychology. But their psychology was part and parcel of their larger philosophical systems, and despite Hume's great insights, they can hardly be said to have made any distinction between philosophical questions and problems of an empirical psychology. Such a distinction, however, soon begins to be noticeable, and it seems proper to assign David Hartley, James and John Stuart Mill, and Alexander Bain to this next phase in the history of thought.

In the mid-eighteenth century, the mind still appeared to consist in large part of sensations and images formed from them. The way in which these ideas are strung together had been suggested but not yet worked out in detail. Philosophers were still vague about how we progress from the raw data of sense impressions to the towering structures of thought of which humans are capable. The first philosopher to take the law of association and turn it into a psychology of association was David Hartley in 1749. As Edwin G. Boring says of Hartley,

He is important because he was the founder of associationism. He was not the originator; that was Aristotle, or Hobbes, or Locke, as one pleases. The principle had been used effectively and greatly developed by Berkeley and Hume. Hartley merely established it as a doctrine. He took Locke's little-used title for a chapter, the association of ideas, made it the name of a fundamental law, reiterated it, wrote a psychology around it, and thus created a formal doctrine with a definite name, so that a school could repeat the phrase after him for a century and thus implicitly constitute him its founder.[11]

11. Boring (1950, pp. 193–194).

Perhaps part of Hartley's success in creating a school of psychology came from his training as a physician rather than a philosopher. For the first time, we are reading a work that does not have a theory of knowledge as its goal but aims toward a theory of psychology such as we are familiar with today. True, it is still armchair theory, far from the laboratory, but there are some new emphases. One of the most important of these is Hartley's interest in physiology, which led him to attempt a crude neurological basis for the psychological theory he was developing and to extend the laws of association to include muscular movements. Although his information about neurology was too imprecise to make this part of his theory of any modern interest, the inclusion of motor phenomena in the theory enormously increased its power and scope. The law as stated in his proposition XX is a clear statement of the associative laws current a century and a half later.

If any sensation A, idea B, or muscular motion C, be associated for a sufficient number of times with any other sensation D, idea E, or muscular motion F, it will, at last, excite d, the simple idea belonging to the sensation D, the very idea E, or the very muscular motion F. The reader will observe that association cannot excite the real sensation D, because the impression of the sensible object is necessary for this purpose.[12]

Much of the characteristic temper of association theory as it was developed during the next century is represented in Hartley's writing. In his proposition XII, for example, the additive nature of complex ideas ("compound impression $A + B + C + D$") is boldly assumed. The simplicity of such an assumption was enormously appealing, but the notion of complex ideas being merely the linear sum of their component simple ideas

12. Hartley (1834, originally published in 1749).

was one of the most vulnerable positions of the theory. On the one hand, the attacks concentrated on the theory's inability to handle the relational and unitary character of ideas and behavior; on the other hand, it seemed patently impossible that all the many complex and abstract concepts could be painstakingly constructed out of their relatively few constituents. From a modern point of view, it seems that the many different associations to be acquired could not be fitted into a human lifetime. Though not directly relevant to our topic, I note that Hartley also accounted for early language learning as an example of the way in which the laws of association covered much of human mental capacities. It is in Hartley's writings that we find the first full development of associationism as a theoretical notion—in contrast to the descriptive use of association that merely observes succession and co-occurrence.

A period of eighty years elapsed between Hartley's 1749 *Observations* and the publication of the major work of his intellectual successor, James Mill. Although no great advances were made in association theory during this time, its basic laws were being adopted by writers in widely varying fields, so that the apparent interregnum of almost a century was actually a time of consolidation of associationistic concepts into the intellectual life of the period. Economics, ethics, and biology were all being influenced by this peculiar brand of empiricism, and even schools of psychology basically opposite in spirit, such as the faculty psychology flourishing in Scotland, were influenced by the laws of association. One representative of the Scottish school, Thomas Brown, attempted an amalgamation between the nativistic approach of faculty psychology and the empirical approach of British associationism. His work, published in 1820, influenced James Mill, but is of interest here primarily because of his discussion of a problem that was to plague any thoroughgoing associationism. It was going to be embarrassingly difficult to explain the perception and the use of relations within a strict associationist framework. How does the idea or image of "small a and large b" become transmuted into the idea of "greater than"? In one sense, Brown's answer is no answer at all, in that he says that this is merely one of the mind's capabilities, an innate capacity or sensibility to perceive relations.[13] Nevertheless, he recognizes the importance of this mental process and that it is fundamentally different from the process of association:

[The] feelings of relation are states of the mind essentially different from our simple perceptions, or conceptions of the objects that seem to us related, or from the combinations which we form of these, in the complex groupings of our fancy.... There is an original tendency or susceptibility of the mind, by which, on perceiving together different objects, we are instantly, without the intervention of any other mental process, sensible of their relation.[14]

The admission of an extraassociational principle, the perception of relationships, to his psychology allowed him a flexibility not to be found in the better-known system developed by James Mill in *An Analysis of the Phenomena of the Human Mind* and published in 1829. Mill followed in Hartley's footsteps in making the concept of association the cornerstone of the mind's operations. From his basic analysis of the laws of association, he proceeds to extend it to every facet of mental life—naming, language development, belief, reasoning, motivation, and the will. From Hartley's beginnings, a complete system has emerged. In one sense, psychology has come into its own. There is an

13. Brown (1820).
14. Brown (1851, p. 288).

optimism about Mill's volumes: the mysteries of the mind have been pried open; in theory, everything is available for study and analysis right down to its roots.[15] Since all aspects of mental life have been built up from simple elements by means of a simple process, presumably nothing stands in the way of eventually analyzing the most complex processes of human thought. We have arrived at the height of the atomistic analysis of the conscious mind, which at this stage of psychology *is* mind. The idea of "everything" is an enormous collection of the organism's past experience, which presumably could be laid bare by careful analysis. In turn, this past experience is in large part potentially recoverable since in memory we rapidly trace back each link in the chain. But in exchange for this grand unifying principle, we must accept vague generalities when it comes to the fine points. Thus Mill can analyze the process of reasoning or ratiocination in a total of three pages and conclude that it is, obviously, a complicated case of association. That brief chapter is appended to the more lengthy analysis of belief. What the problem of reasoning comes down to, then, is what makes us believe in the conclusion we draw from the premises of a syllogism.

Mill's famous son, John Stuart Mill, who edited and annotated his father's works, includes a footnote to the chapter on reasoning in which he points out that reasoning does not consist of syllogisms. Rather, the latter are a means of checking the truth of conclusions drawn from a chain of reasoning—a point already made very clearly by Locke. This note is typical of the younger Mill's contribution to associationism. He takes the bare structure of his father's grand design and wherever possible

15. Mill (1878, originally published in 1829).

makes the analysis both more sophisticated and more plausible. But in so doing, the nature of associationism is subtly changed. Take, for example, the following famous passage from *A System of Logic*:

[The] laws of the phenomena of mind are sometimes analogous to mechanical, but sometimes also to chemical laws. When many impressions or ideas are operating in the mind together, there sometimes takes place a process, of a similar kind to chemical combination. When impressions have been so often experienced in conjunction, that each of them calls up readily and instantaneously the ideas of the whole group, those ideas sometimes melt and coalesce into one another, and appear not several ideas but one; in the same manner as, when the seven prismatic colours are presented to the eye in rapid succession, the sensation produced is that of white. But as in this last case it is correct to say that the seven colours when they rapidly follow one another generate white, but not that they actually are white; so it appears to me that the Complex Idea, formed by the blending together of several simpler ones, should, when it really appears simple (that is, when the separate elements are not consciously distinguishable in it), be said to result from, or be generated by, the simple ideas, not to consist of them.[16]

This view saves us from the difficulties of stating that the conscious idea of white consists of all the colors of the rainbow, an extreme extension of the use of consciousness. At the same time, the facts of psychology that only recently had seemed so clear and obvious suddenly became complicated again. For there is no reason to assume that the laws applying to a mental chemistry will be the same as those of a mental mechanics. Although the laws of association may account for the acquisition of simple ideas, we find a new principle in the way they form themselves into more complex ideas. Instead of simple addition of particles,

16. Mill (1874, p. 592, originally published in 1829).

we are faced with—what? Multiplication? And higher-order laws to go with it?

With James Mill and his son's embellishments, we have reached the zenith of British associationism. What followed was mostly elaboration and problem statement. Psychology was about to break loose from philosophy; observation and verification were to replace the contemplative mode. But the period closed with a flourish. Alexander Bain undertook to subsume all of human mental life under the principles of association, and in his 1855 book *The Senses and the Intellect*, he ranged from simple problems of sensation to artistic creation, from the association of ideas to the explanation of scientific creativity.[17] Bain writes with a disarming sense of comprehension; the world is laid wide open, and if one applies the principles properly, all can be easily understood. In particular, he took up the problem of directed thinking, which had plagued the doctrine of association from the beginning. Why—with all the possible associations available—is one more likely than another? James Mill struggled with the problem, and Bain succinctly states what has been suggested by many others:

Past actions, sensations, thoughts, or emotions, are recalled more easily, when associated either through contiguity or through similarity, with *more than one* present object or impression.[18]

His statement was to remain the major description of direction in thought, and some sixty years later Bain was credited with the invention of the constellation theory by Georg Elias Müller, who developed it to its highest state. Bain also apparently originated the notion of representation. He spoke of experiences—

17. Bain (1868).
18. Bain (1868, p. 545).

the original states of consciousness—as primary states and their revived states as "representation."[19]

James Mill and Alexander Bain were probably the most influential and most widely read of the British associationists in Germany, where the ferment of the new psychology was brewing. They most certainly appear to be the most quoted, and at least bibliographically, they provide us with the link from British to German associationism—from the armchair doctrine of association to its elaboration in the laboratory. But before taking the leap across the Channel, let us take stock of the associationist theory of the higher mental processes.

First of all, from the standpoint of one interested in the higher aspects of mental processes—in the heights of creative and productive thought—the associationists barely got off the ground. One of the most obvious reasons for this earthbound failure lies in the complexities to be found in the rarified atmosphere of creative thinking. But other reasons, perhaps of more interest historically, lie in the contemplative nature of the associationists' attack on these problems. The object of their studies was their own mind; the scientist was using himself as his own laboratory with all its attendant limitations and confusions. The limitations depend on what can be observed by this method. For one thing, the scientist is almost certainly restricted to the observation of conscious processes. Even if they were so sophisticated as to be able to observe gaps in their thought processes or forced to deduce the presence of lacunae by the bare fact of not being able to follow a line of thought, there is not much they

19. Bain (1855). I treasure a marginal remark by one Grace Brubaker in my copy of Bain. She wrote in 1891: "This is a long lesson and little am I the wiser."

can do or say about these unobservables. Furthermore, the confusions involved in the scientist's use of the self as subject are numerous. When working within the manifold of one's own consciousness, is it possible to tell the relevant from the irrelevant, the plain fact from the fact varnished by the theoretical brush of the scientist-observer? These are difficult problems under the best of observational conditions in a laboratory and well nigh impossible to solve without one.

One of the results of the limitation of the study of thought to the conscious mind was the emphasis placed on sensations and images. It is difficult to attack the so-called regulative aspect of thinking—set, motivation, *Aufgabe*—from a point of view unaware of or unwilling to admit unconscious activities. And without these aspects, emphasis tends to be placed wholly on the units of thought themselves—the idea or the image. The static and atomistic analysis of thought that resulted was rather like a giant Humpty Dumpty deliberately and carefully pushed off the wall with all the king's philosophers trying to put him together again. It cannot be said they met with much more success than the soldiers of the nursery rhyme. Once the pieces were broken apart, it was impossible to fit them together in any semblance of a human thought. Once the mechanical laws devised by James Mill to fit units together were found wanting by the younger Mill, it became apparent that some glue was badly needed.[20]

20. In the midst of the British associationist efforts, there appeared J. F. Herbart's (1776–1841) attempt to introduce a rational, mathematical psychology that did not have the influence on his contemporaries that it deserved (Herbart, 1824–1825). However, Herbart realized that the passively associated ideas were insufficient and suggested instead forces of associations that were able to attract and repulse.

Every now and then, these shortcomings became painfully obvious. Reasoning was relegated to the status of a faculty and thus put beyond the pale of explanation, or the will was invoked (or rejected), or all creative, productive processes were relegated (for example, by Bain) to the operation of trial and error plus a little bit of luck. Retrospectively, the time was ripe for the introduction of organizing and directing forces that might not be available to introspection. It would take another fifty years before this advance was achieved, but Wilhelm Wundt first had to open up the possibility of an experimental psychology.

I pause in the tale of successive approximations toward the present with a chapter on the social and political situation at the end of the nineteenth century and beginning of the twentieth, with special emphases on Germany and America—where the major developments in experimental psychology occurred. I also summarize there some of the psychological developments to be discussed at length in later chapters.

3   The Social Context for the New Psychology in the Nineteenth and Twentieth Centuries

Germany and America were the driving forces in the development of an empirical psychology, and I start with the German context for those events. In Germany, the development of modern psychology followed the emergence of a strong industrial basis in the middle of the nineteenth century, generally supported, subsidized, and encouraged by the state in the education-for-industry movement. By the end of the century, large numbers of German youth were being channeled into the universities, and the end of the century also saw general technological advances. The late 1800s produced the major steps of the second industrial revolution (sometimes called the *new technology*), including the effective telephone, wireless telegraphy, the airplane, the development of the German chemical industry (driven in part by Fritz Haber's invention of nitrogen fixing), the diesel engine, and so forth. And together with the new technology and the newly educated masses came new attitudes in many fields, including the sciences, as well as a new psychology.

Johannes Müller, a true polymath, was the towering figure in German science in the middle of the nineteenth century and the guiding spirit in moving German academic theory and research away from *Naturphilosophie* and rationalism and toward an experientially based, empirical natural science—from an *a priori* philosophy of nature to a naturalistic science of nature. He created the Berliner Schule and brought German science up to the empirical standards previously exemplified by England and France.[1] The movement rejected the speculative, vitalistic, and idealistic *Naturphilosophie* as exemplified by Georg Wilhelm Friedrich Hegel and Friedrich Wilhelm Joseph von Schelling. Though focused on the role of science in the universities, the movement was part of a general mid-nineteenth-century tendency toward a materialist (as against the Kantian and Hegelian idealist) interpretation of history and nature. In the universities, that battle was carried out to a large extent by Müller's students Emil Du Bois-Reymond, Rudolf Virchow, Hermann von Helmholtz, and Ernst Haeckel. Once the movement for a naturalistic, experiential science began to pervade much of German thought in the middle of the nineteenth century, it created another ambivalence. A backlash, particularly among its popularizers, was created against science and scientism. This counterflow tried to denigrate science and elevate a vitalistic philosophical, and often blindly destructive, approach in its stead.[2] In part, this was a reaction against a hyperpositivistic point of view created by some of the scientists themselves—a fact-oriented approach that rejected speculation and, as a consequence, also theoretical thought.

Wilhelm Wundt (who is discussed further in chapter 4) benefited from the replacement of the traditional idealism and rationalism of German psychology with a materialistic or empiricist point of view. Wundt's major contribution to history was his

1. Schnabel (1950).
2. Stern (1961).

unequivocal introduction of the experimental method to psychology, though his empirical interests were to a large extent restricted to problems of will, apperception, sensation, and perception in modern terms. Another movement in the same direction that affected the emergence of a quantitative experimental psychology was the introduction of statistical thinking and procedures in the latter half of the nineteenth century.[3] These influences were to create a tension in Wundt's life and career, though not one he easily acknowledged. The young Turks in science were materialists, whereas Wundt was a lifelong idealist who was suspicious of materialist doctrines. He committed psychology both to a *Geisteswissenschaft* (mental or social science) and to an experimental science. By this step, he avoided the materialism of the *Naturwissenschaften* (natural sciences) while at the same time embracing an experimental empiricism. The underlying argument incorporated something like the following reasoning. Laws, like the laws of natural science, were not possible for the complexities of mental life. But if a reductive materialism were to be defended, then thoughts and emotions could be considered to be just collections of neurons and nervous impulses, and the laws of mental life would be natural science laws. Given that there are no such laws of mental life, materialism is indefensible; psychology is a *Geisteswissenschaft* and not a *Naturwissenschaft* (a mental science, not a natural science). And furthermore, it is relatively easy to defend experimentalism from an antimaterialist point of view, since experiments can reveal only sufficient, but not necessary, conditions. A hundred years later, with more sophisticated though not necessarily "better" views of the relations between materialism and science, the

3. Porter (1986).

elusive hunt for a radical reductionist, materialist position continues as always in vain (see chapter 12). At the same time, given the elusiveness of a strict materialist position, the distinction between natural/materialist and mental/antimaterialist sciences has lost both its validity and its force. The success in turning psychology from rationalist philosophy to empirical science, which was originally opposed by traditional philosophers, turned philosophy full circle as—in the early twentieth century —traditional philosophers who had previously considered psychology a necessary part of their domain objected to the inclusion of experimental psychologists in their departments. The creation of independent psychology departments was a natural consequence.

Another development in German scientific culture that affected the character of psychology was the mid-nineteenth-century movement to establish the cultural sciences. Woodruff Smith has extensively and sensitively described this development, which saw an attempt to define the cultural sciences (generally including anthropology, human geography, cultural history, and psychology) and to mold them into a true (nomothetic) field of science. The psychological part of this endeavor was embodied in the field of *Völkerpsychologie* (loosely, ethno-psychology, which was concerned with human groups and their social and cultural achievements). As is shown in the next chapter, this field occupied much of Wundt's activities in his later life. *Völkerpsychologie* as a separate discipline barely survived into the twentieth century, by which time it had split into experimental psychology and ethnology.[4]

4. For a full discussion of these movements, see Smith (1991).

With the failure of the ideals of the German lands' 1848 revolution, young scientists turned away from politics, particularly so after 1866. Instead, they worked for the reform of the authoritarian structure of the German universities, in part to stress the place and importance of natural science. The failure of the hopes of 1848, followed by the triumphs of Prussian hegemony in 1866 and 1871, foreshadowed the general shift in Germany from liberalism to nationalism. Parallel developments tended to suppress the democratic and liberal tendencies in Baden and other states and to terminate their independence. In 1871, following the defeat of France, Otto von Bismarck achieved the unification of the German states and the establishment of the Second Reich. Wundt was to reflect the change in the attitudes of the professoriat that became complete by the end of the century. The scholar was to remain on the sidelines of politics and neutral toward its opinions and interests.[5] A German banker returning in 1886 after a long absence noted the rampant militarism and observed that university professors—the former leaders of liberalism—"now kowtowed to the authorities in the most servile manner."[6] Germany (and the province of Baden, in particular) changed from a democratic, liberal state to an authoritarian, militaristic state. A democratic Germany was emergent in 1848, the 1920s, and again in the 1960s; the authoritarian strand dominated German history in from the 1870s until after World War I and again in the 1930s and 1940s. It was this changing Germany and its varied and ambivalent attitudes in which Wundt grew up and matured and that was reflected in

5. Sheehan (1978, esp. pp. 234–235).

6. Tuchman (1966, p. 307).

Wundt's own transformation from a liberal democrat to a Prussianized older man.

With the new century, a number of different, and sometimes more important, changes would take place in the definition and direction of psychology. Psychology broke with much of its past, just as both European and American society and culture in general exhibited new directions in the twentieth century. The new century brought with it the beginnings of new developments in the arts and the sciences. Whatever the manifest reasons for the outbreak of World War I, the breakdown of old alliances and the unavoidable conflict among the major Western powers apparently created the conditions for changes in areas other than big-power relations and commercial and industrial realignments. The twentieth century brought important breaks in art and architecture with the arrival of the Jugendstil and art nouveau and their rejection of the imitative styles of the nineteenth century. In music, new modes of expression were found in the work of Arnold Schönberg and others, again a sign of the rejection of the old. In France, Henri Matisse and the fauves, followed by the cubists, also rejected mere presentation of nature. And James Joyce opened new doors of expression in literature. The last decade of the nineteenth century saw a cluster of genius emerging in the intellectual life of Europe that would act on intellectual life well into the 1930s. H. Stuart Hughes notes such a "cluster" and draws attention to the fact that an amazing group of thinkers was born in the period between the mid-1850s and 1870s, including Sigmund Freud, Émile Durkheim, Henri Bergson, Ernst Weber, Benedettu Croce, Luigi Pirandello, André Gide, Marcel Proust, Carl Jung, Thomas Mann, Hermann Hesse, and others. All of them participated in the change from a view of humanity "as self-consciously rational" beings to a more limited, irrational (unconscious?) view of human motives and of human freedom.[7]

In the long run, the atomistic and experiential psychology of Wundt was followed by the holistic and experiential psychologies of Otto Selz and the Gestalt psychologists, whereas in America Edward Bradford Titchener was followed by the atomistic and objectivist tradition of behaviorism. This rather surprising bifurcation was, at least in part, a function of new ways of looking at the world in Europe and new emphases on inward-looking strands in the United States. More important, however, was the development of a psychological theoretical language *sui generis*. It was another expression of the rejection of a sheer mirroring of nature and common sense. Psychology participated in the rejection of the "self-conscious rational" nineteenth-century image. When Freud rejected the notion that human motives are self-evident, he needed a new, a psychological language to express this new direction. The general cultural movements toward new ways of expression in art, music, and literature had their parallel in the movements toward a psychological language. Theoretical speculation, both in Wundt and William James, usually consisted of rather vague psychological concepts and a commitment to the notion that true psychological explanation was to be found in the physiological substratum (of the day).[8]

To produce a theoretical language implies the postulation of theoretical entities and processes—and if they were not explicitly neurophysiological ones, then theorists needed what came to be called *mental mechanisms*. Whereas in the last quarter of

7. Hughes (1958, p. 4).

8. A position that was to be mirrored later by B. F. Skinner.

the nineteenth century it was still generally accepted that most or all important mental events were conscious, by the end of the twentieth century it was generally agreed that most important or determining events are unconscious. This shift was part of general trends toward abandoning the view of human rationality (as in Freud) and toward emphasizing theory and its language. Two unrelated developments led to the emergence of a psychological language, and both of them involved the discovery or invention of the unconscious. They are one example of the phenomenon of a way of thinking that was developing independently in more than one place at one time. One development was Freud and his invocation of the unconscious. By assigning to the unconscious psychological functions akin to conscious wishing, willing, and avoiding, Freud invoked a theoretical language that operated as the underlying representation of overt thought and behavior. At the same time, a series of experiments (in retrospect, somewhat unconvincing by themselves) coming out of Würzburg University generated a similar need for a layer of theoretical concepts that were neither conscious contents nor physiological entities (see chapter 5). The "discovery" was that thinking was sometimes unconscious when solving problems, producing associations, and making judgments. The solutions, judgments, and meanings of concepts and words were often given directly without intervening conscious contents. The term *imageless thought*, which has been given to these investigations, is relevant for some instances that lack accompanying imagery, but generally the more appropriate reference is to *unconscious thought*. And it was rapidly followed by the introduction of new categories of consciousness, such as conscious dispositions (*Bewusstseinslagen*), Narziss Ach's *Bewusstheit* (essentially the modern metacognitions), and the notion of the unconsciously registered *Aufgabe* or task. Within a few years, the consensus was that there was a paucity of conscious evidence for complex thought processes. The same conclusion has been attributed to Alfred Binet, who was reported to have commented that one gets a nickel's worth of conscious images for a million dollars worth of thought.

The intellectual turmoil of the first quarter of the twentieth century was reflected in both pre– and post–World War I changes in culture and society. In Germany, the changes in the art world from Jugendstil to expressionism also were mirrored in similar changes in literature and popular culture. In psychology, it was reflected in the dominance of Gestalt psychology and its insistence on structure and the power of the environment. The discontinuity between Wundt and the new psychology reflected in psychology (as elsewhere) the change to twentieth-century modernism. Gestalt ideas ranged far beyond their concerns with perception as they were deployed in Wolfgang Köhler's work on problem solving with primates, Kurt Koffka's concerns with development, Max Wertheimer's and Karl Duncker's contributions to human problem solving, George Katona's contributions to the organization of human memory, and Kurt Lewin's contributions to social psychology. Somewhat buried in the success of Gestalt psychology was the work of Otto Selz, a German psychologist who developed a psychology of thought that was more consistent with later work than Gestalt psychology.[9] Selz was concerned with processes rather than the content of thought and in particular with productive and reproductive thinking within a single system. He was very much the

9. Frijda and deGroot (1981). See chapter 7 for a more extensive discussion of Selz's work.

forerunner of contemporary modelers concerned with operations on knowledge structures.

In the United States, the new century saw basic changes of
values in American society. The new direction was practical and
bureaucratic and concerned with the rationalization of industry
and the establishment of social order. It was also somewhat na-
tionalistic, pragmatic, and inner-directed. American science was
dominated by its pragmatism and its technological emphases,
exemplified in the popular view of Thomas Edison (1847–1931)
as its premier scientist. In Europe, the new century was to see
important new directions in psychology. In contrast to German
industrialism and Prussian authoritarianism, which were tinged
with dreams of empire and romanticism, American society in
the early twentieth century was inward-looking, marked by the
unique American experience of the expanding frontier and the
aftermaths of the U.S. Civil War and imperialist expansion. Internationally, the forces of growth and expansion became loud
and insistent at the end of the century. After the Civil War
reduced the remaining feudal elements of American society,
American industrialists—and isolationists—were preoccupied
with building an expanding country, and the end of the century
saw the beginning of American expansionism and imperial
ambitions. The building of a world-class navy, the annexation
of Hawaii, and the application of the Monroe Doctrine all contributed to a sense of destiny, which culminated in the annexation of the Philippines. The latter is important because older
American values were articulated in opposition to the Pacific expansion. The war with Spain started in 1898 over Cuba. Soon
thereafter the Anti-Imperialist League, which united some of
the finest American public figures, joined the fight in opposition
to the war. However, it was not to be, and first Hawaii and then

the Philippines became American. During the battle in and out of Congress, including William James's opposition, appeals to the inheritors of the ideals of the American revolution failed. The partial success of the imperial adventure and the fissure it revealed in American attitudes on expansion and colonialism led to a more inward-looking atmosphere by restructuring the internal state and producing an intellectual isolationism. Politically, the new century brought a consolidation of American imperialism and a look south rather than across the seas. In science and philosophy, the period was marked by a pragmatic, atheoretical preoccupation with making things work—a trend to find its expression in psychology in functionalism and behaviorism.

The inward-looking period of the turn of the century was reflected in part in the parochialism and the environmentalism of the behaviorist movement. Behaviorism had also responded to the drive of the new technology in the early 1900s. The new movement in America—the revamping of its values—was in part a parallel to the deliberate German encouragement of industry in the early nineteenth century. In America, a new middle class of urban professionals developed the values of "continuity and regularity, functionality and rationality, administration and management" in response to the sense of disorganization following the end of Reconstruction. What was needed was a "government of continuous involvement"[10] that would make possible the further expansion of American capitalism and a sense of order—some control over economic and social forces. Behaviorism was in part a response to this new set of values, and it also was a very American response to the inherited attitudes of the Puritan ethic.

10. Wiebe (1967).

In the next chapter, I spend some time on the major initiators of a modern psychology—Wundt and James—who were both products of the social forces briefly described above. In chapter 6, I briefly dwell on the behaviorist interlude, which had little impact on the study of memory and thought, and expand on the later psychological, particularly German, developments in the early twentieth century.

4   The Birth of Modern Psychology: Wilhelm Wundt and William James

In this chapter, I consider the beginning of modern psychology in the life and work of Wilhelm Wundt and William James. I also discuss Hermann Ebbinghaus, who is important in the development of research in the areas of thought and memory. The birth of modernity will take us to the new century.

Wilhelm Wundt (1832–1920)

Wilhelm Wundt was born in 1832 in the small town of Neckarau in Baden, Germany. His father was a country pastor from an academic family. Young Wilhelm attended the Gymnasium in Heidelberg, and at the age of sixteen he was an active and romantic supporter of the 1848 revolution in Germany. He enthusiastically read Georg Herwegh, the poet of the revolution of 1848; supported the brief republican uprisings during that period; and later regretted the loss into emigration of their leaders and the period of reaction that followed in the 1850s.[1] After Gymnasium, there followed medical studies in Tübingen and Heidelberg, completed in 1855 when Wundt was twenty-three

1. See Wundt's autobiography (1920).

years old. He stayed in Heidelberg until he moved to Zurich in 1874, except for a year in Berlin and occasional periods in Karlsruhe to pursue a short political career.

With the importance of liberal politics in Germany following 1848 and in particular their dominance in the 1860s, the liberals' commitment to the marriage of politics and education motivated scientists and humanists to combine scholarship and politics.[2] In Heidelberg, Wundt and many of his academic colleagues became active in the workers' education movement, and he lectured in Heidelberg and surrounding towns on Charles Darwin and other topics of general interest. In the 1860s, the workers' associations became transformed, in part under the influence of Ferdinand Lassalle and Karl Marx, into more militant organizations that rejected their bourgeois leaders and lecturers. Wundt, who had enjoyed some of his interactions with prominent social democrats such as August Bebel, regretted this shift in the workers' movement and turned toward the center and liberal bourgeois organizations, becoming a member of the *Ständekammer* (representing the various petit bourgeois guilds and professions). He eventually became a candidate of the Progress Party and was elected a member of the second legislative chamber of Baden. There followed four years of great activity in the state capital of Karlsruhe. In the conflict between Prussia and Austria, most of the Baden population was on the side of Austria. Following the defeat of the Austrians in 1866, the situation in Baden was very much up in the air as Otto von Bismarck delayed the admission of Baden to the North German Confederation and Baden rejected all advances from pro-French directions. Wundt found the situation "unbearable" and

2. Sheehan (1978).

resigned from the legislature in 1868 to leave politics and to devote himself to academic pursuits. Two years later, in 1870, following the defeat of France by Prussia and its allies, Germany was united under Prussian leadership.

Wundt had worked briefly in the Heidelberg medical clinic after receiving his medical degree in 1855 but in 1856 moved to the university in Berlin, where he studied toward his vocational goal of doing research in general physiology. He benefited from the physiological research being conducted there under the direction of Johannes Müller and Emil Du Bois-Reymond, eventually moving back to Heidelberg to achieve faculty status (*Habilitation*). Soon afterward he became very ill. His book on muscle movement was published in 1858 and was generally ignored. In 1858, Hermann von Helmholtz moved to Heidelberg, and Wundt became his assistant—a relatively unproductive collaboration that Wundt gave up to write textbooks on general physiology. During his early period in Heidelberg, Wundt saw sensory physiology as his true avocation and soon started work on his *Principles of Physiological Psychology* (*Grundzüge der physiologischen Psychologie*), which was published in 1874,[3] the year he left the university to live in Zurich. Wundt considered the succeeding editions of his work and particularly the sixth edition of three volumes (1908–1911) to represent the substantial part of his life's work. He also developed the justification and basis for the experimental psychology that he was to father, insisting that whereas it was originally called *physiological* because of his background in physiological work, he considered *experimental* not to be restricted to the natural sciences but an important part of an exact mental or social

3. Wundt (1874).

science (*Geisteswissenschaft*) that combined objective methods with self-observation.

At the time, the social sciences (and psychology, in particular) were preoccupied with the distinction, introduced by Wilhelm Dilthey in 1883, between *Naturwissenschaften* and *Geisteswissenschaften*.[4] Dilthey actually makes two major arguments in distinguishing between sciences of the mind (*Geist*) and of nature. He notes that there are two possible perspectives: one can regard everything from the perspective of the natural sciences, or one can regard natural phenomena from the perspective of consciousness. He believed, however, that our physical bodies are governed by the laws of nature. Thus, whereas purpose is a mental phenomenon, it is physically realized in the systems of natural phenomena and laws. On the other hand, Dilthey claimed a more primitive, basic status for the mental sciences since they are in closer contact with the "life nexus" of our experience than are the natural sciences.[5] He also argues for the incomparability of material and mental processes based on the impossibility of deriving mental facts from those of the mechanical order of nature.[6] It was during this period of concern with the nature of the mental sciences that Wundt first reconsidered his interest in social psychological matters, which presented a task "higher" than experimental psychology. Wundt's 1863 book in that direction failed, but the thought was to be taken up later— postponed but not forgotten. The first volume of his *Völkerpsy-*

4. The concept of *Geisteswissenschaften* was a translation of "moral sciences" in John Stuart Mill's *A System of Logic* in 1849 (Makkreel, 1989).

5. Makkreel and Rodi (1989, especially pp. 12–13).

6. Dilthey (1959, p. 11, originally published in 1883).

chologie (on language) was not to appear until 1900 (it is discussed below). A fleeting year of Wundt's first full professorship in Zurich in 1874 was followed by the offer of a professorship in Leipzig in 1875. He quickly adapted to this new environment and made the acquaintance of the two men who influenced his psychological work more than any others—Ernst Weber and Gustav Fechner, the two fathers of psychophysics. In 1874 and 1875, he was given a room for his own experiments in psychology, and in 1879 he moved into a few rooms that constituted the Institute of Psychology and was given a paid assistant. The Institute grew and moved repeatedly—in 1897 to more or less permanent quarters. During the remaining years until 1917, Wundt maintained his interest in philosophy and its history as he directed the new psychology, and starting in 1900 he published the ten volumes of his other ("higher") psychology— the *Völkerpsychologie*. However, his contribution came toward the end of movement toward the field called *Völkerpsychologie*, which by then had been superseded by experimental psychology and cultural studies.

By the time of his death in 1920, when Wundt's autobiography appeared, the once-youthful liberal radical had become the elderly nationalist reactionary. For Wundt, Germany's defeat in World War I was entirely the responsibility of the social democratic and other liberal opposition groups (this was the *Dolchstoss* position that Germany was defeated from within), and he assigned principal responsibility for the war to deliberate planning by England and its leading statesmen under the influence of Benthamite utilitarianism.

The duality of German politics and the parallel development of Wundt's politics are reflected in his psychology, which has produced a split between social and experimental psychology that has been with us in some guise or another ever since. I do not wish to imply a one-to-one mapping of German politics, Wundt's life, and his psychology. Rather, I stress the parallel ambivalences present in all three of these domains that were reflected at various times in Wundt's psychology. His interest in social phenomena, for example, can be seen throughout much of his life, and his concern with rationality and order, though strongest at the end of his life, was present even in his early liberal days. Wundt made a strict distinction between experimental psychology, on the one hand, and ethnopsychological and social psychological topics that were not subject to experimental investigation, on the other hand. The latter were to be approached in a rational and observational manner, whereas experimental psychology was part of the experimental sciences. This distinction reflects in part the duality in German history between a democratic, humanitarian tendency and an authoritarian one.[7] The inquiry into development of the human mind—the social dimension—allowed Wundt to present his humanist, social concerns and to address the contingencies rather than the rules of behavior. Experimental psychology was to a large extent sensory psychology. It was strictly scientific, followed rigid rules of experimentation, and did not allow any "softer" concerns. In the same vein and in part due to the influence of Fechner, Wundt adopted statistical error theory in experimental psychology, though he rejected statistical laws for the historical phenomena treated in the *Völkerpsychologie*.[8] Wundt's topics in experimental psychology were sensory processes,

7. For other dimensions of Wundt's psychologies, see Blumenthal (1970).

8. Porter (1986, p. 67).

perception, consciousness, attention, will, affect, and time and space perception—the classical topics of psychology. He viewed the more complex phenomena as built up from pure sensations and feelings (*Empfindungen und Gefühle*). Whereas his scientific and academic books restricted psychology to its possible experimental foundations, they often introduced the topics of his *Völkerpsychologie*[9]—*Sprache, Mythus*, and *Sitte* (language, mythology, and culture)—without dealing with them at length.

Starting around 1860, Wundt had been concerned with the "higher" psychological functions—the social aspects of human thought and behavior—and this preoccupied him, particularly in the last twenty years of his life. The multivolume *Völkerpsychologie* illustrated Wundt's commitment to the notion that the only source of insight into the development of human thought can be found in its social and historical development. His method was an extensive use of existing ethnographic and anthropological writing, as well as the most widely used extrapolations on language, the family, and other human institutions. It was written from the point of view of a comparative evolutionary perspective. Wundt was particularly concerned with the development of communication systems, starting with a gesture language, developing into "vocal" gestures, and then evolving into language. He related the three broad topics *Sprache, Mythus*, and *Sitte* (language, mythology, and culture) to the individual-psychological aspects of representation, emotion, will, and habit. All these topics are seen by Wundt to be tied to sociality and the historical conditions that give rise to it. The purpose

9. The best translation for *Völkerpsychologie* is "ethnopsychology," which reflects Wundt's belief that the phenomena discussed were cultural products.

was to deal with "those psychological processes that form the basis of the general development of human societies as well as of the creation of common mental products of general validity."[10] In his effort to understand mental structure and development across the development of culture and language, Wundt defended this function against anthropological concerns. He noted that whereas psychology must be based on the results of ethnology and anthropology, mental development may still be the same for different cultures or that similar cultures may, psychologically speaking, represent different stages of "mental culture." In his quasi-summary of the *Völkerpsychologie*,[11] he discusses in detail the early development of human societies, the acquisition of gesture and verbal language (where he was the first to introduce phrase-structure analysis), and the role and development of marriage, myths, and religion. Although his approach was marked by some of the ethnocentric prejudices of the nineteenth century, the analysis of social and cultural behavior and thought was novel and clearly distinguished from the other, experimental, psychology.

Wundt's distinction between experimental psychology and ethnopsychology was in part in the tradition of Dilthey's distinction between *Geisteswissenschaft* and *Naturwissenschaft* (mental and natural sciences). He produced an experimental psychology that was not social and a social psychology that was not experimental.[12] His experimental psychology defined West-

10. Wundt (1900–1909, Vol. 1, pt. 1, introduction).

11. Wundt (1912, 1916).

12. Actually, the aim of the nineteenth-century German interest in the human and cultural sciences was to make them into a nomothetic—that is, natural science (see Smith, 1991).

ern psychology, but his social psychology had little influence in psychology (in Germany or elsewhere), though some sociologists (like Émile Durkheim) were significantly influenced by him. Important in this lack of effects is the fact that only a short one-volume extract of the *Völkerpsychologie* has appeared in English.[13] However, the distinction he made between the two psychologies is still with us. Experimental and social psychologists in the United States, though often trained side by side, often take only superficial note of each other's research, protestations to the contrary and some notable exceptions notwithstanding. Even a philosopher of cognitive science excluded consciousness from being efficacious in cognition but still possibly relevant to resolving conflicts and for planning or for pedagogical or social purposes.[14] It is difficult in this context not to absorb an attitude that makes cognition—however defined—somehow quite different and apart from social concerns and behavior.

To summarize, I stress Wundt's ideas and directions for several reasons. Maybe most important among these is the fact that practically all influential psychologists at the turn of the century were students of Wundt's or were students of his students. Experimental psychology was defined by the experiences of the Leipzig laboratory, and American laboratories were generally opened by his students with imported German instruments. The other reason for stressing Wundt is to stress the duality of his approach. The split that characterized Germany in the nineteenth century between democratic, and even radical, idealism on the one hand and Prussian rational militarism on the other was echoed in Wundt's life and—most important—in his

13. Wundt (1916).
14. Thagard (1986).

psychology. The contrast was between an experimental, tightly reasoned, mathematical psychology and a historical, observational attitude toward those elaborate products of the mind that generate language and culture but that are beyond measurement and beyond experiments. Wundt preached the inaccessibility of those phenomena to experimental and by implication "scientific" study. He asserted their dependence on historical and social influences and determinants. Experimental psychologists sometimes have used the distinction for promoting their exalted status as scientists, whereas social psychologists remained ambivalent about whether they were scientists or could follow Wundt's road into social analysis.

It was Wundt in 1874 who marked out the "new domain of science" and who made the break with self-observation by insisting that "all accurate observation implies...that the observed object is independent of the observer."[15] The psychical processes had to be properly controlled to make objective observation possible. But the transition of psychology to the laboratory also brought with it some Wundt-imposed restrictions on the subject matter of experimental psychology. In the first place, all analytic work in psychology was to be based on the notion that "there is only one kind of causal explanation in psychology, and that is the derivation of more complex psychical processes from simpler ones."[16] Second, experimental study was possible only when external manipulation of conditions was possible—that is, it was restricted to relations between stimulus and consciousness in the simplest sense. Mental products— including complex thought—"are of too variable a character to

15. Wundt (1904, translation of Wundt, 1874).
16. Wundt (1897, translation of Wundt, 1896).

be the subjects of objective observation...[and] gain the necessary degree of constancy only when they become collective." Their study is thus part of social psychology: "[The] experimental method [serves] the analysis of the simpler psychical processes, and the observation of general mental products [serves] the investigation of the higher psychical processes and developments."[17] The nineteenth century thus passed without any significant experimental work being undertaken on these "higher psychical processes."

Wundt's contribution to the establishment of an independent psychological science came toward the end of an epochal period of fundamental change in European natural and social sciences. The mid-nineteenth century saw the contributions of Charles Darwin and Karl Marx, who changed human knowledge about and attitudes toward human origins and the causes of our economic behavior. Major changes occurred in most of the natural sciences, which led one commentator toward the end of the century to assert that physics was "completed." By moving toward independence from the conceptual umbrella of philosophy, psychology took a similar step forward. However, Wundt's brilliant breadth of vision was limited in its lack of attention to the psychological details of human consciousness, memory, emotion, and similar complex phenomena. That slack was taken up thousands of miles away by William James.

William James (1842–1910)

William James was born in New York City, the son of a wealthy father who was interested in the intellectual movements of his

17. Wundt (1897, translation of Wundt, 1896).

time as well as in mysticism, specifically the Swedenborgian movement. Thus William was exposed to the ideas of such contemporary figures as Henry David Thoreau and Ralph Waldo Emerson but also to the mysticism that would influence his interests in later life. The rich intellectual environment in which he lived was further embroidered by his siblings Henry and Alice. Henry James mirrored the family insights into the human condition in his literary career, and Alice James revealed her similar talents in her rich and revealing diary (which was published posthumously). William and his siblings (including two other brothers, Robertson and Wilkinson) were partially educated in Europe, where they traveled extensively. In 1861, William James began undergraduate studies at Harvard University, where he ultimately obtained a medical degree. This was followed by an exploration of the Amazon river basin with the biologist Louis Agassiz. Seeking further study in physiology, James traveled to Germany to study with Helmholtz and met the leading German philosopher psychologists, including Wundt.

In 1872, James joined the Harvard faculty. He previously had been a member of the Metaphysical Club, where he met such noted intellectuals as Oliver Wendell Holmes and Charles Peirce, and in 1875 he started teaching physiological psychology (experimental psychology), just as Wundt had done. When James finally established a laboratory of psychology, it was not for his own use since he never took to doing active research. Instead, he appointed Hugo Münsterberg, one of Wundt's student's, as the lab's first director.

James was not very active politically, though he always expressed his opinions clearly and strongly. During the war with Spain and the proposed annexation of the Philippines at the end of the century, he commented that "the way the country puked up its ancient principles at the first touch of temptation was sickening" and that America was "engaged in crushing out the sacredest thing in this great human world—the attempt of a people long enslaved" to work out its own destiny.[18]

While Wundt was handling the administrative chores of opening his psychological laboratory in Leipzig in 1879, William James was finally settling down. His marriage and his project for *The Principles of Psychology* were both in their second year, the latter not to be completed until 1890.[19] In true Jamesian fashion, however, the work appeared as a stream, published in parts, reworked, polished, and then finally put into the book. Eleven of the twenty-eight chapters were to appear in some form before final publication, eight of them between 1880 and 1887. Just as the *Principles* was to become the major reference text in the decades following its publication, so did the work in progress represent a continuing statement of one set of prevailing views about psychology. To what extent were these principles symptomatic of the age, culture, and society in which they were produced? To what extent did they herald new developments in the twentieth century? William James wrote in a century that was scientifically exciting and socially repressive. A half century that produced Darwin, Marx, and Freud also experienced the dark side of the industrial revolution, enshrined Victorian class-conscious morality, and prepared for the slaughter of 1914. James's world reached for the highest peaks of faith in human rationality and perfectibility, while around it sounded the alarms of revolutions and human misery. The giants of social thought showed the symptoms of these conflicts: Darwin

18. Tuchman (1966, p. 161).
19. James (1890).

combined the inhuman rationality of natural selection with the implied hope of perfectibility, Marx rejected rationality in human affairs but aimed for perfectibility, and Freud seemed to reject both. James was not the psychological giant of the period: that crown went to Freud. But James was a representative of both the scientific and social establishments of his day, as well as a precursor of psychology's new wave—its modernity. The major characteristic of the human sciences in the last half of the nineteenth century was a fascination with physiology and with mechano-physiological models of the organism. This preoccupation, in part a reflection of the technological leaps of the period, informed psychology as much as any other field of inquiry. Explanations of the thought or behavior of organisms were sought in physiological models. If creative theory was to be attempted, it was put into the language or the available "facts" of brain functions. Wundt's psychology was a physiological psychology, just as Freud's models were mechanical models of an imagined physiology. As a result, psychology rarely moved far from the single organism under the controlling influence of its physiology.

Wundt in his *Völkerpsychologie* was one of the few psychologists who transcended this boundary and even then relegated speculations about language and social behavior beyond the scientific pale. Such a stance, together with the emphasis on the individual (and the individual's brain), favored a psychological stance that looked at the mind and the consciousness of the single individual, an approach further reinforced by the uneasiness that a social psychology would have presented for middle- and upper-class scientists who did not wish to (or could not) examine the stresses and strains of their social world. The commitment to the individual organism and to the workings of its brain in more or less isolated transactions with the world also suggests the origins of the commitment of James and the other early psychologists to the British empiricist and associationist view of the mind.

One might have thought that in the nineteenth century a German psychology (and psychologists influenced by German thought) would have strong neo-Kantian characteristics and be concerned with structural aspects of the human mind and holistic interpretations of its workings. Instead, the mainstream of psychology (from Wilhelm Wundt to Edward Bradford Titchener to John B. Watson) as well as the Russian developments (from Ivan Sechenov to Ivan Pavlov to Vladimir Bekhterev) was associationistic in principle and atomistic in practice. Since the physiology of the nineteenth century was tailor-made for associationistic interpretations, it is likely that the commitment to physiological rather than psychological theory drove psychology in that direction. It was not until the beginning of the twentieth century that the Kantian tradition reasserted itself (in the Gestaltist movement) and structuralist views became acceptable. In contrast, it is useful to remember that the French had been characteristically unimpressed by the associationist sirens from across the channel and produced their own independent tradition that culminated in Alfred Binet, Edouard Claparède, and Jean Piaget. They also developed their own structural, localized physiology in the nineteenth century, however, in further contrast to the German and associationist commitment to brain-paths physiology. None of the above implies that William James was only a minor product of his life and times. On the contrary, his uncanny insights into the workings of the private world of consciousness and self speak to the creative fruitfulness of his contribution. James was committed to associationism and to the physiology of the day, but he was no atomist. The *Principles* has often been called primarily descriptive, and it is—to the extent that one is willing to describe James's mastery of the contents of conscious thought as "merely" descriptive. By transcending the atomistic and often artificial introspective method of the Wundtian tradition, he was able to bypass the arid examinations of minute experiences and to speak of the functions of consciousness, of the stream of human thought, of the various functions of primary and secondary memory, of the importance of attention, and of the structure of the individual self.

James's early career in medicine made him particularly sensitive to the natural experiment—the case histories that demonstrated human minds and brains as they functioned in ways different from the ordinary, the "normal." He paralleled Freud in understanding that the unexpected—the errors, the unusual aspects of human functioning—may be more useful than the litany of normal human experience and behavior. James continuously "applies" his psychology. He was full of advice for training the will, memory, attention, self-perceptions, and the like. The two major revolts against Wundtian/Titchenerian introspective atomism were the Selz-Gestalt deviation (introspective and anti-atomistic) and the Pavlov-behaviorist deviation (antiintrospective but atomistic). James surely was, in intent, a precursor of the former, although the historical lines of descent are tangled. James was one of the fathers of American functionalism. His stress on the antecedent conditions of mental life and on action presages both functionalism and behaviorism. James talks about an active organism; he displays a psychology that is influenced by the contemporary evolutionary flavor of the human sciences. Only goal-directed actions that result from some decision process are unequivocally mental (*Principles*, Vol. 1, p. 11). Mental life is seen as adaptive, and, as in the case of the emotions, it is sometimes seen as consequent on skeletal and glandular events: observable behavior becomes an important determinant of mental life. Consciousness and attention are always at the core of James's speculations. Thus, in the rambling chapter on the will, he concludes that "will consists in nothing but a manner of attending to certain objects, or consenting to their stable presence before the mind" (*Principles*, Vol. 2, p. 320). He will not go beyond this reduction; he even maintains that the motor consequences (the willed act) are a "mere physiological incident" (*Principles*, Vol. 2, p. 486). Consciousness is the crux of mental life, yet James avoids Titchener's definition of the mind as "simply the sum total of mental processes experienced by the individual during his lifetime."[20] James avoids a definition of mind altogether, although he is willing to define psychological science as concerned with "thoughts...and their relations to their objects, to the brain and to the rest of the world" (*Principles*, Vol. 1, p. 197). *Thoughts* is his preferred term for designating "all states of consciousness" (*Principles*, Vol. 1, pp. 185–186). With consciousness at the center of mental life, how is James to deal with apparent unconscious events? His treatment of unconscious automatic actions is symptomatic; they are referred to either as a lack of memory of a conscious state or as "split-off cortical consciousness" (*Principles*, Vol. 1, p. 165). In the end, consciousness becomes the primary principle of practically everything. Since thoughts cannot be unconscious, since no unconscious structures or entities are invoked, since consciousness is the root cause of mental life, what follows? "If evolution is to work smoothly, consciousness in some shape must have been

20. Titchener (1896).

present at the very origin of things" (*Principles*, Vol. 1, p. 149). Given this view, James then sees human minds as the most complex aggregation of the "primordial mind-dust" (*Principles*, Vol. 1, p. 150). For a man who calls Immanuel Kant "mythological," this seems to be a rather vulnerable position. What forced James into it? Essentially, the absence of psychological theory. I refer here to the inability of psychologists (and many other scientists) in the nineteenth century to create acceptable, useful, and convenient fictions as explanatory vehicles for psychological observations. Remember that Freud too started with quasi-physiological metaphors. The avoidance of explanatory fictions is not surprising; they had haunted the chemists and physicists for centuries in the form of alchemy, soul-stuff, and mysticism. Science could not afford to be painted with that particular brush. The only theoretical fictions that were permitted to the practitioners of the human sciences were physiological ones. Physiology seemed so far advanced that talk of brain paths and of neural connections and associations did not seem "mystical" or made up. It was "factual." Theory was totally relegated to physiology—as, for example, in this explanation of memory storage and retrieval: "The condition which makes [recall] possible at all ... is neither more nor less than the brain-paths which associate the experience with the occasion and cue of recall" (*Principles*, Vol. 1, p. 655). The ready acceptance of such a statement as an "explanation" illustrates the state of both the psychology and the physiology of the time. With the twentieth century came liberating forces whose origins still seem obscure, but convenient and useful fictions broadened psychology's reach and power.

The absence of psychological theory does make the *Principles* a descriptive work, although James is willing to become more speculative and theoretical when he moves out of the confines of the traditional psychological problem areas, such as memory, sensation, and perception. For example, he speculates that degree of self-esteem is the ratio of people's successes to their pretensions (aspirations). But this kind of endeavor stops short of speculating about social, economic, or political humanity. The avoidance of theory in psychology has pursued us through the behaviorist episode. Even Clark L. Hull introduced useful fictions that were carefully phrased in terms of diminutions of observable stimuli and responses, and B. F. Skinner still wants to leave theory (structure) to the physiologists. William James remains an excellent example of the way in which a social-scientific convention can inhibit creative thought. James did well enough, even within that constriction of theoretical thought. His work on emotion, right or wrong, engendered a rich research tradition and, by way of William Bradford Cannon's later attention, significantly moved the field forward. Only recently have we rediscovered James's important insights on attention and memory. He informed us about the distinction between retention (storage) and recollection (retrieval) long before anyone dreamed of the computer metaphor. Only recently have we rediscovered the concept of the self, and too many of us have still not absorbed James's insights into the distinction among the material, social, and spiritual (conscious) selves (although few of us have had to contend with a Swedenborgian father who rejected all notions of selfhood). His analysis of the subjective perception of time guides our current, still inadequate, attempts.

Finally, one wonders what James might have done with problems of social interaction and development, sexuality, or cross-cultural variation had he been the product of a society and a personal history that made such topics thinkable. The few indications we have suggest that he would have reflected his Victorian privileged social position, but his sensitive wisdom about the human experience would surely have enriched us. William James was a necessary and welcome part of our history. Not a man for all seasons, he was sometimes wise, at others obscure, but usually instructive about psychology, philosophy, and physiology a hundred years ago. In the *Principles*, we find the accumulation of the contemporary wisdom. After finishing them, James essentially went back to philosophy. He had said it all, and it is all there.

Hermann Ebbinghaus (1850–1909)

Hermann Ebbinghaus worked in a variety of different areas of psychology, including vision and ability testing, but his major contribution to the history of psychology was his initiation of the experimental investigation of human memory, enshrined in his 1885 book.[21] He needs also to be remembered for his early insistence on the operation of unconscious processes; his search for psychological, rather than phenomenal or physiological, theory; and the identification of major phenomena of human memory that have been neglected until recently. He also bequeathed us the nonsense syllable and endless lists to be learned and remembered. The former turned out to be not as meaningless as Ebbinghaus intended, and the latter did not lead to an understanding of memory of connected discourse or of events.

Ebbinghaus explicitly stressed the importance of his discovery of the effect of "distant associations." He saw the effect as a

21. Ebbinghaus (1885).

specific refutation of the then conventional wisdom that "ideas become associated if they are experienced simultaneously or in immediate succession." In contrast, he noted that remote associations "must find opportunity to authenticate their existence and to enter into the inner course of events in an effective way."[22] To reject one of the central tenets of the associationists was novel and courageous, and Ebbinghaus knew that he was tackling a resisting establishment. The postulation of unseen and unobservable remote associations, from an empirical psychologist, was more than the simple erection of a useful theoretical hypothesis. The idea that all the important mental events were conscious ones—that these conscious processes represented both the data and the processes that gave rise to them—had to be overcome before fruitful theory could be developed in psychology. Ebbinghaus noted that increasing the strengths of associations among events that are not part of current ideas in consciousness would "favor a more rapid growth, a richer differentiation, and a many-sided ramification of the ideas which characterize...mental life" (1913, p. 109). He concluded, somewhat tentatively, at the end of his monograph that these increases in strengths outside of consciousness included not only remote associations (in a list) but also indirect (related) associations. Ebbinghaus concluded that "if use is made of the language of psychology, then, as in the case of all unconscious processes [*unbewusste Geschehen*], expression can be only figurative and inexact" (p. 112). In other words, Ebbinghaus looked for, but did not quite trust, a psychological language sui generis.

Ebbinghaus's approach to serial order had a lasting effect. It established an associationist analysis as the preferred way to look at the way humans impose serial orders on memorial

22. Ebbinghaus (1913, pp. 108–109).

contents. To be more precise, Ebbinghaus and his descendants were concerned with the way our memory can represent serial orders that are provided for us. As I discuss in chapter 11, it was not until the 1950s that the problem was adequately addressed.

Hermann Ebbinghaus started the first section of his book with a description of three kinds of memorial effects. The first is concerned with the voluntary production of "seemingly lost states" (1913, p. 1). This kind preoccupies him in the monograph and dominated traditional verbal learning and memory research for nearly a hundred years. The second and third kinds of effect are, however, of current interest because it is only within recent years that these memorial phenomena have received intensive attention. The second kind of memory concerns the involuntary production of memorial contents; the spontaneous appearance of a mental state that is recognized as "one that has already been experienced" (1913, p. 2). As Ebbinghaus knew, these memories are "brought about through the instrumentality of other, immediately present mental images" (1913, p. 2). The third kind of effect concerns prior states that provide evidence of their lasting effects indirectly. These mental states do not return to consciousness. However, preoccupation with a certain topic facilitates under some circumstances the later preoccupation with a similar topic.[23] The investigation of conscious contents that occur without deliberate search or occur because of the activation of related topics or materials has been allowed to lie fallow. Now that we are again concerned with how people may be reminded of things, how others (such as amnesic patients) who cannot consciously retrieve material may still demonstrate adequate "memories" due to sheer activation, how

23. Ebbinghaus (1885, p. 3).

categories and topics and (even) words may be primed, we are returning to Ebbinghaus's unfinished agenda that in everyday life memories seem to pop into our minds more frequently than we consciously retrieve them.[24] I have spent some time with Ebbinghaus's contribution because he preceded the major insights of the Würzburg school in their discovery of unconscious thought (to be discussed in the next chapter). He was the only major figure, apart from Helmholtz and his discussion of unconscious conclusions (*unbewusster Schluss*) in perception, to have the courage to move psychology beyond conscious thought.

Wilhelm Wundt's and William James's Heritage: Their Successors and an Interlude in Psychology

I consider the period starting about 1880 and ending in the new century to be an interlude because it was concerned to a large extent with cleaning up the loose ends and leftovers of the nineteenth century. William James was the great summarizer and only to a lesser extent a theorist, and the great period of the British empiricists/associationists came to an end. At the same time, Titchener was playing out a rather idiosyncratic version of Wundt's psychology. During this period, major changes were taking place in the intellectual life in Europe that were to be reflected in psychology in the next century (I refer to these changes in later chapters). Both U.S. and European history and theoretical psychology were in a transitional phase of consolidation in which no major themes emerged. James was not a great systematizer, but his *Principles* was an encyclopedic work, well

24. Mandler (1994).

written and imbued with the American spirit of keeping contact with the everyday practical world. James's novel contributions were his work on emotion and on habit (the "great flywheel of society"), the developments of the notion of the "stream of consciousness," and an analysis of memory that has survived to the present. He made psychology exciting and accessible, not least by his humanity, knowledge, and writing skills. But James was entirely dedicated to an individual psychology and did not consider the human mind as it was molded by society. In a sense, he mirrors the individualism of the American frontier. For James, one moved from physiology to individual psychology, which was a natural science. For Wundt, the road branched after physiology to an experimental psychology that was a *Geisteswissenschaft* and to a social science of the human mind situated in history and society. Both of them were dedicated to bringing about a sharp break with the preceding philosophers of psychology—their rationalism and their abstract theorizing. Both were committed to empiricism, though Wundt's psychology was voluntarist, and James's was less concerned with the will and more concerned with the wheel of habit. In the United States, the commitment to empiricism was one of the new directions of psychology, and an acknowledgment of the influence of Darwinian ideas was the other. While Darwinian thought in the first few decades was often characterized by wild speculation that would put even some contemporary sociobiologists to shame, it did build a slow and solid concern with evolutionary matters in the psychological community.

James was appalled by Herbert Spencer and social Darwinism but represented the beginning of the earliest American biology- (not physiology-) oriented movement—American functionalism. These psychologists—starting with John Dewey and including such people as Harvey Carr, James Rowland Angell, and others—were concerned with the evolutionary functions of behavior on the one hand and with the establishment of empirical relationships on the other. Functionalism was contrasted with structuralism. It asked how a mental process operates, what it accomplishes, and under what conditions it appears. Central to its concerns were mental operations, not elements. Functionalists were concerned primarily with looking for empirical laws—literally, the observation and experimentation with behavior as "a function of." Their last important contribution was in 1942 with John A. McGeoch's book on human learning with chapter headings that actually were "x as a function of y."[25] In the United States, psychology in the late nineteenth century was dominated by Wundt's students, and in the years following the pilgrimage to Leipzig, there emerged a dominant figure in America—the experimental introspectionist Edward Bradford Titchener. Titchener is primarily responsible for the identification of Wundt with a dreary psychology concerned with "introspecting" the contents of mind. Titchener's trained introspectionists whose training defined what could be observed, and the mental contents thus "observed" were proclaimed to be the building blocks of mind.[26] Sheer phenomenal experience was the stuff of psychology, and in the process Titchener identified some hundreds of individual experiential elements that structured mental contents. Titchener prepared the ground for the birth of behaviorism in America in the second decade of the new century. The infertility of much of Titchenerian psychology marks the end of the introspective and atomistic

25. McGeoch (1942).
26. Titchener (1896, 1898).

tradition of experimental psychology, while the Wundtian thought on social and cultural phenomena never effectively reached the American continent—nor did it have any significant following in Europe. With the advent of a respectable experimental psychology—and the opening of the major psychological laboratories in the United States—the nineteenth century came to an end, and the first decade of the new century introduced a modernism that would manifest itself quite differently in the United States and in Germany with the advent of behaviorism and Gestalt psychology.

James and Wundt had initiated a new psychology that broke with the previous tradition of basing psychological knowledge on self-observation by looking at the psychology of the "other"—the subject, the representative of human psychology. It was primarily Wundt who initiated the psychological experiment, whereas James roamed across the psychological landscape. Neither had a solid base on which to build a psychology. They were innovators and therefore sometimes vague, repetitious, inconsistent, and unsystematic. It would be anachronistic to expect anything else or to find general systems or consistency in their work.

5 The "Discovery" of the Unconscious: Imageless Thought

If Wilhelm Wundt opened a new psychology, he also limited it with his pronouncement that experimental procedures were not applicable to "high psychical processes." However, very soon the slack created by Wundt's dicta was taken up with a vengeance at the University of Würzburg. Karl Marbe and Oswald Külpe triggered one of the most active periods in the investigation of human thought. Marbe provided much of the experimental and conceptual impetus; Külpe, though credited with the leadership of the Würzburg school, was more concerned with philosophical questions and generally encouraged the direction of the laboratory investigations. The first paper to come out of this new school was by August Mayer and Johannes Orth in 1901.[1] They, like the other members of the Würzburg group, had adopted much of the associationist theory that preceded them, but in the course of a study of qualitative aspects of the associational process (initiated by Marbe), they stumbled across an unexpected finding. While examining the thought processes

1. Mayer and Orth (1901). In brief, they discovered what, in English translation, has been called "imageless thought." "Imageless thought"—often but not always related to the absence of images—was generally thought without specific conscious representations.

intervening between a stimulus word and the subject's reaction, they found that subjects frequently reported a kind of conscious experience that was neither an image nor an awareness of an act of will or choice. They also noted that sometimes associations were made to the stimulus word without any conscious processes whatsoever, and although this finding might seem to be troublesome for a theory of thinking based on the association of images, this aspect of the problem seemed not to bother them. They were struck, however, by those conscious processes that seemed to be completely imageless. Since their subjects could not describe these processes beyond saying that they had them, Mayer and Orth were in turn helpless to say anything about them. As a solution, they coined a phrase, *dispositions of consciousness (Bewusstseinslagen)*, took note of the occurrence of these states, called them states of consciousness inaccessible to further analysis, and let it go at that.[2]

This seemingly negative finding was an extremely important one. First of all, it was an entering wedge into the closed ranks of association theory. For if thinking consists of associations between images—which had been asserted since Aristotle's time—how can there be thought with no images present? What mediates the obviously meaningful response to the stim-

2. These dispositions are not, as some have implied, entirely equivalent with "imageless thought." The best translation of the *Bewusstseinslagen* is "states of consciousness" that are not acts of will, images, or perceptions; they cannot be further analyzed. See Humphrey (1951, p. 34 n.) for suggesting "state of consciousness" in contrast to the earlier use of "attitudes," which ordinarily imply direction. The current English use for *Bewusstseinslagen* in everyday discourse is "attitudes," which sometimes confuses technical psychological discussions. "Imageless thought" is a more general term that includes *Bewusstseinslagen* but is not restricted to them.

ulus word? Perhaps even more important, however, was that Mayer and Orth were forced to invent, albeit reluctantly, a new theoretical term. In the face of their subjects' inability to describe what was going on, the psychologists were forced to remove themselves from the subjects' theorizing and to invent a term of their own. This is not to say that theoretical terms were necessarily alien to psychologists or that they were invented by the Würzburgers. Rather, this was the major step toward letting the subjects' behavior dictate the necessity for inventing such a term. Just as in other fields of psychology, the theory of thinking was forced to invent theoretical concepts to bridge an introspective void.

Alfred Binet (1857–1911) apparently came upon the imageless-thought problem independently, and he neither cited nor is cited by his German contemporaries. He discussed imageless (unconscious) thought at length in chapter 6 (*La pensée sans images*) of his 1903 book,[3] which apparently has never been translated. Binet gave extensive examples of thought processes without (conscious) imagery. He also noted that elaborate images such as those found in daydreaming were incompatible with the rapid processes of thought. As he put it, thought is an unconscious act that needs words and images to become fully conscious.[4] In contrast to the German investigators, he looked to William James for further information but found that whereas James was struck by the small part played by images in human thought, he elided the issue by suggesting that words take the place of images—that is, substitute for them.[5] Binet rejects

3. Binet (1903).
4. Binet (1903, p. 108).
5. James, *Principles* (1890, Vol. 1, p. 265; Vol. 2, p. 58).

the argument primarily because thought precedes words and also because such an argument would deprive one of sensory images.

It was an uneasy transition in the history of thought. Neither Mayer and Orth nor Marbe, with whom they were working, were able to do much with this new phenomenon, but Marbe was startled to find a similar problem in his studies of judgment. Marbe had set himself the task of determining, with the help of the new experimental method of controlled introspection, what conscious processes were involved in the act of judgment. The judgment was considered to be the most basic unit of rational thought; it had been studied intensively by logicians for centuries, and thus it was clear that a great deal was known about it. But exactly what? No distinction had yet been made between the judgment as a human act and the judgment or proposition as a statement of fact. The intertwining of logic and psychology in the history of thought frequently led to facile interpretations of reasoning and judging, such as was present in James Mill's treatment of the problem. But Marbe set for himself a genuinely psychological problem when he asked: What goes on in consciousness during the act of making a judgment? The psychological importance of Marbe's monograph on judgment, published in 1901, lies in the fact that it was the first unified study of complex thought processes. Although the monograph has also been credited with introducing the concept of *Bewusstseinslagen*, in it Marbe makes little use of that category. Having ventured into the area of judgment, he finds it necessary to justify his method in an introduction and repeats the, by then, traditional complaints against the armchair psychologists. He finds his results astounding; his subjects fail to discover any state of consciousness that is coordinated with the judgmental act. Again and again he stresses this negative finding: for example, "The present data are quite sufficient to draw the conclusion that no psychological conditions of judgments exist.... Even...the observers concerned...were extremely surprised to note the paucity of experiences that were connected with the judgmental process."[6] Marbe's major conclusions lead to the theory that judgments could not have any conscious correlates since they are based on knowledge. Like practically all his predecessors, Marbe too had difficulties with the problem of knowledge. To know something implies that we can judge the correctness of a judgment, but the judgment of correctness depends on knowledge that Marbe then relegates to a psychological disposition, a faculty. Knowledge is built into people; they either have it or not. The next major attack on knowing was to be undertaken by Narziss Ach, who introduced the notion of *Bewusstheit*, an awareness of knowledge without palpable content.[7]

In the meantime, comprehensible or not, the "dispositions of consciousness"—or *Bsl's*, as they were soon called—were here to stay. In fact, an interesting thing soon happened to them. Because subjects and experimenters were pretty much interchangeable in the Würzburg laboratories, the term Bsl found its way from the theoretical language into the protocol language of the introspecting subject. The infestation of the language of the subject with the theoretical concepts of the psychologist is beautifully illustrated in a 1906 article by August Messer.[8] The abbreviation *Bsl* in Messer's protocols refers to the fact that his subjects, who were also his colleagues working on problems of

6. Marbe (1901, p. 43).
7. Related to the contemporary notion of metacognition.
8. Messer (1906).

thinking, actually used the word *Bewusstseinslagen* (states or dispositions of consciousness) in reporting the effects of a particular stimulus.

The general nature of Messer's experiments was typical of the Würzburger school. The subject is given a task (*Aufgabe*) and then a series of stimulus words. The task may be to give the first word that the subject can think of, to give a coordinated concept for the stimulus word, or to make a judgment about a sentence. After a description of some of the quantitative (reaction-time) results, some of the images evoked by the reactions, and a long section on the psychology of judgment, Messer discusses the *Bewusstseinslagen*. Imbedded in the protocols of that section, we find examples of the following order:

Subject 4:   *"Bsl*, containing two thoughts: 1. You have to wait, 2. The coordinated object will come to you." *"Bsl*, for which I can give the thought: that's easy." *"Bsl*: There is a subordinate concept somewhere, but you can't formulate it very easily."

Subject 6:   *"Bsl*: don't say that." *"Bsl*, my father always used to mispronounce that name." *"Bsl*; you could say that at anytime."

Subject 4:   *"Bsl*: Can't I think of anything? Is that a coordinated whole? Then I remembered the word *anvil*. Then for a time being an emptiness of consciousness and then a further Bsl which went in the direction of the questions: What are you supposed to do now: Are you supposed to test or to search?"

Subject 2:   *"Bsl*: Let's take the other meaning!"

Subject 3:   *"Bsl*: Why not think about something else!"

Messer bravely attempted to classify or order this endless array of *Bsl* and came to the conclusion that what he was dealing with was not a peculiar type of conscious experience occurring now and again during the thinking process but rather was thought itself. Thus his task of classification became no less than to put order into the entire range of thought. One of the prominent aspects of his classification is the emphasis on relations. The experiencing of relations had always posed difficulties for classical associationism. How are relations among images perceived? A consistent associationist, such as Hermann Ebbinghaus was trying to be, had to say that in perceiving two tones, for example, we perceive their equality just as directly and in exactly the same way as we perceive the tones and their various qualities themselves. The difficulty of this position had been frequently criticized, perhaps most succinctly by William James, who, in the *Principles*, pointed out that the perception of A followed by the perception of B is not the same thing as the perception of B following A. With the advent of imageless thought, it was at least possible to tackle this problem, although a satisfactory solution was not to be reached until Otto Selz and later members of the Gestalt school addressed themselves to these questions. Messer seems to be groping to the conclusion that much of the thinking process goes on below the conscious level, with conscious processes attending it with varying degrees of clarity. Consciousness is beginning to take shape as the visible portion of an iceberg, with much of the work of the thinking process going on below the surface. Eventually, Messer concluded that the *Bsl* term might as well be abandoned. In a footnote, he suggests a solution that Binet had advocated previously and that Karl Bühler was to adopt in the following year:

It would probably fit language usage best if we were to restrict "thoughts" to those *Bsl*'s whose content can only be formulated in one or more sentences, while the *Bsl*'s concerned with the meaning of single words or phrases should be designated as "concepts."

In 1906, Messer only mentioned the unconscious aspects of thought *en passant*, but Ach had already treated the problem in 1905.[9] Ach worked out both an ambitious experimental program and a comprehensive theory. He proclaimed the heuristic and scientific value of "systematic self-observation," which was his phrase for the experimental technique used in the Würzburg laboratory. His theory depends a good deal on unconscious mechanisms of thought, but first I concentrate on his development of the concept of the *Bsl*. For Ach, the *Bsl* was one type of imageless thought, fitting into his larger schema of *Bewusstheit*, or awareness. The *Bewusstheiten* were described as the imageless knowing that something is the case. Although in themselves they were unanalyzable experiences, they served the purpose of bringing the elementary experience of knowing, or knowing the meaning of something, into consciousness; they are what the familiar "Uh-huh" of daily recognition is about. Around these knowings or awarenesses, Ach wove a somewhat vague physiological theory to explain when images will arise to consciousness and what degree of intensity they will attain.

To develop his theory, Ach used a wide variety of reaction experiments. The subject might be instructed to flex his right index finger when a white card was presented, to give a motor response only to a certain class of stimuli, or to name the stimulus (one of several cards of different colors) when it was presented. In more complex situations, the response might be conditional—that is, the motor response was required only when a red card was presented to the left of a white card, or a discrimination was required in which the subject reacted to one color with the right thumb and to another with the left thumb.

9. Ach (1905).

In addition, there were purely verbal tasks, such as free associations or judgments, or tasks that required the subject to give the name of the river on which a given town was situated. The introspections collected after the completion of the task dealt primarily with the main period—that is, the interval between the perception of the stimulus and the completion of the response.

In his theory, Ach noted that qualitative characteristics of the presentation are due to unconscious (that is, not conscious) effects. Determining tendencies are unconsciously acting attitudes (*Einstellungen*) that are derived from the meaning of the goal presentation and, directed toward the future coming presentation, result in the spontaneous appearance of the determined presentation. Ach is attempting to explain and utilize in his theory what were to him clear facts derived from his experimental findings: meaning, or recognition, may sometimes be carried by visual images, but at other times it occurs without their presence or before any images have crystallized. Yet his "facts" and those of Marbe and Messer were soon to be bitterly disputed. Wundt, for one, was not the man to admit the appearance of an experimental psychology of thinking that he had declared as impossible just ten years previously. And in 1907, Karl Bühler published the *nec plus ultra* of the Würzburger method in a study that did not fail to point out Wundt's previous misgivings.[10] Bühler's investigation was much more ambitious than those of his colleagues. His stimulus materials were complex questions requiring extensive thought processes that terminated in yes or no judgments; the subjects then gave a retrospective account of the processes intervening between

10. Bühler (1907) (*Würzburger Habilitationsschrift*).

stimulus and response. Bühler concluded from these protocols that there were basic unanalyzable units in the thinking process, which should simply be called *thoughts*. These units could, however, be classified into types, and three of the most important were (1) consciousness of a rule (*Regelbewusstsein*) by knowing that one can solve a problem and how it is done without actually having the steps in mind; (2) consciousness of knowing the meaning of something by "intending" it (*Intentionen*) without having the meaning content clearly in mind; and (3) consciousness of relations (*Beziehungsbewusstsein*), an awareness similar to Ach's conception. The following passage illustrates Bühler's conception of these "thoughts" and also presages the concern with the unit of thought that was to reach full flowering in the next decade.

What really is the consciousness of a rule? It is a thought in which something, that from a logical point of view we call a rule, comes to consciousness. But this does not quite unequivocally determine the concept. I could simply designate a rule just as I designate any other object. But consciousness of rule is not such thinking *of* a rule; rather it is thinking a rule or thinking according to a rule. The object of the consciousness of a rule is not the rule, but rather the state of affairs, the object, that the rule describes, on which it is used, from which it might possibly be derived. Using a distinction of Husserl's, we might say: Consciousness of a rule is a thought with which we can adequately think certain objects that the logician calls laws. There are at least two ways, . . . and not just one, in which objects can be adequately represented in consciousness, in perception. Perception is image; the other self-sufficient (adequate) object-consciousness is the consciousness of a rule. . . . One thing seems to me to be certain, that consciousness of a rule is a very frequent experience in scientific thinking.[11]

11. Bühler (1907, pp. 339–340). See also Bühler's companion articles (Bühler, 1908a, 1908b).

There is a greater emphasis in this analysis of thinking on processes than on contents, and it illustrates the influence of "act psychology" on Külpe and thus on others of the Würzburg school. In their eager attempts at classification of imageless contents, some of the Würzburgers at times had ignored the obvious active processes occurring in their thinking subjects and seemed to be harking back to the static classificatory schemes of the early associationists.

Unfortunately for Bühler, his retrospective technique of introspection, plus some incautious remarks on the necessity of sympathetic interaction between the subject and experimenter, brought swift retribution. That same year, Wundt thundered from on high. He defended his earlier position, criticized the Würzburger methods, questioned their data, and rejected their conclusions. After some fifty pages of detailed analysis, he concludes:

1. The inquiry experiments are not real experiments, but rather self-observations with handicaps. Not a single one of the requirements set for psychological experiments is met by them, on the contrary they realize the opposite of each of these requirements. 2. They represent the most inadequate of the older forms of self-observation; they occupy the attention of the observer with an unexpected, more or less difficult, intellectual problem and demand of him in addition that he observe the behavior of his own consciousness. 3. The method of inquiry must be rejected in both of the forms in which it has been used. As an inquiry prior to the experiment, it subjects self-observation to the unfavorable influence of examination pressure; as an inquiry after the experiment, it opens wide the door to the interfering influence of suggestion. In both forms the method vitiates self-observation most severely in that the subject who is to observe himself is at the same time subjected to observation by others. 4. The representatives of the method of inquiry ignore the well tried rule that in order to solve complex problems one must first master the simpler ones which the former presuppose. As a result they

confuse attention with consciousness and fall victim to a popular error in believing that everything that occurs in consciousness may easily be pursued in self-observation. This last error alone would be sufficient to explain the lack of results obtained by the inquiry experiments.[12]

Perhaps the success of the Würzburger attack can be measured by the virulence of the reply. In any case, a more dispassionate examination of their results was soon mounted by Edward Bradford Titchener. In 1909, Titchener gave a series of lectures, printed in book form as *Lectures on the Experimental Psychology of the Thought Processes*,[13] in which he summarized and analyzed the work of the Würzburg school in detail and included his own forceful objections to some of their conclusions. Primarily, he disputes that there are such things as imageless thoughts. The quarrel is a curious one. It rests on two distinct yet related problems. The first problem is to be found in the nature of introspection itself, and the second in the nature of theories of mind or thinking that would be acceptable to the two schools. If one carefully observes one's own thought processes, does one find imageless thinking or not? At first glance, this seems to be a factual question. And yet we have already noticed how the Würzburg subjects, as they became practiced in their techniques and familiar with the theoretical notions abroad in their laboratory, gradually began to describe their mental processes as imageless thought, whereas originally the term was invented to define an unexpressable experience. The *Bsl* became more and more common and eventually came to pepper the protocols. That is not to say that there was no such experience (the term was invented to fill a gap in the common language) but rather to point out the

12. Wundt (1907, p. 358).
13. Titchener (1909).

vulnerability of introspection to the theoretical language in vogue. It is quite possible that Marbe and Ach experienced the *Bsl* and that Titchener did not. Perhaps it should not be said that Titchener did not believe in imageless thought because he could not observe any such process in himself but rather that he could not observe any such process because he did not believe there was such a thing.

What is probably more important, however, is the disagreement about the kinds of statements that are to be acceptable, not only in the theoretical language of psychology but in its protocol language as well. For Titchener, as for the Würzburgers, the essence of the psychological experiment was controlled *introspection*. But he carried this principle to its ultimate conclusion, and as frequently happens to principles stretched to the breaking point, it led him into absurdities. If our experimental technique is introspection and if this is all the material we have to work with, then psychology must remain the analysis of the conscious mind. Other, unconscious processes may be taking place within the organism, but strictly speaking they are not psychological; they fall rather within the realm of physiology. What does this imply for the protocol language, the language the subjects use? First of all, rather than implicitly suggesting, Titchener directed his subjects as to the language they must use. They were explicitly trained to reduce their experience to the most basic terms possible, and these terms were prescribed—*sensations* and *affections*. The goal was "to describe the contents of consciousness not as they mean but as they are." Thus, meanings—that is, objects, relations, recognitions, and so forth—are not to be admitted to the protocol language (the "stimulus error") but are to be built up by the experimenter-theoretician out of the raw sensations as given to him by the subject. To confuse the mental process and the object—to describe the object in commonsense terms of everyday language—is to commit the "stimulus error." What Titchener required was to report the conscious content of an experience. An "apple" is not an apple so far as introspective report is concerned but is the hues, brightness, and spatial characteristics of that stimulus object. Nor should one say that one is afraid, for this is merely an interpretation; one must describe the conscious content.

The difficulties inherent in carrying out this edict are enormous. To learn to describe our familiar three-dimensional meaningful world in terms of patches of colors and vague kinesthetic images is not only difficult to the point of impossibility but also introduces some degree of distortion of the basic data. The Würzburgers before Titchener and the Gestaltists after him were at great pains to show that such sensations are not the raw data of psychology but theoretical abstractions of a high order. Indeed, when the sensationalist position is carried to its extreme, it seems literally impossible to commit the "stimulus error." As George Humphrey states in his careful analysis of Titchener's position:

[The] sensationist position endeavours in effect to analyze all experience (save affect) into pure sense datum. But such sense datum can, of itself, give no indication concerning its occasion (stimulus, as Titchener uses the word). To take a single example: Nobody experiencing simply "blue visual image . . . vague kinaesthetic image," etc., would be in the position to commit the stimulus-error of maintaining that he thought about a woman coming in secretly. [This refers to a previously given protocol.] How does he know to what these "pure" images refer unless there is something present in consciousness to tell him, and something which is of necessity of a non-sensory nature, since a complete inventory of sensory process has already been made? The *reductio ad absurdum* of the sensationist position is surely given in the following quotation from

Titchener: "I was not at all astonished to observe that the recognition of a gray might consist of a quiver in the stomach." What is there *in this particular "quiver"* to indicate that it is a recognition "quiver," or even to allow the stimulus error to be made from it? The sensationist hypothesis is in the position of precluding the error with which it taxes its opponent.[14]

What exactly did Titchener and his subjects find when they introspected on the same thought processes that the Würzburgers had investigated? What was the manner of the squabble going back and forth across an ocean via the psychological journals? Despite the quarrel about the allowable language in the protocol statements and about permissible conclusions to be drawn from these protocols, the actual descriptions elicited by subjects are highly similar, and the practical conclusion drawn is almost identical: there is "a paucity of conscious contents in much of our thinking." The theoretical conclusion is of course entirely different, but the protocols themselves, drawn from Marbe, Messer, and Ach on the one hand, or from Edmund Jacobson, T. Okabe, H. M. Clarke, and other students of Titchener on the other, could be interchanged with little noticeable difference. To take just one example from Jacobson's study in 1911 in which he visually presented words and sentences to subjects who were instructed to report everything that occurred in consciousness, Jacobson found that at least in some instances subjects reported that the sentences were meaningful to them while the visual and auditory sensations from reading the stimulus were the only conscious contents they had. He adds a footnote about his own experiences in this regard:

The writer finds that he can converse or think in words or in incipient verbal articulations, with the meaning present, while for considerable

14. Humphrey (1951, pp. 126–127).

periods of time he can discern no vestige of sensations or images other than those from the words themselves. There are, in the background, sensations due to bodily position and to general set; but while it is introspectively clear that these play an important part in the whole experience, they do not seem to vary correspondingly with the verbal meanings, as the conversation proceeds or the thought goes on.[15]

This statement is adduced as evidence for the purely sensory content of consciousness, yet it could equally well be used as a perfect illustration of imageless thought. In either case, the paucity of consciousness involved in understanding a sentence is manifest. Faced with this scarcity, Titchener seems on occasion to drop his context theory of meaning and relegate meaning to the unconscious or the physiological substratum. But once there, meaning is out of Titchener's experimental psychology, and the experimental study of thinking has reached a dead end. Indeed, the backwater in which Titchener soon found himself seems due not so much to a return to atomistic associationist principles per se as to the restriction of psychological research to the realm of consciousness and the restrictions on the theoretical language. At this point, let us return to Würzburg and meet the next problem to be faced there—that of *Aufgabe* (task), or more generally, of motive and purpose, a problem that places us squarely into the realm of the unconscious.

The unconscious was "discovered" in these studies only in the sense of noting phenomena that seemed to call for its invocation. References to unconscious processes as such go back to the antique, and its importance was underlined in significant ways from the early nineteenth century on—a topic to which I return in chapter 13.

15. Jacobson (1911, p. 572).

6 The Early Twentieth Century: Consolidation in Europe and Behaviorism in America

In the previous chapter, we saw how the new tradition attacked one of the stumbling blocks of the British associationists—the problem of elements, the atomistic conception of complex thinking being made up of simple ideas, and the dependence on the Aristotelian dogma of "no image, no thought." However, there was still left another associationist heritage—the problem of direction. Why does one train of thought rather than any other occur? What determines the direction of thinking? There was no a priori reason that an associationistic psychology should ignore problems of motivation or purpose in thinking. As noted before, the question of direction or force was already addressed by Johann Friedrich Herbart some 150 years earlier. In fact, these topics occurred occasionally throughout the various journals and books, but the mention tends to be casual, as in Thomas Hobbes's *Leviathan*, and even when James Mill introduced such concepts as desire or end to deal with directed thinking, the notion is nonetheless given a subsidiary and secondary role. For a long time, it seemed that the associative play of sensory elements would be sufficient—that no directive or motivational concept would be needed to explain the flow of thought. Even when directive notions were considered, they were couched in associationistic terms, as when James Mill speaks of a pleasurable idea of the future being associated with the means to that end. Nevertheless, by the end of the nineteenth century various extra associational principles to account for the directional aspects of thought and action began to appear. In 1889, Georg Elias Müller and Friedrich Schumann published a paper on motor set;[1] in 1900, G. E. Müller and Alfons Pilzecker talked about perseverative tendencies;[2] and in 1893, Oswald Külpe, in his *Grundriss der Psychologie*,[3] mentioned the importance of the subject's preparation in determining reactions to various stimuli.

The major credit for introducing a directional concept to the psychology of thought goes to Henry J. Watt, who wrote his doctoral dissertation at Würzburg in 1904 on this topic.[4] He investigated experimentally the effects of the task (*Aufgabe*) and demonstrated its vital importance to the course of the associations that took place in his reaction experiments. His work and that of Narziss Ach on the similar concept of determining tendencies, which was done at about the same time, created a true milestone in the history of thought. As Edward Bradford Titchener put it, their work made it impossible for any future psychologist to write a theory in the language of content alone. The beginnings were modest enough. Watt gave his subjects specific tasks to perform. When they saw the stimulus word, they were either to name an example of the class to which it belonged, to name a whole or a part of it, or to solve some similar simple problem. Not surprisingly, he found that these tasks

1. Müller and Schumann (1889).
2. Müller and Pilzecker (1900).
3. Külpe (1893).
4. Watt (1905–1906). His thesis was originally published in Watt, 1904).

were at least as important as any associations or reproductive tendencies in determining the subject's response to the stimulus word. At first, then, as the name *task* implies, the directive concept was an external or situational one. It might be conceived of as an independent variable, controlled by the experimenter and presented in the form of instructions in the same way as other stimuli were presented. Sophistication quickly set in, however. One of the first things Watt noticed was that the subject was completely conscious of the task at the beginning of an experiment but it gradually seemed to drop out of consciousness, at the same time losing none of its effectiveness in determining the course of the reactions. Here then was another glimpse of the submerged portion of the iceberg; both large parts of the content of thought and a vital controlling factor were found outside of consciousness. Watt was unwilling to commit himself on the status of this factor, stating firmly that the ideas he has propounded in his thesis do not imply "notions like the unconscious"; in fact he implies that the concept of unconscious operations is unnecessary. Rather, the *Aufgaben* seem to hold the same status as the reproductive tendencies (associative bonds); they are extraconscious rather than unconscious. The one concept provides the material of thought, and the other a kind of steering or guiding mechanism. A certain theoretical confusion is evident here, wherein *Aufgaben* can move from consciousness and the protocol language out of consciousness and into the theoretical language. Such slippage from one universe to another, common in many psychological treatises of the time, was to be criticized with growing sophistication by Kurt Koffka (see below) and later writers. Whatever the exact status of the *Aufgaben*, however, their introduction provided much needed flexibility for an associationistic theory of thought.

Whether or not Watt was ready to take the plunge into the unconscious, it was not long before others did. By the turn of the century, the unconscious was part of the Zeitgeist. The new concepts of evolutionary theory, economic theory, and Freud's work in psychological theory were all eroding the supremacy of the conscious mind in determining thought and action. While the belief in human rationality holds sway, the conscious mind must remain king. But as the belief in rationality began to be undermined, other concepts rose up to fill the breach. Behaviorism found root in this soil, and so did the unconscious. August Messer, as was shown in the last chapter, during his struggles to classify the *Bsl* came to the conclusion that much of the thinking process went on at an unconscious level. When he tackled the problem of the *Aufgaben*, he expanded the role of the unconscious, noting that their role was primarily an unconscious one. The importance of the unconscious, however, was voiced most convincingly by Ach in 1905.[5] Working at the same time but independently of Watt, he developed the concept of *determining tendencies*. The concept is very similar to that of *Aufgabe* but placed within the framework of a more elaborate theory. The unconscious nature of the determining tendencies was dramatically illustrated by his use of posthypnotic suggestions. Although the determining tendencies are similar in nature to the *Aufgaben*, there are some differences in emphasis, and they play a more complex role in the thinking process. The concept is a more truly motivational one, in the modern sense of the term; that is, it is less an external stimulus than an internal condition of the subject. Its directing functions have been expanded. In one experiment, for example, Ach demonstrated that the deter-

5. Ach (1905).

mining tendencies could influence perception as well as the course of associations. He also pointed out that a determining tendency could form a new association or reproductive tendency where none was before.

The next step in building a consistent theory of directed thinking was taken by Otto Selz, but his developments do not belong properly into the history of the Würzburg school. That movement had done its work in a period of barely more than a decade. The isomorphism between conscious experience and the processes of thinking had been rejected, and never again would psychologists insist that thinking must be amenable to detailed self-observation. Nor would it be possible for anyone to ignore the importance of directive influences on the train of thought. The importance of the Würzburg movement and the hopes for the future were summarized by Külpe in an address to the Fifth Congress of the German Society for Experimental Psychology in Berlin in 1912. It was published initially in an article in a monthly magazine on science, art, and technology.[6] The importance he ascribed to this paper is shown by his republishing of it as an appendix to his book of lectures.[7]

The new findings from Würzburg were both startling and provoking to most psychologists interested in thought, whatever their theoretical stance. And while all this ferment was in progress, the association psychologists could not and did not sit idly by. We have seen already how one sophisticated defender of the classical position (Titchener) reacted to the notion of imageless thought. At the time, the major defender of an associationist theory of directed thought was Georg Elias Müller. He published

6. Külpe (1912).
7. Külpe (1922).

an extensive critique in 1913 in which he took the Würzburgers to task—that is, after the major findings of that movement were available to him. Apart from chiding the association critics for prematurely jumping to conclusions, he quite properly indicated the vagueness of the concepts that psychologists such as Ach were trying to substitute for associative mechanisms. The tenor of Müller's critique of determining tendencies, for example, was to be echoed many years later in the criticism of so-called cognitive concepts, such as "hypothesis," by the stimulus-response theorists of the 1940s and 1950s.[8] The history of psychology in the twentieth century has repeatedly produced the phenomenon of the classical associationists keeping the cognitive rebels honest by demanding strict definitions and deductive theories.

Müller harked back to the atomism of the British associationists and gives Alexander Bain credit for originating the constellation theory of directed thinking. Later, that was to be a basis for Müller's own *Komplextheorie*, in which associative clusters combine into new complexes. However, the inadequacy of the associationist position that tries to build complex thought out of simple associations was still illustrated by Müller's argument that goal representations (images) of the new are quite adequate to account for the appearance of novelty in thought. His argument there is as vague as some of the passages for which he excoriates the Würzburgers.[9] However, Müller, like his antagonists, resorts to a concept (goal representations) that, like tasks

8. Müller (1913).

9. In the same volume in which he attacked these new developments, Müller also explored mental processes that are not strictly variants of associationism (see chapter 10).

and determining tendencies, encompasses a much larger unit of consciousness (or behavior) than do images or sensations.

We should note that Georg Elias Müller's attack on the Würzburgers was primarily motivated by his unease with the variety of concepts that they had invented to come to terms with the notion of unconscious processes. He defended a general associationism, and in his work with Schumann he developed the concepts of both retroactive and proactive inhibition.[10] What was missing was a theoretical model to replace the mere associations of his predecessors. We note some of Müller's broader conceptions in chapter 10.

While German psychologists were absorbing their new psychology, behaviorism—an entirely different development—was germinating in America. A discussion of behaviorism is important for a book on memory and thought because of the developments that it prevented in the United States. I discuss later some of the motivations of the movements that were instrumental in excluding significant parts of psychology. The stage for this epoch in American psychology was set by John B. Watson in 1913 when he advocated a "purely objective" method for the "control of behavior."[11] Behaviorism rejected Titchener and the German tradition as being irrelevant to the daily concern of people, and it would have nothing to do with the elaborate theoretical fictions arising in Germany and France. It was a psychology stripped to the bare essentials—pragmatic, at times antiintellectual, self-consciously Puritan American. Like the reformist response to Catholicism, the fancy, complex elaborations of a basic faith were rejected: behaviorism was a call for fundamentals.

10. Müller and Schumann (1894).
11. Watson (1913).

Watson's manifestos in the nineteen-teens rejected analyses of consciousness and theoretical invocations and stuck with observables—both in the environment and in behavior. Thought was subliminal speech, and (particularly with the adoption of the Pavlovian approach) complex behavior was to be understood from the combination of simple behavior rules—true of all mammals within the context of a simplistic evolutionary perspective. Watson directly tied behaviorism to the wider American concerns by stressing behaviorism's native character—that it was "purely an American production."[12] Erwin Esper noted how extraordinary that statement was, coming from a pupil of the (German-born) protobehaviorist Jacques Loeb, a student of Herbert Spencer Jennings and (the British) Charles Scott Sherrington who picked up much of his experimental method from (the Russians) Pavlov and Vladimir Bekhterev.[13] So much for the "myth of the immaculate conception of American behaviorism."

The initial success of behaviorism spawned a variety of different strands and directions. Central to nearly all of them was a preoccupation with simple mammalian rules that enthroned *mus norvegicus* as the major focus of research. In contrast to the radical behaviorists, some theoretical entities entered the fold, including Edward C. Tolman's influential cognitivist labors, deviant from the dominant associationist thinking.[14] But even when theory was invoked, it never strayed far from a language

12. Watson (1919, p. vii).

13. Esper (1964, p. v).

14. Though the physicalism of behaviorism was not universal. Skinner used a functionalist, nearly cognitive-informational, definition of stimuli and responses.

tied to stimuli and responses, as in Clark L. Hull's ambitious, but in the end failed, system. It may still be too early to determine which of the various strands that influenced the development of behaviorism was more important than any other. Suffice it to say that the movement itself was consistent with a number of old and new American cultural and social values. It also had its kindred movements in such developments as the drive for scientific management and the time-and-motion studies of Frederick W. Taylor designed to make the American worker more productive at less cost.[15]

In the early twentieth century, the United States was turning inward to a new American consciousness. In science and philosophy, the new twentieth century was marked by a pragmatic, antitheoretical preoccupation with making things work—a trend that was to find its expression in psychology in John B. Watson's behaviorism. I add a remark of Alexis de Tocqueville's that is apposite of the behaviorist development and relates its origin to a more lasting tradition of American democracy: "democratic people are always afraid of losing their way in visionary speculation. They mistrust systems; they adhere closely to facts and study facts with their own senses."[16]

Relevant to the topic of memory and thinking are some arguments of Watson's that have often been neglected. Watson's dismissal of the introspectionism of his predecessors is well known and documented.[17] In addition, another part of his attack against the established psychology contained the seeds of the failure of his program. In his behaviorist manifesto of 1913,

15. Taylor (1911); see also Schwartz (1986).
16. Tocqueville (1889, p. 35).
17. See, for example, Baars (1986).

Watson, who had been doing animal experiments for some years, claimed to be "embarrassed" by the question of what bearing animal work has on human psychology and argued for an investigation of humans that is the same as that used for "animals." In the first paragraph of his 1913 manifesto, he asserted: "The behaviorist, in his efforts to get a unitary scheme of animal response, recognizes no dividing line between man and brute."[18] The manifesto was in part a defense of his own work, a way of making it acceptable and respectable. Watson's preoccupation with marking his place in American psychology was also noticeable in his treatment of his intellectual predecessors. He referred to "behaviorists"—that is, his colleagues in work on animal behavior—but there was no acknowledgment that animal researchers such as George John Romanes, C. Lloyd Morgan, or Jacques Loeb were his conceptual predecessors and pathfinders. He did give credit to Walter B. Pillsbury for defining psychology as the "science of behavior."[19]

Watson's continuing argument was clothed primarily in the attack on structuralism and Titchener's division of experience into the minutiae of human consciousness.[20] However, he expanded the argument for behaviorism on the basis of using animal experiments as the model for investigating human functioning. The following year, in his banner book,[21] Watson complained even more strongly that his work on animal learning and related topics had not been used in our understanding of human psychology. Watson's unification of human and non-

18. Watson (1913, p. 158).
19. Watson (1913).
20. Titchener (1910, especially pp. 15–30).
21. Watson (1914).

human behaviors into a single object of investigation prevented a psychology of the human from being established, and in particular it avoided sophisticated investigations of human problem solving, memory, and language. Eventually, behaviorism failed in part because it could not satisfy the need for a realistic and useful psychology of human action and thought.

Watson's goal was the prediction and control of behavior, particularly the latter when he equates all of psychology with "applied" psychology. There is the reasonable suggestion, made *inter alia*, that we need to be (as we have since learned to call it) methodological behaviorists—that is, concerned with observables as the first order of business of our, as of any, science. Postbehaviorist psychologies did not ask for the feel or constituents of conscious experience but rather were concerned with observable actions from which theories about internal states could be constructed.

Watson's influence was probably most pervasive in his emphasis on the stimulus-response (S-R) approach. The insistence on an associative basis of all behavior was consistent with much of the empiricist tradition. The exceptions were Tolman's invocation of "cognitive maps" and B. F. Skinner's functional behaviorism. However, most behaviorists seriously attempted to follow Watson's lead in insisting on the action of stimuli in terms of their physical properties and on defining organism response in terms of its physical parameters—the basis for a popular reference to behaviorism as the psychology of "muscle twitches." The position was a direct result of working with nonhuman animals, for whom it was at least difficult to postulate a "cognitive" transformation of environmental events and physical action. Skinner, on the other hand, used functionalist definitions of stimuli and responses as eliciting/discriminative conditions and operant behavior.[22] However, his initial focusing on the behavior of pigeons and rats also alienated him from research on specifically human functions, and it is likely that Noam Chomsky's (somewhat misleading) review of Skinner's *Verbal Behavior* put him beyond the pale of the burgeoning cognitive community.

One of the consequences of Watson's dicta was the switch to animal work in the mainstream of American psychology. The following table shows the shift over decades into animal work as well as its subsequent decline in the primary journal, the *Journal of Experimental Psychology*:

Articles in the *Journal of Experimental Psychology*

Year	Number of Articles	Percentage of Nonhuman Subjects	Editor
1917	33	0%	John B. Watson
1927	33	6	Madison Bentley
1937	57	9	Samuel W. Fernberger
1947	50	30	Frank I. Irwin
1957	67	22	Arthur W. Melton
1967	87	15	David A. Grant
1977*	20	10	Gregory A. Kimble

Note: * These data are for *JEP*'s successor journal, the *Journal of Experimental Psychology: General.*

This rise and decline in animal research took place independently of the interests of the editors, the majority of whom were in fact not doing research on nonhuman subjects. It also

22. Skinner (1995).

illustrates the basis of the developing unhappiness among the many psychologists who were doing research on human memory and related topics at being shut out of the most prestigious publication outlets (see below). When human subjects were used, they frequently participated in studies of eyelid conditioning and related topics in uncomplicated (noncognitive?) conditions and environments. For example, in addition to the 30 percent animal studies in the 1947 volume, another 14 percent were on conditioning.

At the theoretical level, very little of Hullian theory was applicable to complex human behavior. John Dollard and Neal Miller[23] presented a major attempt to integrate personality theory (mostly derived from Freud) into the Hullian framework, and Charles Osgood tried to explain much of human action in terms of associationist mediation theory.[24] The major attempt to apply Hullian principles to more complex human behavior was in the volume on a mathematico-deductive theory of rote learning.[25] Apart from a somewhat naive and rigid positivism, the theory generated predictions (primarily about serial learning) that were patently at odds with existing information, its logical apparatus was clumsy, and predictions were difficult to generate. The book generated no follow-ups of any influence nor any body of empirical research. It was irrelevant. The proposals developed few consequences, and together with the insistence that thought processes could be reduced to implicit speech, it was generally accepted that the Hullian approach had little to offer to an understanding of human thought and action.

23. Dollard and Miller (1950).
24. Osgood (1953).
25. Hull et al. (1940).

There is a wealth of anecdotal information about the difficulty of getting research on complex human functions into print during the behaviorist period. Much of the work was eventually reported in relatively obscure (and essentially unrefereed) journals like those of the Murchison group (such as the *Journal of Psychology* and the *Journal of Genetic Psychology*) and *Psychological Reports*. One example of work sidelined into secondary journals was research on clustering (categorical and otherwise) in memory organization and related activities. Weston Bousfield started these major deviations from the stimulus-response orthodoxy with a paper in 1953.[26] When James J. Jenkins and associates sent Arthur Melton, a major establishment stalwart, one of their (later influential) papers, they were told by Melton, scribbled across their submission letter, that "this would be of no interest to my readers."[27]

As I have indicated, one of the reasons that stimulus-response behaviorism and research on human memory and thought were incompatible was the physicalism of the S-R position. The eliciting stimuli were defined in terms of their physical characteristics, and, in principle, responses were either skeletal/muscular events or their equivalents in theoretical terms. Such concepts as the "pure stimulus act" and rg (r for the implicit response and g for the anticipated goal) were theoretical notions that were to act implicitly in the same manner as observable behavior and were intended to do much of the "unconscious" work of processing information.[28]

26. Bousfield (1953).

27. Personal communication, James J. Jenkins.

28. Greenwood (1999) has discussed in detail the shortcomings of Hullian psychology with respect to representation and conceptual processing.

In the absence of mainstream interest in those areas, research on *human information processing*, as the cognitive movement was called early on, moved to new or neglected areas of research (such as free recall and problem solving) rather than attacking research with nonhuman animals.

The Würzburg school had successfully changed the psychology of thought. The next developments—which were mostly concerned with the unit of thought—went in new directions and represented the psychology of the first half of the twentieth century in Europe.

7 The Interwar Years: Psychology Matures and Theories Abound

New approaches to empirical psychology were conceived and developed during the years between the two world wars. Most of the developments took place in Europe. The major players were the German successors to the Würzburg school, such as Gestalt theory, as well as advances in the francophone countries. I stress the dominant German psychologies whose glories were, with the advent of German fascism, soon followed by their shame.

I start with the flourishing of new ideas up until the 1930s, starting with the notion that, at least since the days of John Locke, assumed that mental life went from the simple to the complex and that complex operations were painstakingly constructed out of elementaristic components. As was shown earlier, David Hartley made explicit the notion that complexity equals summation. This seemed such an obvious formulation that it was difficult to combat, and it was not until the beginning of the twentieth century that serious consideration was given to the proposition that complex units and operations may be acquired and used in one fell swoop. Unhappiness with atomism had been around for some time, however, and it seemed patently obvious to some writers that thinking could not be reduced to a conglomeration of images and ideas. William James, for example, had clearly posed the problem in 1890 in relation to perception:

We certainly ought not to say what usually is said by psychologists, and treat perception as a sum of distinct psychic entities, the present sensation namely, plus a lot of images from the past, all "integrated" together in a way impossible to describe. The perception is one state of mind or nothing.[1]

And in discussing the stream of thought, he cuts the Gordian knot that had made the concept of "relation" such a puzzle for the associationists:

There is no manifold of coexisting ideas; the notion of such a thing is a chimera. Whatever things are thought in relation are thought from the outset in a unity, in a single pulse of subjectivity, a single...feeling, or state of mind.[2]

No part of the new psychology of thinking produced a greater departure from tradition or a more revolutionary attitude than the notion that the elementaristic particles of association psychology could not in principle do justice to the problems of complex thought.[3] To abandon once and for all the conception of larger units of consciousness being glued and pieced together out of atomistic ideas and sensations meant to create a new vocabulary and new theories. Slowly, the conviction that the mind contained such new and wondrous things as tasks, sets, and goal representations had gained adherents. Even the associationists admitted these new entities, though often in the role of *dei ex*

1. James, *Principles* (1890, Vol. 1, p. 80).

2. James, *Principles* (1890, Vol. 1, p. 278).

3. In America, it was John Dewey who carried on James's battle against elementarism during the early twentieth century.

machina. The new theories used these new units as their building blocks, not as crutches. Environmental inputs set into motion a vast apparatus of complexes, structures, and directing mechanisms—none of which were to be found in consciousness, and many of which represented whole trains of ideas or sensations and replaced these particles with complicated hypothetical processes that restructured, organized, and molded the process of thinking.

Probably the major turning point in the history of thinking came with the work of Otto Selz. Although Selz studied with some of the Würzburg psychologists, his *magna opera* were written elsewhere and published in 1913 and 1922.[4] Not only does he deal in these two volumes with the problem of directed thinking, but he is the first psychologist who is both willing and able to deal with the problem of productive thinking under the same rubric as reproductive thought. Neither his original two volumes of work nor the summary of his theory of productive and reproductive thinking[5] received adequate attention during the ensuing years. Selz himself restricted his work in subsequent years, spent in a minor academic position in Mannheim, to a restatement of his position, and much of the psychology of thinking between 1920 and 1950 might have advanced faster had his work been used more extensively. He was killed during the 1940s in a German concentration camp.

Selz's primary reaction was against the constellation theory of the associationists. His major source of data and concepts can be found in the essentially descriptive work of the Würzburg school. However, he also represents the confluence of another

4. Selz (1913, 1922).

5. Selz (1924).

point of view insofar as some of his ideas can be traced to the act psychology of Franz Brentano and to Alexius Meinong[6] in particular. It seems plausible that one of Selz's main contributions—the notion of the actively processing mental apparatus—derives from the influence of the German philosophers, whereas the content of his theory is more clearly influenced by the psychology of association and the Würzburg school. Whatever his antecedents, Selz was the first voice in the early twentieth century to call for a psychology of thinking that dealt primarily with processes rather than with contents. Instead of posing problems for a theory of thinking, he saw his task as the construction of a predictive and explanatory theory that related environmental events to the products of human thought. As Adrian de Groot has phrased it, Selz constructed "a conceptual model for thought processes.... [He] sounds much like modern model builders, who first of all strive for a system of general laws, logical consistency, and precision—if possible even in axiomatic form."[7] This very search for precision and explicitness earned him the epithet "machine theorist" from some of his successors, such as the Gestalt theorists Wilhelm Benary and Kurt Koffka.

Starting with a critique of the constellation theory, Selz advanced his theory of specific acts—responses that are specific to the structured complex of the task before the subject. Responses (thoughts) exist within systems that produce the missing links in reproductive thinking and that attain the assimilation of new responses in productive thinking. The existing structure of responses in a sense demands a particular comple-

6. Meinong (1904).
7. de Groot (1964).

tion by the use of anticipatory schemas rather than permitting a haphazard trial-and-error search in a welter of all possible response tendencies. Different systems, determined by the task and other experimental conditions, will be completed by different specific responses. Thus, the unit of thought becomes a structured system of responses or thoughts rather than a string of elementary particles. In 1927, Selz published a summary of his system.[8] In some passages, such as his notion of operations, he reads like a contemporary writer on thought, and the modernity of his ideas was attested by work in midcentury that tied Selz's theory to work on problem solving and computer simulation.[9]

The line of development that stretches from the Würzburgers to Selz and to the Gestalt school is nicely illustrated in a dispute over priorities. In 1925, Koffka published an article on psychology in a general handbook of philosophy.[10] In 1926, Karl Bühler and Selz[11] critically evaluated Koffka's article and charged that Koffka had "borrowed" his theory of thinking from Selz without giving the latter adequate credit. The attack was both strident and pertinent enough to move Koffka to publish a reply in 1927[12] in which he defended himself against the accusation on the grounds that "since Selz's theory is essentially ... different from mine I cannot very well have borrowed my theory from Selz." The essential difference apparently lies in Koffka's

8. Selz (1927).

9. Newell, Shaw, and Simon (1958). See also de Groot (1964) and de Groot's (1946) earlier exposition and use of Selz's theory.

10. Koffka (1925).

11. Bühler (1926); Selz (1926).

12. Koffka (1927).

insistence on the emergence of new qualities: *meaning* is the essential quality of the natural process *thinking*; *structure* develops out of processes and is not produced by external factors. He calls Selz's theory a machine theory that leaves little or no room for the inherent emergence of novel productions and processes. Eighty years later, it seems that the difference is a minor one and that modern thought has tended to prefer Selz's "machine" position against the nativism of the Gestaltists. The growth of the psychology of thinking, however, need not be evaluated in terms of priorities. The important aspect is that a structural psychology of thinking was being developed in contrast to the constellation theory.

Starting with Christian von Ehrenfels in 1890,[13] the notion of Gestalt qualities had made some inroads into sensory psychology, but it was not until the 1920s that Gestalt psychology became concerned with problems of thinking. I return to this aspect of the Gestalt movement later. For the time being, it is useful to stress another aspect of the contribution of Gestalt psychology. It is quite apparent that by the time Selz wrote his theory of thought, psychologists had abandoned the notion that all the concepts used to explain the thinking process must be found in consciousness. Tasks, determining tendencies, and anticipatory schemas were all theoretical notions constructed from the data available to the psychologist. But this development had taken place nearly unnoticed, and soon the Gestalt psychologists were to come along with Gestalt qualities and the laws of organization—none of which were even remotely "given" in consciousness. With this step, the break with a tradition that demanded that thinking be explained in terms of

13. Ehrenfels (1890).

introspective evidence was practically complete. However, one other traditional attitude had to be changed before psychology would come of age. In 1912, Kurt Koffka argued convincingly for a distinction between descriptive and functional concepts.[14] Koffka's analysis of imagery clearly states the difference between the data of immediate experience and the concepts constructed by the scientist. Koffka pointed out that many of his contemporaries had been unable or unwilling to make such a distinction, which was to become diagnostic of the age when behaviorism was being born in America. The Gestalt school's commitment to this distinction was underlined by Koffka's expression of debt to Wolfgang Köhler and Max Wertheimer for many useful discussions.

Koffka's preoccupation with the nature and use of theoretical concepts was not only reflected in the work of the Gestalt school. In 1917, Edouard Claparède, for example, who was to stress the importance of "hypotheses" in problem solving, used a method of thinking aloud as an experimental technique. He was careful, however, to distinguish between these protocols and introspection, and he warned against treating them as identical.[15] In the same year, in *The Mentality of Apes*, Köhler made the subject-scientist distinction, although perhaps his subjects gave him an unfair advantage in arriving at this conclusion. Speaking of insightful solutions to problems given to his apes, he says that

[it] often follows upon a period of perplexity or quiet (often a period of survey), but in real and convincing cases, the solution never appears in a disorder of blind impulses. It is one continuous smooth action, which

14. Koffka (1912).
15. Claparède (1917).

can be resolved into parts only by abstract thinking by the onlooker; in reality they do not appear independently.[16]

In some ways, Köhler's book is more relevant to the studies of animal learning that had begun to appear in the early twentieth century than it is to the topic of this book. Much of his argument against blind trial-and-error behavior is focused on Edward Lee Thorndike's version of association theory, and even in 1917 it was already outmoded as an argument against associative models of human thinking. He did, however, formulate the concept of "insight," and in so doing laid out a battleground to be well littered during the next decade with the reputations of both human and animal psychologists. In retrospect, much of the controversy seems to have been unnecessary and was due in large part to an inadequate understanding of what was meant by the term *insight*. Although Köhler himself later changed its definition, it is clear from the following passage what was meant at the time:

We can, in our own experience, distinguish sharply between the kind of behavior which from the very beginning arises out of a consideration of the structure of a situation, and one that does not. Only in the former case do we speak of insight, and only that behavior of animals definitely appears to us intelligent which takes account from the beginning of the lay of the land, and proceeds to deal with it in a single, continuous, and definite course. Hence follows this criterion of insight: *The appearance of a complete solution with reference to the whole lay-out of the field. . . .* How one is to explain that the field as a whole, the relations of the parts of the situation to one another, etc., determine the solution, belongs to the theory. Here we have only to exclude the idea that the behavior of the animals is to be explained by the assumption according to which the solution will be accomplished without regard to the structure of

16. Köhler (1925, p. 191, originally published in 1917).

the situation, as a sequence of chance parts, that is to say, without intelligence.[17]

"The theory" was in the process of being worked out by Köhler, by Wertheimer, and by Koffka. Most of the work, both theoretical and experimental, was carried on in the field of perception and on related problems of recall and memory. Throughout this time, the theoretical tools were undergoing a profound change. A vocabulary of wholes and structures was in the making, but these were not merely new elements to be associated as sensations once had been and to be held together by directional forces such as the determining tendency. Directional concepts were to be allowed no special status. For example, in his treatise on problem solving, Karl Duncker explicitly rejected this aspect of the work of Norman R. F. Maier,[18] who had suggested that thinking consists of combining previous experiences in new patterns under the influence of an organizing principle of direction. Duncker refuses even this remnant from the associationist approach:

There exists as little fundamental difference between "direction" and "the elements to be combined" as between "direction" and "problem." For these elements combine with one another with only apparent simultaneity. In reality, they usually follow upon one another in a sequence in which each element possesses problem-character (thus "direction"-character) with respect to the following, and solution-character with respect to the preceding elements.[19]

The new units were to be basic, and the laws of association to be considered subordinate. The elements of any mental process

17. Köhler (1925, pp. 190–191, originally published in 1917).

18. Maier (1930).

19. Duncker (1945, p. 17).

are not discrete units combined into complex structures. The structures are given in the first place, and the laws of association of any part with any other are determined by the laws of the total structure—not vice versa. As a result, association by contiguity is recast in the light of meaningful contiguities within structures, and problems of recall and other memory functions are based on association by similarity, which in turn is a function of the structural requirements of a percept. It is clear, therefore, that not the associative processes but the structures themselves needed study, and to this end Gestalt psychology turned primarily to the field of perception, secondarily to the study of changes in percepts over time, and only finally to other processes. One of the early essays concerned with a Gestalt analysis of thought is Wertheimer's disquisition in 1920 on syllogistic reasoning.[20] The goal of this undertaking was most ambitious; Wertheimer wanted to know no less than "How does thinking really work?" Though the ambition sometimes outdistances explanatory achievement, whatever one might think of such terms as "recentering" and the "inner necessity of the whole," at a descriptive level Wertheimer's account challenges any theory of thinking. Gestalt theory may not have significantly advanced our understanding of the structure of the cognitive apparatus, but its representatives did have the courage to tackle the most difficult problems.

Wertheimer's interest in "thought processes in actual affairs" illustrates (just as Köhler's previous emphasis on insight did) one of the distinguishing characteristics of the Gestalt school—a concern with the determinants and functions of intelligent behavior. Not until the second half of the twentieth century was

20. Wertheimer (1920).

there a revival of general interest in the mental processes involved in intelligent behavior, a field kept fitfully alive after the promising beginning made by such men as Alfred Binet and Claparède in the first part of the century. Jean Piaget was probably the most insistent in promoting this view of intelligence. Ironically, Binet's very success with his intelligence test tended to obscure for many years his more fundamental concern with the problem of intelligence.

The most detailed and thoroughgoing attempts to extend Gestalt theory to the field of thinking were published by Karl Duncker in 1926 and 1935.[21] Duncker started his analysis of productive thought processes within a framework very similar to Selz's. The latter had recognized the difficulties association theory faced in dealing with relations such as "part of," "cause of," and "equal to," and he had included these relations among the experimental structures to be learned, to be incorporated into larger complexes, and to be applied to new problems. Duncker used the basic units of Gestalt theory to handle these relations. He did not consider them as learned, but rather, for the most part, as dynamically and perceptually given by the nature of the problem and the structure of the mind. Although he granted that types or classes of solutions can be acquired and then applied by *resonance* (a term taken from Claparède and denoting association by similarity) to new situations, he thought that this approach left certain basic questions unanswered. If the solution is correct, how is it achieved, why is a particular schema brought to bear on the problem? If it is incorrect, why has that particular mistake been made? Mistakes or successes may be traced to the blind applications of previously

21. Duncker (1926, 1935).

learned principles, but if we are to understand how, aside from chance, correct solutions are reached, we must discover what is demanded by the situation as given. In short, we must examine the structural requirements of the problem if we are to understand the subject's behavior within that situation.

Thus, Duncker's entire work becomes an explication of *insight*, although he places no particular emphasis on that term. Duncker applies the organization and dynamics of structures to problems of thought, but he is equally interested in the problem of the logical relation of a problem to its solution. He asks how human thought can obtain information about the nature of a conclusion from the nature of the premises. This is a very different question from that asked, for example, by David Hume. Duncker's question is not epistemological but primarily psychological. I have touched only briefly in these pages on the relation of logic to thought, in part because it represents a different tradition from the one followed here but also because until theories of thinking began to approach the sophistication of theories of logic, there was little hope of disentangling the two. It was only when logic, thought, and logical thought were clearly demarcated in modern times that the real argument over the relationship of each to the other began. Only after the rift had become a chasm did it seem requisite to begin fitting them together again. This time, however, it was the psychologist who explored the nature of logical relations as they influence thought, not the philosophers using the psychology of thought (such as it was) to construct their logic. These problems have stayed with us until the present, influencing points of view ranging from cognitive development to computer simulation. In this sense, Duncker, as well as Wertheimer, was influenced more by Kant than by Hume. There is the implied assumption that the mind is constructed in such a way that certain logical relations are imposed on the world, rather than being built up out of our experience of the world, though Duncker himself expressed the opinion that he differs from Kant on this point.

There was an aura of optimism hovering over Duncker's work, as if the hope of rationalism had again touched the psychology of thought. Both the world and the mind are constructed in such a way that the processes of interaction between the two can be laid bare by careful analysis. Thought, in its very nature, tends to be intelligent—that is, insightful—though it must be added that, as they are used by Duncker, these terms have lost much of their commonsense and therefore controversial meaning. Thought is insightful when it understands what it is thinking about, and the basis of that understanding is to be found by structural analysis. Although lip service is paid to the role of past experience, the history of the organism is underplayed in favor of analysis of current processes. The aura of optimism became a positive halo in Wertheimer's *Productive Thinking*. Wertheimer, a major source of inspiration and concepts for the Gestalt school, worked on and off during his lifetime on problems of thinking but barely completed his theory shortly before his death. His book[22] was published posthumously in 1945, but unfortunately the conclusions that he reached were more programmatic and hortative than theoretical. The experiments reported in his book are similar in nature to the problems with which Duncker worked; indeed they formed the basis for much of Duncker's work. In any case, Wertheimer's influence on the history of thinking as such extends well beyond the period covered in this volume. As we have suggested earlier, Wertheimer posed

22. Wertheimer (1945).

problems and questions for the associationists of the mid-century just as Bühler had done for Wilhelm Wundt and his followers. With Wertheimer, and some time earlier with Koffka,[23] the Gestalt theory of thinking had reached its peak of development—and probably also of influence. The problems that Köhler, Duncker, and the others had posed were to remain important goads for any theory of thinking. But the concepts of Gestalt theory have failed to catch fire. The reasons for this failure are probably threefold: first, the evidence failed to materialize that the Gestalt laws of perception could be easily incorporated into the theories of other areas of psychology; second, right or wrong, the nativism of the theory was alien to the prevailing empiricism and genetic approach of the period; and finally, there was an increasing demand for theories that permitted unequivocal statements and elegant deductions, two demands that Gestalt theory could not pretend to fulfill. The best available history of the background and development of Gestalt theory has been presented in a thorough and insightful treatment by Mitchell G. Ash.[24]

However, the basic issues and problems remained whatever the fate of Gestalt theory, and the emphasis on structural factors and the intensive analysis of situational determinants was to be carried forward by other thinkers, just as Kurt Lewin's demands in these respects fruitfully influenced other fields of psychology. In retrospect, it is clear that the history of thinking from early associationism to the Gestalt period unfolded drastic changes in theoretical stance and also in the kinds of questions that were being asked. From an examination of the flow of images and

23. Koffka (1935).
24. Ash (1995).

thought, we have moved to the analysis of problem solving. With the departure of conscious contents as the privileged subject matter of psychology, it has become possible to conjecture what processes might intervene between the asking of a question and the production of an answer and also between the posing of a problem and its solution. Just at the time that the results of the Würzburgers became common coin, the marriage between behaviorism and associationism produced a stream of development that was to interfere with the normal development of a psychology of thinking. Some of the battles that Georg Elias Müller and Selz fought were to be staged all over again some thirty and forty years later. But behaviorism also encouraged the interest in problem solving, which seemed to be less tarred with the introspectionist brush than other fields of thinking. Another area of research that slowly became identified with the psychology of thinking developed during this period—concept learning and attainment. When we look retrospectively at the problem of thinking in the first four centuries, we can see that, like much of philosophy, it fathered many independent empirical offspring and problems. Early theories of thought developed into problems of sensation and perception, nineteenth-century associationism gave rise to studies of human memory, questions about the nature of intelligence gave way to the intelligence tests, and the determining tendencies flowered into problems of motivation and attitude.

Once the problems of war and reconstruction were overcome, new concerted attacks were being launched on the elusive central problems. The notion of structure gained acceptance, though the structures that Piaget, for example, found in his subjects were derived from the active interplay between organism and environment and not from postulated qualities of the mind. Rigorous theorizing has been made possible—and sometimes mandatory—by the availability of the modern computers. The battle over associationism is continuing, though *sotto voce*, but the new theories of thinking have often benefited from, if not explicitly acknowledged, the various successes and failures of the psychologists discussed in these initial chapters. Before we proceed to the new psychologies that were generated by the information age and the cognitive revolution, we must consider the ravages of the fascist dominance in Europe, as well as their consequences.

8 The Destruction of Psychology in Germany, 1933 to 1945

This chapter and the next are—in some sense—a diversion. They do not discuss the content or the development of psychological theory and practice; rather, they deal with historical events and their specific effects on the history of psychology. The effects of Adolf Hitler and his ideologies are only rarely detailed in histories of psychology. I believe they are an integral part of that history, in part because of the destruction of a discipline by a fascist ideology and in part because the center of gravity of experimental psychology shifted from Germany to the United States. In the next chapter, I repair the previously neglected need to document the shift from Europe to America. The account concentrates on the background of the psychologists who came to America as their influence prepared the background for the American psychology of the second half of the twentieth century.

The destruction of psychological science during the early years of Germany's National Socialist (NS) regime is an important part of psychology's history. Given the preeminence of German psychology during the early years of the twentieth century, it is important to understand how psychology in Germany was destroyed as a viable field of knowledge with the advent of the

National Socialist regime in 1933. The intellectual and moral fiber of German psychology were undermined and disabled by the brutal ideology of the regime with the connivance of influential leaders of German psychology. My discussion is based mainly on the proceedings of the congresses of the German Society for Psychology.[1]

The 1933 Congress

Psychology started the National Socialist era with a postponement. Hitler was appointed German chancellor in January 1933. The Thirteenth Congress of the German Society for Psychology was scheduled for that year in Dresden in April, which had been the traditional month of meeting of the biannual congress. However the thirteenth congress was postponed until October and took place in Leipzig from 16 to 19 October.[2] I first examine the changes in the executive board of the society and the accompanying *Gleichschaltung*[3] of the psychological establish-

1. Most of this chapter is taken from Mandler (2002d), which was based on the *Proceedings* of the Society. For more detailed discussions and a more extensive bibliography of relevant sources and elaborations, see the original article. I use the original German when dealing with National Socialist terminology and neologisms, together with the appropriate translation. In particular, *Volk* needs to be read as "German race," rather than just "folk." I use the abbreviation *NS* rather than the colloquial *Nazi* to refer to the ideology of the National Socialist party (NSDAP).

2. Klemm (1934).

3. The term *Gleichschaltung* can be translated literally as "synchronization," but the term represented a widely used threat used to bring public and private institutions and firms into conformity with National Socialist doctrines and requirements. The best translation is probably "enforced conformity."

ment. Tracing its development, we find that in 1929, at its meeting in Vienna, the board had seven members: Karl Bühler, William Stern, Hans Volkelt, Narziss Ach, David Katz, Johannes Lindworsky, Walther Poppelreuter.[4] Volkelt and Lindworsky left the board for unknown reasons, and in 1931 the board consisted of the remaining five plus Felix Krueger. Until 1933, the tradition was that each congress was to be chaired by the local academic luminary: Bühler in Vienna, Stern in Hamburg, and Gustav Kafka, the professor in Dresden, was added in anticipation of the Dresden congress. In 1933, there were five new members of the board (Otto Klemm, J. Handrick, Erich Jaensch, Oswald Kroh, Johann B. Rieffert), all of whom had already expressed their loyalty to National Socialist ideas and leadership early in 1933. Poppelreuter, Rieffert, and Volkelt appeared at the congress in the brownshirt *Sturmabteilung* (SA) uniform. Kafka had strongly opposed any notion that any of the Jewish members of the society be excluded from the Congress, and he delayed its preparatory work. At the same time, an article in one of the more vicious NS journals (*Freiheitskampf*) announced that appropriate measures to cleanse the organization would be undertaken and that one could not guarantee the congress an undisturbed meeting. The congress was postponed and shifted from Dresden to Leipzig under the chairmanship of Krueger after Kafka resigned from the board, as did Bühler (whose wife was Jewish), Stern, and Katz (both of whom were Jewish). We do not know whether these resignations were voluntary or forced by threats. Ach and Poppelreuter continued from 1929

4. Whenever lists or serial mentions of people appear, I cite them in the order in which they appear in the *Proceedings*. When no other source is given, page references refer to the relevant volume of the *Proceedings*.

to 1931 and 1933. Handrick was a curious addition. He was a nonacademic, a *Regierungsrat* (higher administrative functionary) in the labor ministry in Berlin and in 1931 was director of the *Berufsamt* (employment bureau) in Dresden. He had just (in 1933) become head of the German Society for Applied Psychology, in another NS takeover, and was apparently the first government official to become a member of the Society's executive board.

The retention and appointment of some of these men becomes obvious when we examine their contributions to the congress. In general, the theme of the 1933 congress was changed from the psychology of the unconscious and shifted to "central questions of the current German experience." Following the opening address by the NS minister for education of the state of Saxony in which the new Germany and the "great psychologist Adolf Hitler" were invoked (p. 5), Krueger gave his welcoming and theme-setting addresses, which ended in a tribute to the new leaders of the nation, with Adolf Hitler—"the farsighted, courageous and deeply empathic Chancellor"—at their pinnacle (p. 36). The seven main addresses were given by Ludwig Ferdinand Clauss (on the Germanic soul with the usual pictures of the preferred "Aryan" types), Jaensch, Karl Wilhelm von Isenburg (on racial purity), Philip Lersch (on character typology), and Rieffert. The addresses given by members of the board either were on NS themes or included appropriate tributes to the new order. Jaensch spoke on the countertype (*Gegentypus*) to the German culture: how the new German movement was dedicated to healing and enriching the culture and how finding an end to the countertype (primarily of mixed race) would solve the task of healing for Germany and the world (p. 58). Klemm sees the promise of a new technology brought to fruition by the bearers of a new will. Poppelreuter—an NS party member since before 1933—started by stressing how psychology must serve the new state. He then showed his NS *bona fides* by relating how already in 1931 and 1932 he had taught political psychology on the basis of *Mein Kampf* and finally asserted that the predicted century of psychology will have been seen to have properly started with the Hitler movement (pp. 59–60). Rieffert ends his address by asking that German psychology plan actively to be put in the service of the new German National Socialist development. Ach gave a minor address on the *Führerproblem* that ended with a definition of the "heroic leader" (p. 112). Krueger, Wilhelm Hartnacke, and others claimed *Ganzheitspsychologie* as embodying the aims of the new regime. It is an approach not generally familiar to the Anglophone reader and has common roots with Gestalt psychology. In the NS context, it was used to emphasize the unity of experience, transcending immediate or personal preoccupations and consistent with the notion of the new German *Volk* community. The individual is seen as part or a larger unity (*Ganzheit*) of the nation and social structures.[5]

What had happened? German psychology quickly adjusted itself to the National Socialist government. Faithful followers of the NS party line were brought into the executive committee and together with a very few others immediately spouted the racial, political nonsense of their leader. This was an immodest haste. Psychological journals immediately dropped the Jewish editors of their editorial boards (before this was required by law), and the Leipzig congress was planned to identify psychology

5. For discussions of the role of *Gestalt-* and *Ganzheitspsychologie* in NS Germany, see Ash (1995), Graumann (1985), and Prinz (1985).

with the new regime before a single university lecturer had been dismissed. The steps taken by the psychologists amounted to a *Selbstgleichschaltung* (a voluntary adaptation to the new regime) that went "far beyond" the official requirements.[6]

For the Anglophone reader, some of the foreign support shown for the new psychological order is of direct interest. We read that Goodwin B. Watson "expressed, primarily in the name of the younger American psychologists, his understanding and sympathy for the new Germany" (p. 6). In 1934, Watson published his own account of the meeting that he was "privileged" to attend. Coming from one of the leading liberal psychologists of the following decades, Watson represented a curious ambivalence, as if he did not want to believe the worst. He describes the absence of "non-Aryan" leaders of German psychology and the "politicalization" of psychology. His criticisms sound muted as he speaks of the German "revolution."[7] Elsewhere in the proceedings, we are told of a speech by Charles Spearman—given on another occasion (not otherwise specified)—who by coming to Germany and by presenting remarks that seemed sincere had demonstrated his ties to German psychology. Spearman was elected to and accepted honorary membership in the society in 1934 and permitted his name to be used as such at least until 1939. Subsequent proceedings note the presence of foreign delegates, from Sweden and the University of Buenos Aires in 1934, nineteen foreign delegates not otherwise identified in 1936, and "several" in 1938 with special attention given to the speeches of the Swedish, Hungarian, and Latvian delegates and particularly the glowing tributes of a Greek psychologist.

6. Jaeger (1993).
7. Watson (1934).

In German political life, Hitler had been chancellor since January, the Reichstag fire provocation occurred in February, and the enabling laws that established the one-part state were passed in March. But Paul von Hindenburg was still president of the country, and large sections of the intellectual opposition believed that Hitler's reign might well be temporary. Except for the targeting of socialist, communist, and militant democratic leaders and activists, there was little in the way of political terror and practically none for anybody who was not Jewish and kept relatively quiet. In other words, one did not need to be a hero or to risk one's life and liberty to express opposition or distance from the regime.

There were several roads an active academic could choose to follow with the advent of the National Socialist regime. He (and I use the masculine form since all the major players were men) could continue an active career as an NS member or sympathizer, such as Jaensch, Poppelreuter, Rieffert, Kroh, and others. He could continue to be an active member of the opposition, such as Karl Duncker and later Kurt Huber, who was executed as a member of the *Weisse Rose* resistance group. He could emigrate because he was Jewish or married to a Jew and forced to leave his profession. He could keep quiet and neither support or oppose the regime publicly, certainly a defensible position and taken by many good people. Finally, he could stay on trying to find an accommodation between his conscience and the regime.

Of special interest is the career of Wolfgang Köhler, who at the time was the director of the Berlin Psychological Institute and editor of the *Psychologische Forschung*. He was also a traditional conservative German politically, as was Thomas Mann, who reacted similarly to the National Socialist regime. One of his acts was to dissociate himself from the regime, which had required all university lectures to be started with the "Heil Hitler" greetings. He gave the greeting and then told his students that this was an act that was required of his position but in no way expressed his agreement with the sentiments it represented. In April 1933, he published a letter in a Berlin newspaper in which he deplored the dismissal of people who were not to the regime's liking as well as the effects of the anti-Semitic policies of the government. Some contemporary ambivalences occurred in parts of the article in which he agreed that Jews had played an undue role in German life but stated that this was no reason to consider Jews inferior or to deprive them of their livelihoods. Whether these statements were made as a publicly acceptable declaration or whether they echoed the sentiments of his class, they were no different from the sentiments of many conservative British or American academics of his age and status. Even some of his best friends were Jewish. Köhler's later actions were decisive ones. He defended his associate's Kurt Lewin's continued tenure in his post (though on leave of absence in the United States), which was allowed since Lewin was a war veteran. He defended Duncker, Otto von Lauenstein, Hedwig von Restorff, and others in their posts and refused to dismiss them for political or racial reasons. He also took over the formal direction of the doctoral work of students of Hans Reichenbach (who being Jewish had to leave the university). Köhler was important to the regime. Having lost the Jewish professors, the regime needed to hold on to the remaining internationally known psychologists. Köhler tried to resign in 1933, but his resignation from the university was not accepted until 1935, by which time his continuing skirmishes with the university administration and the government had become too much for the regime.

To repeat, living in the Third Reich, particularly during its early years, required neither heroic deeds nor public declarations of adherence to the worst of National Socialist ideologies. But for the psychologists in charge of their professional organization, the latter seemed proper and important to express quickly their loyalty to the new regime. Of the forty talks given at the Thirteenth Congress of the German Society for Psychology, many others felt no need to kowtow to the new powers in Berlin. Among the more prominent dissenters from the regime, both Wolfgang Köhler and Karl Duncker gave scientific papers at the 1933 congress, and dozens of psychologists continued their work for years to come without proclaiming obedience to the new order. During the early 1930s, at least, it was possible to remain a decent human being in Hitler's Germany.

The 1934 Congress

The Fourteenth Congress of the German Society for Psychology took place in 1934, only a year after the 1933 congress, though after 1934 the two-year interval was again respected. The chair of the congress was Oswald Kroh, and it took place in Tübingen. The theme of the 1934 meeting was *Gemeinschaftsleben* (not fully expressed in a literal translation of "communal living"); the intention was to emphasize collective German cooperation and consciousness.[8] Krueger's main opening address is devoted to various expressions of community—family, student groups, army, and so on. In contrast to his 1933 speech, it is sparing in its tributes to the National Socialist regime; the concern is more in bringing psychology into line with the political goals and

8. Klemm (1935).

tasks of the new state—forming the new *Volk* community and responding to the morality of the NS movement. The three main themes of the congress were the origin of social forms (race and genetics and social behavior), theory of social behavior (building communities, military *Führer* skills, consolidating forces, childhood and youth), and education for community (dynamics of community life, family and school, and character development). The intent is to demonstrate the serious relevance of psychology to the main themes of National Socialist Germany. It is as if psychologists had been waiting to demonstrate their wares in support of German unity and community.

The 1936 Congress

The atmosphere changed significantly at the fifteenth congress in Jena, chaired by Friedrich Sander. The dedicated Hitler follower Jaensch became the new chair. At the same time, there emerged the dominance of *Wehrmacht* (armed forces) personnel.[9] The head of the German army's division of psychology, Colonel Hans von Voss, was made an honorary member (he joined Karl Groos, Friedrich Schumann, and Charles Spearman) and some thirty-five members (out of 289) are identified in the membership list as armed forces psychologists (no other speciality is identified). At the membership meeting, Krueger announced his retirement as chair of the executive board, and the following September he appointed Jaensch as his successor, who in turn appointed the new executive board consisting of himself, Klemm, Kroh, Krueger, and Max Simoneit (head of *Wehrmacht* psychology).

9. Klemm (1937).

The general topic of the congress—feeling and will—was not new to German psychology. It had been a major topic in nineteenth-century German psychology, including the new experimental tendencies under Wilhelm Wundt. On the other hand, these are rubrics to which the NS regime responded very positively, and the general notion of the will of the German *Volk* received appropriate attention. In his opening addresses, Krueger paid fulsome tribute to the *Führer* and his infinite wisdom, and Jaensch in a special public address found room for a specific attack on Jews and their evil influence, apparently the first for these congresses. The elevation of Voss to honorary membership during the opening session underlined the commitment of the psychologists to the building of the *Wehrmacht*.

The 1938 Congress

The Sixteenth Congress of the German Society for Psychology was held in Bayreuth in 1938 and chaired by D. Kolb. It was the last one before the fall of the National Socialist regime.[10] With the advent of the war, no other congresses were held under NS leadership, though the theme for the 1940 congress was announced to be the relation of psychology and race theory. The 1938 congress was marked by an unusually large representation of governmental and party leaders and representatives. There was a special section on *Wehrmachtspsychologie*, and Colonel von Voss had advanced to major general and was again a central figure emphasizing the unity of party and armed forces. The board has been enlarged with the addition

10. Klemm (1939).

of Ach (rejoining the board), Lersch, Walther Moede, Gerhard Pfahler (he was an early NSDAP member), Sander, and Otto Tumlirz.

The theme of the congress was character and education, and there were repeated references to the German racial basis. As with the topic of will, concerns with typologies—personality and ethnic types—were old ones in German psychology but are of special interest in the NS context in which positive judgments of the acceptable, northern, Aryan character are contrasted with negative comments about the despicable character of Jews and some Slavic types. Of special note was Jaensch, who gave the thematic opening address and lost little time to attack the "Jewish psychoanalyst" Alfred Adler and the "Jewish intelligence tests" of William Stern. He urged psychologists to seek the truth just as Hitler, like a natural scientist, searched for the truth. He found it necessary to attack the Dutch journal *Acta psychologica*, which included "practically all of the emigrated psychologists," and asked whether the future of the field should be left to Jews and emigrants (p. 25). Konrad Lorenz reported on research with domesticated animals and noted that our genetically determined social behavior is important for the exclusion of those types whose dangerous virulent propagation threatens to invade the body of the nation. He urged further genetic research to discover the facts that solidify "our holiest racial [*völkisch*] and human heritage [*Erbgüter*]" (pp. 146–147).

In looking over the content of the politically unaffected papers, it is obvious that—with the departure of the leaders of the Gestalt movement and other outstanding psychologists (such as David Katz and Otto Selz)—German psychology had left the mainstream of early twentieth-century psychology. It

took some twenty years or more for German psychology to re-
cover after the end of the war.

The Postwar Congresses: 1948, 1951, and 1953

As did other professionals psychologists recovered slowly from
the devastation of Hitler's war and the postwar ruins and economic depression. Nothing particularly outstanding occurred in
the postwar congresses. In 1933 and 1934, some ambitious men
were in a hurry to declare their allegiance to the new order, but
in 1948 and later, there was no room apparently for a discussion
how one could overcome the problem of the Hitler Reich or of
problems of democratic education of the young (in contrast to
the 1930s' discussions of the education of the young for the
new Germany). The post-Hitler board of governors spent too little time trying to find politically unembarrassed psychologists.
There were some psychologists who had not been supporters
of the Nazis and who presided over the society in the postwar
years, such as Heinrich Düker, Kafka, and Hubert Rohracher
(from Vienna). But in 1953 Lersch and Kroh were again part of
the five-member board, in 1954 Lersch was chair and Sander
(who had published openly National Socialist and anti-Semitic
material) was vice-chair, and in 1955 Kroh presided again over
the society. Albert Wellek, who was active during the NS period
in the Society but apparently not in a political role, became
prominent in the postwar period. One other "survivor" is worth
mentioning. Wolfgang Metzger had, with the departure of its
founding members, taken over the leadership of the Gestalt
movement during the NS period. It behooved Metzger, however,
also to speak and write positively of the new Germany and the

NS movement and to point out parallels between Gestalt theory and National Socialism in their opposition to the spirit of the West. These depressing signs of the lingering power of the NS system can be contrasted with refreshing signs of rejuvenation and rebuilding.

I conclude by noting that the members of the generation of German psychologists who welcomed Hitler and his ideology, who acceded to his criminality, and who finally failed to welcome his downfall and demise are long gone. The postwar generations are like a breath of fresh air, and one often feels that the young German professionals are less likely to succumb to totalitarian lures than some of their colleagues in some other democratic countries.

9   The Success of Gestalt Theory and Its Translation to the United States

With the destruction of any viable psychology in Germany (and Austria), most of its most creative practitioners moved to the United States. Though the major theme of this volume is the experimental psychology of memory and thought, I expand significantly from those topics to include a number of individuals who influenced the new directions in American psychology. The purpose is to illustrate the pervasive shift in the United States, which affected all aspects of psychology and in turn fed back on each individual field. The influences and directions are best illustrated in a discussion of individuals. In a sense, there were few uniquely influential immigrants, just as the total number of immigrants in psychology was very small. The story deals very largely with Gestalt psychology. It deals with the transformation of the movement from Germany to the United States, though some space is given to psychologists who were not strictly members of the Gestalt movement.[1]

1. The account to follow is a distillation of an extensive chapter that Jean Mandler and I published in Mandler and Mandler (1968). In that publication, we have expressed our appreciation and thanks to the many people and institutions that were helpful and generous in their contributions to our work. The reader is directed to that chapter for

To the extent that German psychology, as represented by its immigrant scholars, affected the American scene, its influence was the result of interactions between two very different and essentially disparate intellectual traditions. If, in 1910, somebody had told a group of American psychologists that twenty-five years later the arrival of some of the major representatives of German experimental psychology would create a tension between two different intellectual forces, he would have been ridiculed. In 1910, American psychology was an outpost of German experimental psychology. The promising young psychologist who wanted to make his way was practically guaranteed recognition or at least acceptance into the establishment—small though it was at the time—if he had spent some time at one of the major German laboratories, particularly Wilhelm Wundt's in Leipzig. Pilgrimage to Germany was necessary for any American psychologist who could afford it financially or intellectually. German experimental sensationism and atomism—as exported through the returning travelers or by the sheer intellectual force of the grand old man of American psychology, Edward Bradford Titchener (a German-trained Englishman)—was the dominant force. William James had ably and eloquently resisted the German tradition, but though James was partially successful at Harvard University, the major thrust of American psychology was German in origin and method.

By 1930, the situation had changed radically. During the first quarter of the century, behaviorism not only challenged

more detailed discussions of the people and events presented here. All the correspondence and communications we received have been deposited with the Archives of American Psychology at the University of Akron.

the philosophical traditions prevalent in the nonexperimental departments; it also overwhelmed an experimental psychology that depended on introspectionist evidence and subverted the functionalist school, which was intellectually indebted to John Dewey and developed in Chicago under the leadership of James Rowland Angell and Harvey A. Carr. The alliance among behaviorism, functionalism (with its comparative, evolutionary, pragmatic, and empirical emphases), and the remnants of British empiricism dominated philosophical conceptions of the structure of the mind. The new Pavlovian rumblings from Russia also helped to create in America an experimental psychology that rejected introspective evidence as an empirical basis for a scientific psychology, emphasized comparative (animal) research, and reinstated a naive empiricism and associationism that, as has been shown in previous chapters, had already been rejected by some of the more sophisticated associationists in England and Germany, such as Alexander Bain and Georg Elias Müller.

In addition, or as a result of these tendencies, the investigation of complex human thought and perception was postponed. What was in fact an actual rejection was frequently represented as a postponement, with the claim that the investigation of complex human mental events must be relegated to the future when the basic elements of behavior—that is, the conditioned reflex and other simple responses in simple animals—would be understood. These responses were to be the building blocks for an eventual science of the higher mental processes. This promissory note, or rubber check, dominated American thinking. It did not exclude other trends, and countervailing forces did exist. The prevailing atmosphere was antitheoretical. The paucity of theoretical thought among the early behaviorists was coupled

with the failure of functionalism, which started as a grand enterprise designed to accommodate psychology to Charles Darwin.
It used *function* in his sense but ended up as a label for dustbowl
empiricism, narrowly concerned with some limited set of response variables operating as a "function" of an even more limited set of environmental events.

In the area of human thought and language, American
psychology continued Hermann Ebbinghaus's simpler formulations, again betting on the eventual understanding of complex
language and thought through the investigation of simple learning of simple events. Explicit theory was absent, and years of
diligent research dealt with the effects of easily manipulated environmental variables. The complexity of language and the complexity of thought were rarely approximated or even admitted.
When theory was attempted in the behaviorist camp, such as
the ambitious and grand theoretical attempts of Clark L. Hull,
there was always the injunction that theoretical constructs
must never again lead one to mentalism and complex mental
structures. Even Hull, when building a theoretical model,
reminds himself that it is not theory that is dominant but the
observable. Thus, the decade arond 1930 finds in America an
antimentalistic, comparative, pragmatic psychology. German
hegemony had died with Titchener, and American psychology
was to a very real extent American.

In the early 1930s, as conditions in Germany became threat-
ening to scientists, the American economic situation was one
stumbling block to the settlement and placement of refugee psychologists. Still, there is no doubt that the German psychologists
(particularly the Gestalt group) were seen as intruders and
alien to the prevailing psychological atmosphere. American empiricism rejected the nativism of the Gestalt school, American

functionalism rejected the frequently obscure theorizing of the Gestaltists, and American behaviorism neither wanted nor was able to handle complex problems of cognitive processes. On the whole, the American establishment in psychology—firmly based at Harvard, Cornell, Princeton, Yale, and Chicago—rejected the new psychology from Europe, particularly a psychology that had taken as one of its aims a determined opposition to behaviorism. Behaviorism was too new, too successful, too exciting an enterprise not to fight back spiritedly against the foreign invaders.

In contrast, by the third decade of the century, Gestalt psychology had become one of the leading forces in German psychology. In a departure from the earlier chapter where I stressed the Gestalt approach to thinking and memory, in this section I talk more generally to include perception and allied topics. The acceptance—in various forms—that much of psychological processing did not take the forms of conscious thought naturally led to the readiness to accept theoretical structures, unconscious and directive, and prepared the ground for the Gestalt movement. To a very large extent, it was the latest and most successful development in experimental German psychology. It must be remembered that the experimental, empirical tradition in psychology was only about fifty years old by then, and even today some corners of psychology are committed to a philosophical approach to their subject matter. The birth of Gestalt psychology proper can be dated fairly precisely to Max Wertheimer's investigations of apparent movement in 1910, first published in 1912.[2] Wertheimer showed that the perceptual experience of motion was not some additive result of successive sensations of position but rather that perceived movement

2. Wertheimer (1912).

produced a new unitary outcome that could not be split up into successive stationary sensations. This insight was to revolutionize the experimental investigation of visual perception, but it also, in the wider forms of the Gestalt movement, changed the conception of the unit of psychological analysis. Sensationism, structuralism, the stress on the analysis of elements in psychophysics as the basis of psychology receded into the background, and the new analysis of the functional units of thought and perception (units not analyzable or definable in terms of their constituents) preoccupied the experimental psychologists in Germany. To say that Gestalt psychology was successful in this revolution is to say too much and too little. Many of the specific theoretical notions that accompanied the insight that higher-order units of perception and thought are important in psychology failed to survive beyond the field of visual perception. However, the acceptance of the notion that these higher-order units are the psychological events that must be investigated is the success that Gestalt psychology has had and that no psychologist after the 1930s in Germany and after the 1940s in America and elsewhere was able to ignore. In that sense, current psychology has relived the Gestalt revolution at a different level and with different emphases.

The so-called production theory of the Austrian psychologists that preceded the Gestalt movement probably better represents current attitudes. The production school insisted that Gestalt qualities result from complex mental operations imposed on sense data. In the same way, it is Karl Bühler's emphasis on the learning of rules and Otto Selz's notion of mental operations that are recognizable today. Wertheimer at Frankfurt first excited Kurt Koffka's interest, and in 1915 Koffka wrote the article that recorded what Wertheimer then and subsequently was hesitant to commit to public print—the principles of Gestalt psychology. Just at a point when further collaboration might have developed, Köhler went to Tenerife in the Canary Islands to study chimpanzees. Köhler was forced by the war to stay in the Canary Islands for more than six years and during that time continued his research, which then was under the influence of both Wertheimer's ideas and those of Max Planck. This wedding of the psychology of perception and physical field theory was to influence all of Köhler's subsequent work. Köhler was, by all means, the most prolific and, from an American point of view, the most forceful agent of the movement. However, the triumvirate representing the intellectual aegis of Gestalt psychology came into being after Köhler's return to Germany.

Gestalt psychology had developed to an important internationally known movement in German psychology by the early 1920s. The close relationship among the triumvirs, their attraction for the best brains in psychology, and their obviously superior ability to attract thought and disciples created a nucleus of psychology in Berlin, much of which eventually emigrated to the United States. Not only were the three founders in Berlin at one time or another, but Kurt Lewin also became part of the group, Fritz Heider spent some time there, as did George Katona from Hungary and some of the younger generation who were all to come to the United States later, such as Rudolf Arnheim, Hans Wallach, and Karl Duncker. German atomism, sensationism, and associationism had been supplanted as a source of inspiration in psychology. Remnants of nineteenth-century German experimental psychology were still alive in the United States, particularly in association with the American behaviorist revolution. Franz L. Neumann, a nonpsychologist, described the difference in the two atmospheres: "the German exile, bred in the veneration of theory and history, and contempt for empiricism and pragmatism, entered a diametrically opposed intellectual climate: optimistic, empirically oriented, ahistorical, but also self-righteous."[3]

There is little evidence that psychological organizations in the United States took immediate cognizance of the threat to academic and scientific freedoms or of the threat to the individual livelihoods and lives of psychologists. I describe in the previous chapter how quickly the *Gleichschaltung* of German psychology proceeded within the fascist regime. Despite Albert Wellek's protestations to the contrary,[4] organized German psychology accepted with equanimity both the dictum that this "Jewish" field was in for a major upheaval and the removal of its leaders. The active flight from Germany started in 1933; in many cases, that flight was made easier by prior, primarily nonpolitical departures for America by such men as Koffka and Heider. In the United States, there is little evidence of any concerted action for the first five years of the Nazi regime.

In 1937, the International Committee of the International Psychological Congress awarded the Twelfth International Congress to Vienna. In March 1938, Austria was occupied by German troops, and the following month the Midwestern Psychological Association, meeting in Madison, Wisconsin, passed a resolution that requested the International Committee to select a meeting place "in a country which permits the unhampered development of psychology and of other sciences" and that asked the International Committee to add Karl Bühler, who had been briefly arrested in Vienna, as an associate. The res-

3. Neumann (1953).
4. Wellek (1968).

olution condemned "the Nazi dictatorship, which has subordinated the integrity of science and of scientists to a political creed."[5] The Congress was to be held in 1941, but the cascade of events overtook those plans before then. Whether influenced by an awareness of the political significance of a congress to be held in the Third Reich or generally driven by the pressure of events, in the fall of 1938, the American Psychological Association appointed a committee "to survey the problem of psychologists displaced from their positions and livelihoods in other countries and seeking asylum and professional opportunities elsewhere." And throughout its history, the committee was faced with the difficult problem of trying to import psychologists into a country where many American psychologists were unable to find positions. Other national organizations provided funds for the support of the displaced psychologists, but the meager funds available from psychologists themselves helped in very minor aspects of the work of this committee, largely due to the work of Barbara Burks. In retrospect, it seems ludicrous to talk of the influence of some hundred-odd psychologists, assisted by an organization that spent less than one thousand dollars over a period of five years in helping to integrate them into American psychology and to assess the influence this handful of people had on a profession that today has some many thousand members and a multimillion-dollar budget. But one other organization must be mentioned briefly because of the impact it made on American academic life and psychology—New York's New School for Social Research and

5. Documents related to this resolution and to the work of the Burks committee (below) are available in the *Archives of the History of American Psychology*.

particularly its graduate faculty, which practically determined the receptivity of the intellectual world of America to the scholars from abroad. Alvin Johnson selected the first group to come to the "University-in-Exile" and, throughout the 1930s and early 1940s, was involved in the recruitment and selection of faculty. Among the experimental psychologists who taught or studied there were Max Wertheimer, George Katona, E. M. von Hornbostel, Rudolf Arnheim, Kurt Goldstein, Hans Wallach, and Martin Scheerer. In the following, I discuss highlights of the lives and American positioning of the major players in the transition of German psychology to the United States.[6]

Foremost in the migration of the Gestalt school to the United States was the move of its leading triumvirate. Kurt Koffka, the first, was born in 1886 and received a Berlin Ph.D. in 1908. In the spring of 1925, he and Köhler, representing the Gestalt school, participated in a conference at Clark University in Worcester, Massachusetts. In 1926 and 1927, Koffka was at the University of Wisconsin and in 1927 was appointed for a five-year period to the William Allan Neilson Chair at Smith College, where he remained until 1941 and his death. Koffka's position in Germany had become at least difficult. He had been the major, most bitter, and sometimes vituperative exponent of the Gestalt school. It was Koffka who attacked its opponents in print and by word of mouth, and it was Koffka against whom much of bitter hostility to Gestalt psychology in Germany was directed. I should emphasize here that the critique was generally unrelated to the later adoption of *Ganzheitspsychologie* (Gestalt's sister theory) as the leading identification of Nazi psychologists. The latter was an adoption for purposes of political expediency of a

6. For details, see Mandler and Mandler (1968).

theory that in its principles had little ideological overlap with German fascism. Koffka directly affected one important contributor to the American scene: Harry Helson was moved to embark on an extensive exposition and critique of Gestalt psychology, and James J. Gibson regularly attended Koffka's seminar. Koffka was writing his *Principles of Gestalt Psychology*:[7] one of the undergraduates with whom he discussed the manuscript was Mary Henle, and Molly Harrower was one of his doctoral candidates. Among the psychologists Koffka had brought from abroad were Fritz Heider, Alexander Mintz, Tamara Dembo, and Eugenia Hanfmann.

Max Wertheimer was born in Prague in 1880, the oldest of the triumvirate. His early interests were in poetry, literature, and music. His music brought him into contact with Albert Einstein, with whom he played chamber music. Wertheimer went to the University of Berlin, where he studied psychology with Carl Stumpf and Friedrich Schumann, ending up at the University of Würzburg, where he received his Ph.D. with Oswald Külpe in 1904. Wertheimer had been mulling over the inadequacies in the associationist analysis of psychological phenomena and had been searching for a perceptual example to demonstrate his new ideas. The report of the Phi phenomenon of apparent movement was presented at the 1911 meeting of the *Gesellschaft für Experimentelle Psychologie*. From 1916 until 1929, the period that was to become the high point of the development of Gestalt psychology, Wertheimer worked at the University of Berlin, and during this period American psychologists still found it desirable and necessary to read the German literature in psychology. Thus, the creation of a new journal, the

7. Koffka (1935).

Psychologische Forschung, was an important event in Germany and throughout the psychological world. The journal was started by Wertheimer, Koffka, and Köhler, together with Kurt Goldstein and Hans Gruhle. In 1929, Wertheimer accepted the chair at the University of Frankfurt, where he stayed until his departure from Germany. Wertheimer left Germany secretly the day before Germany voted the National Socialists into power in March 1933. One of Hitler's speeches had so disturbed Wertheimer that he decided to depart secretly the next morning to Czechoslovakia. While in Czechoslovakia, Wertheimer received an invitation to join the faculty of the New School for Social Research and went to the United States in September 1933. Where Koffka's influence was largely through his first and partly through his second book, Wertheimer's was practically completely personal. His influence was exerted through his seminars, which included Rudolf Arnheim, Solomon Asch, George Katona, Abraham S. Luchins, Abraham H. Maslow, David Rapaport, Martin Scheerer, and Herman Witkin. Wertheimer died suddenly in 1943, having left unfinished a work that became influential in American psychology—*Productive Thinking*.[8] Wertheimer's book, and the studies of his student in Berlin, Karl Duncker, laid the foundation for much of the later American work on creative thinking. Wertheimer was one of the pioneers in the study of teaching students to attack problems creatively and to understand their structural characteristics. His work and that of his student Catherine Stern on structural arithmetic presaged the change in teaching methods in mathematics and science that has changed elementary and secondary education.

8. Wertheimer (1945).

Karl Duncker's studies in Berlin resulted in Duncker's brilliant study on thinking, *Zur Psychologie des productiven Denkens*, published in Berlin in 1935 and posthumously translated into English in1945.[9] Duncker's political views forced him to escape to England. In 1938, he was invited to Swarthmore, and, depressed by the outbreak of the war, he committed suicide there early in 1940. He may have been the most brilliant of the Gestalt group. His main contribution has made a continuing impact on the psychology of thinking, both in the United States and elsewhere; his monograph was as a touchstone of theoretical insight and empirical thoroughness.

Probably the most influential student of Wertheimer's was Solomon Asch. He expanded classical Gestalt thinking into social psychology and was an active and effective proponent of the Gestalt view in the psychology of memory. In the same area of the experimental psychology of thinking, mention must be made of George Katona, who was also a member of the immigrant group. His influence has primarily been out of the purview of this book—industrial psychology. I discuss in chapter 10 his early contribution to the psychology of mental organization. Another important influence on the American scene through Wertheimer is Rudolf Arnheim. Arnheim did his dissertation with Wertheimer in Berlin, and he exerted his influence on American psychology primarily outside of experimental psychology. Arnheim's investigations in the psychology of art within the Gestalt framework became the dominant influence in the psychology of art, but American psychology of the 1930s had little interest in problems of aesthetics.

9. Duncker (1935, 1945).

If the mythical average American psychologist or student of psychology were to be asked what single man represented the Gestalt movement in the United States, he would undoubtedly answer Wolfgang Köhler. Köhler wrote more and influenced more people in the United States than any other member of the triumvirate. Of all the immigrant psychologists, only Kurt Lewin had more of a general impact on academic psychology in the United States. Köhler outlived all the major figures who came to the United States in the 1920s and 1930s by more than twenty years. He was born in 1887 and received his doctoral degree at Berlin in 1909. From 1909 until 1913, he was at Frankfurt. Between 1913 and 1920, at Tenerife, he researched problem solving in apes and perception and produced theoretical work in Gestalt psychology. I described earlier Köhler's actions under the Nazis when he assumed the chair at Berlin previously held by Carl Stumpf. He remained in Berlin until 1935. He was thus at Frankfurt at the beginning of the movement and in Berlin during its flowering and was the last of the big four (to include Lewin) to come to the United States. Köhler was active in many aspects of Gestalt psychology during the Berlin years and gradually assumed the role of its major spokesperson. He was becoming known in America both by visits of American students to Berlin and by his own trips to the United States. He visited Clark University and Harvard in 1925 and 1926 and was invited to give the 1934 William James Lectures at Harvard.[10] William McDougall had vacated his chair at Harvard in 1927, and Köhler was one of the leading candidates for the position. Köhler would have affected American psychology quite differently from within a university that was part of the es-

10. Köhler (1938).

tablishment than from a smaller college on its periphery. The appointment to McDougall's chair was delayed for some years, but with the succession of James Bryant Conant to the presidency of Harvard in 1933, the decision was finally made in favor of Karl Lashley. Köhler was appointed at Swarthmore College in 1935. Robert B. MacLeod, who had gone to Swarthmore to develop a new department, had had prior associations with the Gestalt group when, in 1928, he did some of his graduate work in Berlin. Köhler not only helped create at Swarthmore one of the major centers of psychological research and scholarship in the United States but also attracted a large number of postdoctoral and predoctoral research associates. Among them were David Krech, Claude E. Buxton, Richard Crutchfield, W. Dewey Neff, J. C. R. Licklider, Herman Witkin, Mary Henle, Richard Held, Jacob Nachmias, Henry Gleitman, and Ulric Neisser.

In 1936, one of Köhler's most eminent students, Hans Wallach, was increasingly under pressure to leave Germany and was offered an appointment at Swarthmore. Wallach's collaboration with Köhler significantly influenced the field of visual perception. With Wertheimer at the New School for Social Research, Koffka at Smith College, and Köhler at Swarthmore, the Gestalt triangle in the Northeast became a center of intense activity. Major figures of American psychology would visit Swarthmore, the New School, Smith College, and Lewin at Iowa, including such notables as R. H. Wheeler, Karl Lashley, Edward C. Tolman, Karl Muenzinger, Egon Brunswik, Donald Adams, and Karl Zener. At Swarthmore itself, Köhler, Asch, and Wallach carried on the traditions of the Gestalt movement. One should not lose sight of the fact that some of the impact of Gestalt psychology as a new movement had been made prior to the arrival of its major figures in the United States. Thus, in a sense, the influence of Köhler and others was a continuation of a trend established by the time Köhler himself came to the United States. But after the blossoming of the movement before and after the war, Gestalt psychology had become an American movement.

The rule of the Gestalt movement by the triumvirate was unquestioned, although a fourth member of the Berlin group was not strictly a Gestalt psychologist but was one of the major figures to come out of Berlin in that period. Kurt Lewin was the youngest of the four, born in 1890. He did his doctoral work in Berlin under Carl Stumpf and received his Ph.D. in 1915. Another one of his teachers was Georg Elias Müller. Much like the rest of the group, Lewin was a product of classical German experimental psychology. At no time could he be called an orthodox Gestaltist, but he was part of the movement and influenced it as much as he was influenced by it. From the beginning, his interest was not strictly in the experimental laboratory but rather in social variables, social events, and the world beyond the ivory tower. In 1921, he was appointed to the University of Berlin and taught there until 1933 (he and Duncker were two of the four junior appointments under Köhler). Lewin attracted a large group of very able graduate students, some of whom later came to the United States and became prominent psychologists in their own right. Among them were Maria Rickers Ovsiankina and Tamara Dembo. Throughout this time, Lewin was less involved with introspective experiments than his Gestalt colleagues. In that sense, he was much better prepared for the objective experimentation of American psychology than were the other major figures. His concepts—generally referred to as *field theory* and specifically in opposition to the atomism of association theory—dealt with energies, tensions, and needs. During the late 1920s, most of the experiments were concerned with problem solving, interruption and completion of tasks, and related topics. These series of experiments easily adapted to the American tradition and are to this day fruitful starting points for experimental investigations of the level of aspiration, effects of success and failure, and environmental effects on problem solving. Probably Lewin's first impress on American psychology was the publication of a paper by J. F. Brown in the *Psychological Review* on Kurt Lewin's methods.[11] Other visitors of Lewin's were Donald MacKinnon, Karl Zener, Donald Adams, and Norman R. F. Maier.

Lewin had been invited in 1932 to spend six months at Stanford University, and in 1933 he left California by way of the Pacific and through the Soviet Union. On 20 January, Hitler came to power, and by the time Lewin arrived in Moscow he was certain that there was no room for a Jew in Nazi Germany. He resigned from the University of Berlin before he was removed by the new regime, and shortly thereafter R. M. Ogden offered him a position at Cornell University, where he arrived in August 1933. The experimental social psychologist and theoretician was invited by the School of Home Economics at Cornell for a two-year appointment. Just as with Köhler, Wertheimer, and Koffka, his first appointment was at the periphery of the American academies. In 1935, he spent a brief period in Palestine, and his friends in the United States feared that he would move there permanently, but Lawrence K. Frank persuaded the Iowa Child Welfare Research Station at the University of Iowa to offer him

11. Brown (1929).

an appointment there, and Lewin moved to Iowa in 1935. His long-time associate, Tamara Dembo, went with him, as did Roger Barker and Herbert Wright.

It was at Iowa that a long stream of American students began to gather around Kurt Lewin. Among the Americans at Iowa, either permanently or on a visiting basis, were Dorwin Cartwright, Alvin Zander, Robert Leeper, J. R. P. French, Alex Bavelas, Leon Festinger, Sybille Escalona, Ronald Lippitt, and Erik and Beatrice Wright. Lewin's interactions with his students, his generosity with his time, and his insatiable interests made him one of the central figures of American psychology. In 1938, Kenneth W. Spence came to Iowa, and Spence was for a time a transmission station between Kurt Lewin and Clark L. Hull on suggested variations and changes in Hullian theory. In 1938 and again in 1939, Lewin spent some time at Harvard, primarily at the urging and invitation of Gordon W. Allport and Henry A. Murray. When war came, Lewin was a consultant for the Office of Strategic Services, the Office of Naval Research, and the Public Health Service. In the early 1940s, Lewin was ready to start an institute to deal with problems of group dynamics and to go further into what he termed *action research*. MIT was the successful bidder for the institute, and in 1944, Lewin moved from Iowa to Cambridge, where he founded the Research Center for Group Dynamics, the crowning glory of his career in the United States. Lewin had moved far from his initial work on associationism under Stumpf and his work with the Gestalt group in Berlin to the leadership of American social psychology in 1947. Lewin's interests and methods of tackling problems fitted in with traditional American interests and methods, not so much in the limited field of experimental psychology itself as in the characteristic social temper of American life in the twentieth century.

Certainly in a broad sense, America was ready for Lewin when he arrived. American social psychology, developmental psychology, and experimental psychology all changed significantly because Kurt Lewin wrote and taught in the Unied States. To list his students and associates at the Research Center in Group Dynamics at the Massachusetts Institute of Technology is to list an honor roll of social psychology.

Fritz Heider was bom in Vienna in 1896 and grew up in Graz, where he received his Ph.D. with Alexius Meinong in 1920. In Munich, he took courses with Karl and Charlotte Bühler in child and experimental psychology. From 1921 to 1924, Heider lived in Berlin, where he had some contact with Köhler and Wertheimer and also extensive contact with Lewin. In 1927, he went to the University of Hamburg with William Stern and Heinz Werner. He was at the Bonn congress of the German Society for Psychology in 1927, when Georg Elias Müller and Köhler met head-on in a public confrontation of Gestalt and associationistic complex theory. In 1929, Koffka contacted Stem concerning an opening at Smith that Heinz Werner had turned down and that was then offered to Heider. In 1930, Fritz Heider came to the Clarke School for the Deaf with a nominal appointment at Smith, where he started teaching on a part-time basis in 1931. In December of 1930, he married Grace Moore and, partly as a result of this union of Austrian and American psychology, never again left the United States permanently. Heider stayed at Smith until 1947 and during that period developed one of the most influential theoretical conceptions in current social psychology—*balance theory*. In 1947, Roger Barker asked Heider to join the reorganized psychology department at the University of Kansas, where he remained until his death. From the 1930s on, Heider had been working on his magnum opus, which was finally published in 1958.[12] Heider's influence was delayed by some twenty years after his arrival in the United States, but next to Lewin's contributions his theories today are the most alive of those stemming from the German and Austrian immigration.

Another though somewhat peripheral member of the Gestalt school was Kurt Goldstein, who was born in 1878 and died in New York City in 1965. Goldstein had a medical degree from Breslau in 1903 and after various medical appointments was appointed professor of neurology at the University of Frankfurt, where Wertheimer was a colleague. In 1930, he moved to the University of Berlin but was forced to leave the country in 1933. The Rockefeller Foundation supported him for a year in Amsterdam, during which time he wrote his major book.[13] In 1934, he reached New York, where he was appointed clinical professor of neurology at Columbia. In 1938 and 1939, he gave the William James Lectures at Harvard and a graduate seminar (with Sylvan Tomkins as teaching assistant) at the Harvard Psychological Clinic. In 1940, he became clinical professor of neurology at Tufts College Medical School. He had close contacts with Gordon Allport and Karl Lashley and collaborated with Eugenia Hanfmann and Maria Ovsiankina.

Two men represent the influence on the immigration from the University of Vienna—Karl Bühler and Egon Brunswik. Bühler was born in 1879 and started his career with an M.D. degree in 1903, followed by a Ph.D. from Strassburg in 1904. In 1906, he went to Würzburg and followed Oswald Külpe to Bonn in 1909 and to Munich in 1913. In 1918 he went to the University

12. Heider (1958).
13. Goldstein (1939).

of Dresden and in 1922 was appointed to the professorship at Vienna. He stayed there until 1938, when he was arrested by the German government for a brief period. In 1939, he came to the United States. His first position was at St. Scholastica College in Duluth, and from 1940 to 1945, at the College of St. Thomas in St. Paul. Then, at the age of sixty-six, he moved to Los Angeles, where he held appointments at the University of Southern California Medical School and at Cedars of Lebanon Hospital. He died in 1963. Bühler, whose major contributions to psychology all predate his arrival in the United States, was truly one of the casualties of the immigration. A man who had been considered for McDougall's chair at Harvard in 1928 and who in 1927 and 1928 was a guest professor at Harvard, Stanford, Johns Hopkins, and Chicago, he was never given due recognition when he came to the United States on a permanent basis. Unfortunately, none of his major works written prior to his immigration was translated into English until later.[14] Bühler influenced American thought primarily through the many Europeans and Americans who had studied with him in Vienna, including Egon Brunswik, Edward C. Tolman, Rene Spitz, and Else Frenkel-Brunswik. His wife, Charlotte Bühler, fifteen years his junior, was much more influential in developmental psychology and had a major impact on that field.[15]

Egon Brunswik, born in 1903 in Budapest, started out in engineering but completed his formal studies as a student of Karl Bühler's in Vienna, where he received a Ph.D. in 1927. In 1933, Edward C. Tolman spent a year at the Psychological Institute in Vienna, and partly through his good offices Brunswik received

14. Bühler (1926, 1934).
15. Bühler (1934).

a fellowship at the University of California at Berkeley in 1935 and 1936, where he remained, joining the faculty in 1937. He died in 1955. Brunswik was the only major figure in the immigration who followed a more or less traditional career in American academics. Else Frenkel, another student of Bühler's in Vienna, became Brunswik's wife in 1937, and she made significant contributions to personality and social psychology. Brunswik's most important notion, the *probabilistic view of the environment* (the uncertain flux of the organism's environment that affects its behavior and mental processes) is present in much of modem American psychology. At the University of California at Berkeley, there was a fruitful interaction between Tolman and Brunswik. His notion of representative design and his brilliant, though sometimes obscure work on the conceptual history of psychology have both challenged and intrigued generations of psychologists. In 1966, Kenneth R. Hammond noted that whereas Tolman, Clark L. Hull, and Lewin left their ideas and doctrine to a sturdy and determined second generation, there were, in effect, no heirs present at the reading of Brunswik's intellectual will. Brunswik's ideas have become part of the American Zeitgeist. He published relatively few experimental articles, but most of them were seminal.[16] He did early work on probability learning and concept formation with probabilistic cues, on social perception, and on the influence of values on perception. Many of the students at Berkeley were profoundly influenced by him, including Roger Barker, Donald T. Campbell, Kenneth Hammond, Jane Loevinger, Murray E. Jarvik, Julian Hochberg, and Max Levin.

16. Brunswik (1952, 1956).

A group of psychologists came to the United States from the University of Hamburg. I have already discussed one of them, Fritz Heider. Three others, though not strictly experimental psychologists, were William Stern, Heinz Werner, and Martin Scheerer. Stem, born in 1871, was a student of Hermann Ebbinghaus, under whose direction he received his doctorate in 1892 at Berlin. In 1897, he followed Ebbinghaus to Breslau. In 1916, he was appointed director of the Psychological Laboratory and professor at Hamburg. In 1933, he left Germany, spent some time in Holland, and in 1934 went to Duke University to the department then headed by William McDougall. He died in 1938 at the age of sixty-seven. Stern's primary interests were in personality theory and in individual differences. His major influence has been on Heinz Werner, also at Hamburg, and on Gordon W. Allport. Stern himself did not live long after his arrival in the United States, and it is primarily through these men that his influence has been felt in American psychology.

Werner was born in Vienna in 1890 and received his doctoral degree from the University of Vienna in 1914. From 1915 to 1917, he worked at the University of Munich and in 1917 was appointed to the Psychological Institute at Hamburg, where he worked under Stem. He was appointed to the Hamburg faculty in 1921 and in 1933 was dismissed by the Nazi regime. Walter Pillsbury invited him to come to the University of Michigan, where he stayed from 1933 until 1936, though not on a regular faculty appointment. In 1936, while still at Michigan, Werner was appointed as senior research psychologist at the Wayne County Training School, where he stayed until 1943. He received his first regular faculty appointment at Brooklyn College as an instructor in 1943. It is noteworthy that a man of

Werner's stature was not able to get an appointment at better than the instructor level. Finally, in 1947, Clark University invited him as professor in the department of psychology and education, and in 1949, he became chair of the independent department of psychology. Under Werner's leadership, Clark University again attained the high reputation it had achieved some years earlier under G. Stanley Hall. Werner died in 1964. While Werner was part of the tradition that developed Gestalt psychology in Germany, his interests, going back to his days in Munich, were in developmental psychology and as such were in contrast to the ahistorical position of the Gestaltists, particularly Lewin. However, like the Gestaltists, his accommodation to America was easy in the one respect that made all of them acceptable: they were experimentally oriented and concerned with empirical investigation. His later research ws concerned with language and with perception, where he collaborated primarily with Seymour Wapner while in the area of language he worked primarily with Bernard Kaplan.[17]

Martin Scheerer, who was born in 1900 and died in the United States in 1961, received a Ph.D. at Hamburg in 1931, and though not an experimental psychologist, was important in the development of cognitive theory and symbolic processes. He was at Montefiore Hospital from 1936 to 1939 and became a professor at the University of Kansas in 1948, where he was an important member of the quasi-Gestalt group there.

If the total effect of the German immigration on American psychology is diffuse, there is no doubt that the German immigration did leave German psychology denuded. Certainly, few German psychologists (with several important exceptions such

17. Werner and Kaplan (1963); Werner and Wapner (1952).

as Köhler) significantly protested the Nazi regime. In his evaluation of the impact of the German immigration on American
psychology, Albert Wellek overemphasized the effect of the German immigration on American psychology as much as he overemphasized the resistance to Nazism of those who remained
behind. The full force of a statement such as "American psychology of the present would not be what it is and could not
become what it yet promises to be, without the ferments and
instigations of the German emigration" overstates the case.[18]
Apart from the various important indigenous American trends,
there were other influential names in American experimental psychology—for example, Georg von Bekesy, a postwar
immigrant from Hungary. Edwin G. Boring coined the phrase
that Gestalt psychology died of its success, but it is difficult to
know whether that success was a personal or a programmatic
one.

Gestalt psychology in the United States flourished briefly, and
it was an important set of ideas that unified an immigrant group
that might have fallen apart much faster had it not been held
together by the common experience of the immigration. The
German movement did bring the traditions of German experimental psychology of the turn of the century to America, and it
did produce a leavening of American psychology by reminding
it of its philosophical past. During the predominance of behaviorism, it provided a movement in a minor key that stressed
mental organization and structures so that in the 1960s many
American psychologists within or outside the Gestalt tradition
could come back to the problem of mental structure, a problem

18. Wellek (1968). See chapter 10 for the primarily American and other
European sources of the current scene.

originally stressed by an American—William James. Methodological behaviorism, the commitment to objectivity, was an American movement that had strong roots in pragmatism and in American philosophy. By becoming part of the American scene in the long run, the German immigrants pushed a young science to greater maturity in an atmosphere conducive to such development, where behaviorism, pragmatism, and the open marketplace of ideas made it possible for psychology to become respectable. The fact that the immigrants were assimilated into the American scene is important for the history of psychology, and it was done despite opposition and xenophobia. Gestalt psychology is no longer recognized as a major active school that attests both to the limited utility of its system and to the fact that we have adopted some of its ideas into the fabric of American psychology. Gestalt psychology—an early and partial information-processing approach—is still a useful tool for some psychological questions such as memorial and perceptual organization.[19] Many of its original ideas have survived in other guises and theories. In the long run, the Gestalt immigrants added to the brew of information-processing, cognitive, and constructivist psychologies that made up the "cognitive revolution" within a generation of their arrival.

19. See, for example, Rock and Palmer (1990).

10 A New Age of Psychology at the End of World War II

The topic of this chapter would generally considered to be the cognitive revolution in the United States of the 1950s. As I emphasize, the revolution was an idiosyncratic American event because that is where behaviorism had taken hold, and if there was a revolution at all, it was against the limits that behaviorism had proscribed for experimental psychology. The changes in American psychology have been sometimes referred to as a paradigm shift, Thomas Kuhn's account of major changes in scientific approaches, procedures, and theories.[1] However, psychology is not a mature science. There were American, Russian, English, German, and French psychologies—and no internationally recognized paradigm. If anything, it was a miniparadigm shift, applicable parochially only to the United States. On the other hand, one might argue that with the beginning of the twenty-first century a true international psychological paradigm was developing.

For a full understanding of the revolution, the reader would benefit from any and all of the other accounts that have

1. Kuhn (1970).

appeared in the literature.[2] An excellent overview—based on interviews with many of the participants—is provided by Bernard Baars's book that covers most aspects of the period. George A. Miller has written his own account, stressing his personal (r)evolution during the 1950s and emphasizing events in information theory, artificial intelligence, computer theory, and linguistics. Howard Gardner has described the emergence of the new cognitive science in an extensive review that covers most of the relevant issues and movements. Allen Newell and Herbert Simon presented their perceptions and experiences as an addendum to their book on problem solving, stressing developments in logic, cybernetics, linguistics, and, of course, problem solving. J. D. Greenwood has added a philosophical perspective to these accounts but also stresses the precurors of modern cognitive psychology. A more focused account is David Murray's, which tells a somewhat unidimensional story that argues that is was primarily, if not uniquely, Gestalt psychology that made the cognitive period likely or possible. Gestalt psychology was one of the many influences and, by the 1950s, was already on the wane.

Precursors for a "Revolution"

By the 1920s and 1930s, the new developments were in place—Gestalt psychology in Germany, behaviorism in the United States, and Pavlovian psychology in the Soviet Union. But radical changes had taken place in the overture to World War II. The Gestalt psychologists were driven from Germany, and most settled in the United States, and behaviorism had enunciated the

2. Baars (1986); Miller (2003); Gardner (1985); Newell and Simon (1972); Greenwood (1999); Murray (1995).

aspirations of American psychology for a single encompassing system that would eventually understand all of human and animal behavior. However, an academic pause was impelled by the war from 1939 to 1945. The war quieted any serious theoretical activity as the most active people were absorbed in applied work in support of military needs and goals.

The postwar changes in culture and technology came relatively slowly but were no less drastic than previous ones. In technology at large, Alan Turing had prepared the ground for the computer age, John von Neumann imagined the digital computer, the dormant development of television became a reality, and radar and its related cousins—born in the war—contributed their novelties. The changes accelerated with the invention of the transistor in 1947 and the later development of integrated circuits. With the end of war, the information revolution, tentatively started in the 1930s, became a reality. The start of the information revolution is probably best placed in 1936 with Turing's path-breaking publication of the notion of the "Turing machine," the ancestor of future computer developments.[3] Both industry and the scientific/intellectual establishment exhibited the symptoms of a new way of social organization centered on knowledge acquisition and transmission. Clande E. Shannon and Warren Weaver[4] popularized information theoretical analyses, and von Neumann,[5] Oskar Morgenstern, and others produced notions of computation and game theory and other ideas from engineering and physics staked

3. In Turing (1936), more fully developed in the 1950s by von Neumann (1958) and also by Turing's (1950) exploration of the "thinking machine."

4. Shannon and Weaver (1948); Shannon (1948).

5. Neumann (1958).

claims to an understanding of human behavior—including, of course, Norbert Wiener's cybernetics.[6] Since all major cultural changes are overdetermined, I try to do justice to various strands that signaled the change in psychological research and theory. At this point, one cannot give pride of place to any one of these developments; we are too close in time to those changes to decide which, if any, were central and which peripheral.

In the midst of the military activities of the war can be found one such strand. The war effort had contributed in part to the changes in psychological theory and research by bringing together a number of people in a number of efforts. Of special interest to later developments was a group at Harvard that included J. C. R. Licklider, S. S. Stevens, Ira Hirsh, Walter Rosenblith, George A. Miller, W. R. Garner, and Clifford Morgan. Their primary concern was psychoacoustics and noise research, but they also worked in signal detection and related topics. With the creation of the Lincoln Laboratory at MIT in 1951, this early deviation from behaviorist dogma prepared the ground for mathematical models and the commanding influence of signal-detection theory in perception as well as memory and other fields.[7] By the time the revolution started, these strands were ready to contribute to a new psychology. Similar war time accumulations of talent occurred in other military activities in both the United States and the United Kingdom (for example, the military's interest in vigilance phenomena influenced Donald E. Broadbent).

American psychology was to assimilate much of European psychology. We have already discussed at length the German

6. Wiener (1948).
7. Green and Swets (1966).

psychologies prior to 1930. The most extensive growth of a cognitive psychology during the behaviorist interlude occurred in Britain. It is of particular interest since no language barrier would have prevented these ideas from being generally adopted in America—but it was not to be. The early stages in the British history of cognition[8] were set by Fredevic C. Bartlett in the 1930s and by the brilliant Kenneth Craik, who died in an accident in 1945. Craik suggested in 1943 that the mind constructs models of reality:

> If the organism carries a small-scale model of external reality and its own possible actions within its head, it is able to try out various alternatives, conclude which is the best of them, react to future situations before they arise, utilize the knowledge of past events in dealing with the present and future, and in every way react to a much fuller, safer and more competent manner to emergencies which face it.[9]

Craik was the first director of the Applied Psychology Unit in Cambridge which for another half century would be a leading center for cognitive psychology. He was succeeded by Bartlett and Norman Mackworth. In 1958, Donald E. Broadbent became the APU director. Broadbent also anticipated the American revolution with his early work on attention in the 1950s and his work on communication.[10] Another important influence in Britain was George Humphrey, whose two books on the history of and data on thinking summarized the field and pointed to new directions.[11] The development toward a basically theoretical

8. See also Collins (2001).

9. Craik (1943, p. 57).

10. For the major British influences, see Bartlett (1932), Broadbent (1958), and Craik (1943, 1966).

11. Humphrey (1948, 1951).

(cognitive) psychology that had started in Great Britain produced less immediate general influence. This slow start may in part be due to the lack of a highly motivated opponent in the behaviorist tradition, which was essentially absent in Great Britain.

The contribution of French psychology has been largely overlooked, which is unfortunate since the work of Edouard Claparède, Alfred Binet, and others was closely related to modern cognitive approaches. For example, in the same two decades that Wolfgang Köhler published his work on insightful solutions, Claparède was studying problem solving, culminating in the notion of the hypothesis as central to problem solving and incidentally producing psychology's first protocol analyses.[12] The important contribution of the francophone Jean Piaget was also delayed at the international level until the 1960s, when his innovative use of the concept of the schema became important in cognitive psychology. However, the mutual isolation of French and American psychology prevented the significant influence that the French psychologists would have deserved. They too, of course, had no behaviorist antagonists.[13] I should add to the discussion the francophone developmental psychologists in the early twentieth century. The major figure was Piaget, only some of whose work was available in English in the 1920s.[14] Similarly, Claparède's work with children had been

12. Binet (1894, 1903); Claparède (1934); Pollack and Brenner (1969); Köhler (1925, originally published in 1917).

13. After 1933 to 1935, no work of impact was done in Germany, and the postwar recovery lasted too long to have any significant influence on the events of the 1950s.

14. Piaget (1926).

translated, but his major contribution to the problem of hypothesis formation was not available in English. Binet's work on intelligence testing was well known early on, but his other major work was not.[15] However, there was little early interest in a theoretical developmental psychology, and the interest in cognitive development did not take off until well after World War II.

In the United States, it was not until another half dozen years had gone by before the rejection of behaviorist dicta hit full stride and established a firm basis for the "new" cognitive psychology.[16] In the United States, the rejection of behaviorism during that earlier period had the flavor of a counterrevolutionary movement, with all the perquisite fervor displayed on both sides. The opposition to the behaviorist hegemony in the United States had been carried mainly by the Gestalt psychologists and their allies. But in 1949, there appeared a major alternative to the mainstream of behaviorism. Canadian psychology had been only partly influenced by behaviorism, and the Canadian D. O. Hebb published his refreshing and itself revolutionary *The Organization of Behavior*.[17] The book was given less attention than it deserved to the eventual embarrassment of the conventional wisdom but found enough support to become the core of a small counterrevolutionary movement. Hebb introduced notions of organization (such as organized rather than atomistic stimulus-response chains) but also cut the knot of the link between physiology and psychology. Being a physiologist by "birth," Hebb coined the phrase *conceptual nervous system*

15. Binet (1894).

16. Though it should be noted that there had been several announcements of "new" psychologies in the previous two hundred years.

17. Hebb (1949).

(CNS), noting that the invocation of quasi-physiological concepts, such as cell assemblies, was not necessarily a commitment to physiological reduction but rather a halfway house between the disciplines, where such concepts could be used as theoretical terms by psychologists.

Another discernible strand in the development of the new psychology was the resurrection of old conceptual directions that had lain dormant. Apart from the concept of organization, which I discuss later, there was the notion of the schema and of cognition itself. The schema concept, originally introduced by Immanuel Kant, has remained essentially unchanged in its use by Piaget, in its implication in Bartlett's work, and in its current incarnation.[18] The schema has not only become scientifically respectable but has also provided a link to connectionism. The term *cognitive psychology* had currency prior to its current incarnation but was seen as a fuzzy, vague approach, often categorized (probably incorrectly) with personalistic, phenomenological approaches.[19] All of these strands and tendencies produced the setting for the major changes in experimental and academic psychology by the mid-1950s. New and old ideas now found the fertile ground necessary for their development. The importance of the right time and the right place can be illustrated by important and influential papers written several years earlier that did not make an impact until "the time was ripe." Lashley's paper on serial order (discussed in detail in the next chapter) was published in 1951 but did not have any significant following until about 1960. Finally, an important influ-

18. Kant (1929, originally published in 1781); Bartlett (1932); Piaget (1953); Rumelhart (1977); Mandler (1984).

19. See, for example, Snygg and Combs (1949), but note Moore (1939).

ence on the new psychology (despite its origins at Clark L. Hull's Yale) was Carl Hovland's work on concept formation, attitude change, and related phenomena.[20]

No single event or group of events can be seen to be causally responsible for that period of activity. Two potentially influential books failed to have any important effect at the time. One was Katona's book on organization; the other Hull's et al. book on an attempt to bring S-R psychology to rote learning.[21] Katona's book was ignored as being irrelevant and beyond the reach of contemporary psychological science. The Hull volume was in the mainstream of psychology but conceptually and methodologically useless. As a result, neither had any effect at the time, but Katona was rediscovered in the 1960s when U.S. memory psychologists "discovered" the importance of organization (see below). The lessons seems to be that one can be ignored by being "out of time" or by being "wrong"; being "right" is useless until the culture is ready.

The "Revolution" Takes Hold

The major events of the miraculous five years between 1955 and 1960 occurred in memory, language, and problem solving. Much of the activity was a recapitulation of the missing theoretical years. Psychologists rediscovered the British psychologist Fredevick C. Bartlett and the importance of schemas and hypothesis in human thought and began to read Piaget as something other than a peripheral Swiss interested in the irrelevant behavior of his children. Donald E. Broadbent made *attention* a

20. See, for example, Hovland (1952).
21. Hull et al. (1940); Katona (1940).

respectable word rather than (as in the United States) a hidden metaphor for the forbidden consciousness and wrote about the importance of communication. The problem of mental organization—forgotten since the teens—was reawakened and became a major theme of the first decade of cognitive psychology. Piaget's work, translated late in its development and ignored by the behaviorists,[22] ignited the explosion of efforts in cognitive development that, ironically, replaced the behavorist dominance of learning problems and became our major source of insights into human learning.[23]

Consideration of structure and of information processing in the wider sense preoccupied other human sciences during the same period. It can be seen in Noam Chomsky's transformational grammar, in early attempts at artificial intelligence, and in the exploration of kinship structures in cultural anthropology. Whatever causes may eventually be definitively identified as the moving energy behind this wide-ranging reorganization, it certainly cannot be said that any one field or any one investigator started the changes or even predated them. The choice of the term *cognitive* was in part fortuitous. For most of that period and in keeping with the culture that fostered it, the new theories were information-processing theories, but *cognitive* had been used occasionally to describe a psychology that imagined an active human organism operating on the information in the environment. The influx of the mathematical psychologists and of the computer made the new psychology much more hard headed, and by the mid-1960s (when George A. Miller and Jerome Bruner started the Center for Cognitive Studies at Harvard

22. Piaget (1953).
23. See chapter 13.

and when Ulric Neisser published his then definitive *Cognitive Psychology*), the name had been chosen and stuck.[24]

The facts of the cognitive revolution in psychology in mid-twentieth century have been well documented.[25] I summarize some of the major factors in its development. The adoption of, or return to, cognitive themes occurred in psychology but also in other disciplines—for example, in linguistics and other social sciences. In general, the following four arguments can be advanced to explain the events surrounding the cognitive resurgence: (1) part of John B. Watson's program (and its insistence on human and animal equivalences) prevented the success of behaviorism and contributed to its replacement; (2) the change toward cognitive approaches occurred slowly in different subfields over some ten to fifteen years without an identifiable flashpoint or leader, so the term *revolution* is probably inappropriate because there were no cataclysmic events; (3) the behaviorist dogmas against which the revolution occurred were essentially confined to the United States, and while behaviorism reigned in the United States, structuralist, cognitive, and functionalist psychologies were dominant in Germany, Britain, France, and even Canada; (4) stimulus-response behaviorism was not suddenly displaced but, as a cognitive approach evolved, behaviorism faded because of its failure to solve basic questions about human thought, action, and memory in particular.

24. There had been an earlier *Cognitive Psychology* by T. V. Moore in 1939, but it was the wrong time. The volume attempted to shape the contemporary research into a Thomist framework and did not invoke an information-based psychology. It also surprisingly failed to even mention William James's psychology. For an appreciation, see Suprenant and Neath (1997).

25. See footnote 2.

As S-R behaviorism faded, there was little in the way of revolutionary Jacobin sentiments for radically rooting out previous dogmas. Certainly, a few of such sentiments found their way into print. Much was said in colloquia and in congress corridors, but the written record does not reveal a violent revolution. If anything qualifies as a Jacobin document, it was Chomsky's attack on B. F. Skinner's *Verbal Behavior*, though the attack was not intentionally aimed at the dominant Clark L. Hull–Kenneth W. Spence position.[26] Conversely, it might also be argued that Chomsky failed to distinguish between the stimulus-response analyses of Hull-Spence and the functionalism of Skinner.

If behaviorism represented only an interlude in the normal flow of the development of psychological science, what was interrupted and what replaced the behaviorist position once it was shown to be inadequate? J. D. Greenwood has discussed the tradition that developed out of the work of the Würzburg school and the psychology of Otto Selz, as well as later content- and rule-based psychologies.[27]

What about the psychology in Europe that coexisted with the behaviorism of the United States? The important aspects of European psychology of the time were that Europe was essentially unaffected and uninfluenced by behaviorism and that the developments in Europe became part of the American mainstream after the decline of behaviorism. There was both a general opening up of America to European ideas and an influx of European psychologists into the United States. If there was little influence from the United States to Europe, so was there relatively little leakage of psychological theory across European frontiers. In

26. Chomsky (1959); Skinner (1957).
27. Greenwood (1999).

the nineteenth century, William James was read in Europe, and Wilhelm Wundt was an international figure up to the beginning of the next century. But in the early twentieth century, the various national groups were relatively insulated.

In summary, there was a plethora of nonbehaviorist ideas available in the world in the 1930s and 1940s. Some of them were heard in the United States, but none of them was rigorously or widely followed. It was not until the late 1950s that the failure of behaviorism made room for these "foreign" notions. As I noted previously, the influence of Gestalt psychology as such was subtle, and many other influences, particularly from England, shaped the coming cognitive psychology. The Gestalt psychologists had little effect in other European countries, so it was not the case that their writing helped "prevent the spread of behaviorism in Europe."[28] Behaviorism held very little if any appeal against the indigenous psychologies.

The Interlude of Organization Theory

In the nineteenth century, experimental psychology of memory was initially dominated by German psychology, which had embraced British empiricism and associationism to a large extent. Hermann Ebbinghaus had introduced the serial and associative learning paradigms that were to dominate the field for many decades. With minor perturbations, the Ebbinghaus tradition smoothly merged into the functionalist tradition of the early twentieth century[29] and then into the behaviorist methodologies. The research was behaviorist in style, emphasizing

28. Murray (1995, p. 3).
29. McGeoch (1942).

stimulus-response connections and some concepts (such as reinforcement and stimulus generalization) imported from the Hull-
Spence tradition. Thus, an often atheoretical neo-Ebbinghaus
tradition survived the war and continued into the 1950s. The
preoccupations of the verbal-learning psychologists were focused on associations—their nature and strengths. Was there
an alternative conception?

A recurrent theme appears and disappears in the history of
psychologies—the notion of organization. Not unexpectedly, it
recurred again during the flowering of the cognitive revolution
—the rebirth of a theory-rich psychology. I review the history of organization theory here and place it in the context of
twentieth-century psychology.

To start, we need to define what organization theory wanted
to replace—the fundamental tenets of association theory. I discuss the purported explanatory function of associations, not
their descriptive function. The latter applies to all instances
where events occur regularly in succession or as cooccurrence.
However, it is sometimes difficult to distinguish between the descriptive and explanatory uses of associations. Consider the
types or laws of association, some of which have been with us
since Aristotle but have been amended by practically every association theorist since then. Such "types" as association by contiguity, similarity, contrast, temporal, and spatial proximity made
it difficult to decide which are purportedly explanatory or
merely descriptive. Generally, association incorporates the notion that any set of words, items, or mental representations
(depending on one's particular theoretical predilections) could
become "associated" by one of the functions listed as "types"—
that is, being given one would produce, generate, and arouse the
other one(s). The rejection of association theory—rare as it

was—generally was based on the claim that the theory was reductionist, mechanical, and not in keeping with apparent complexities of human memory.

The critique of associationist approaches that appears central stresses that they are ineffective in handling problems of meaning. The characteristic of the human mind is that it can handle the simultaneous but selective access to various aspects of a single event. People can differentiate among meanings. For example, the name *James* may suggest

- a man's name;

- a boy who was a classmate in primary school, but such a memory maybe devoid of any other content (just "there was a James");

- one's brother-in-law James, about whom one has a highly developed structural appreciation as to character, appearance, and preferences;

- a vague memory and image of a Mr. James, a professor in college who taught a single course that one remembers well;

- a recollection of the psychologist and philosopher William James and some of his work on memory, without any imagery as to what he looked like.

To differentiate among the various "associations" that the name *James* evokes, one has to invoke a number of different sets, constellations, links, and other steering mechanisms, and one has to use different ones at different times. Organization theory, in contrast, would focus on an integrated meaning representation for each of these uses. The point is that one can access any one of these scenarios individually without any reference to any of the others *and* one can recite (as above) all the

James references in a somewhat haphazard order. We can differentiate meanings.

Associationism had been found wanting for some time. I note in chapter 2[30] that John Locke had already asserted that association of ideas was an inadequate explanation for human reasoning. The latter needed semantic connections among ideas derived from our experience.[31] Others have noted the inability of association theory to handle integrative, spatial, and temporal relational concepts. In the premodern period, it was Johann Friedrich Herbart who wanted something other than cooccurrence to explain association. Herbart considered mental life to consist of a more or less organized *Komplex* of representations (*Vorstellungen*). As noted in chapter 2, he also wanted to expand the notion of associations by invoking specific forces that would direct specific associative links.

The next important step to find a theoretical underpinning for the observed associations came with Georg Elias Müller— next to Wilhelm Wundt, the other father of modern German psychology. In his wide-ranging exploration of memory between 1911 and 1917,[32] he not only berated the facile invocation of concepts to take the place of unconscious thought (see chapter 6), but he also explored a variety of memory phenomenon generally ignored by his predecessors and contemporaries, including the experiences of everyday (nondeliberate) memories[33] and the feats of memory experts. The latter led him to ex-

30. See also Greenwood (1999).

31. Locke (1690), originally published in 1689, Vol. 2, xxxiii, 5).

32. Müller (1911, 1913, 1917).

33. Though Ebbinghaus had made similar noises, generally ignored by his audience.

plore linked memory complexes in his *Komplextheorie*, which is related to if not actually derived from Alexander Bain's constellation theory and also related to some of Herbart's notions about the combination of conscious representations (*Vorstellungen*). Together with his collaborators, Müller had earlier made some attempts to explore the effects of simple pairing of stimuli on their recall, an early instance of George A. Miller's chunking.[34] There is no question that Müller was one of the forerunners of organization theory,[35] though he was not a systematizer but a sensitive and ingenious experimenter and observer.[36] In any case, the field was prepared to accept organizational concepts. Wolfgang Köhler later concluded from Müller's work that "intentional memorizing amounts to intentional organizing," which may well serve as the motto for this discussion.[37]

In the process of the cognitive (r)evolution, a variety of notions were offered that were to replace both stimulus-response behaviorism and its blood cousin—classic associationism. Most of the post-1950s developments rejected the associationist S-R behaviorist approaches, called themselves *cognitive*, and had aspects of organizational principles in their structure. The levels-of-processing approach[38] was one of these attempts and was a

34. Müller and Pilzecker (1900); Müller and Schumann (1894); and see Miller (1956).

35. With Gestalt theory in full flower, Müller (1923) contrasted his approach with theirs, though it was too late to influence the field significantly.

36. For an English summary of Müller's central contributions, see Murray and Bandomir (2000).

37. Köhler (1929, p. 263).

38. Craik and Lockhart (1972).

specific important instance of a movement to reinstate the notion of meaning and its progenitor—organization.

The concept of organization in human memory first appeared as a specific statement by Karl Duncker (noted in chapter 7) in his insistence on the structuring and restructuring of mental representations and also in his suggestion that we construct mental models of the world on which the appropriate operations are then carried out.

The major presentation of the Gestalt principles to problems of memory was carried out by George Katona. Katona, who used many of Müller's insights on organization in his book, followed Max Wertheimer[39] in considering memorial material to be meaningful when the existence and quality of the parts are determined by the structure of the whole. The culmination was the publication of his book on memorizing and organizing.[40] Katona spent much time in explicating, both experimentally and theoretically, basic principles of Gestalt psychology such as understanding, grouping, whole relations, and the function of meaning. The final message is clear: "[O]rganization is a requirement for successful memorization. It must be present in some form in all kinds of learning."[41] Organization refers to the establishment or discovery of relations among constituent elements. Katona's book characterized the organizational movement. It was typical of the behaviorist interlude that in 1941 Arthur W. Melton, one of its gatekeepers, dismissed Katona's book as lacking operational definitions and producing unreliable results.[42]

39. Wertheimer (1921).
40. Katona (1940).
41. Katona (1940, p. 249).
42. Melton (1941).

Not surprisingly, the attempts to introduce notions of organization into American psychology were not successful.

Another presentation of organization theory and attack on associationism by Köhler noted that "whatever factors favor organization in primary experience must at the same time favor association, retention, and therefore recall."[43] In general, *meaning*, *organization*, and *structure* are used interchangeably in these suggestions. Take, for example, Garner's similar approach, though not in the field of memory: "By structure I mean the totality of the relations between events. Meaning... refers to the entire set of relations... [and] meaning as structure [implies] that the structure itself is meaningful."[44] In his approach, Katona emphasized grouping and the notion that organization is a process that establishes or discovers the formation and perception of groupings; it is a requirement for memorization.

Independently of the Gestalt movement, the movement toward organization theory was characterized by Bartlett's work with schemas and his insistence that memory was constructive not reproductive[45] and by the associationist Edward Lee Thorndike's experiments demonstrating that *belongingness* ("this goes with that") was a major factor in determining what was learned and retained.[46]

Some of my own work was instrumental in introducing the next stage of interest in organization. A limited approach to the problem of organization in 1967 argued for organization and the hierarchical organization of words, in particular, as

43. Köhler (1941, p. 492).
44. Garner (1962, p. 141).
45. Bartlett (1932).
46. Thorndike (1932, p. 72).

determining factors in memory for sets of words.[47] The definition of organization postulated the formation, availability, and use of consistent relations among the members of a set or subsets such as groups, concepts, categories, and chunks. This was accompanied by a series of experiments that demonstrated how people imposed organization and categories on sets of items and how the use of these categories constructed hierarchies and determined memorial performance. In support of the notion of hierarchical organization, Gordon Bower concluded that such "schemes...are particularly effective retrieval plans."[48]

The organizational approach rejected associationist approaches and brought the problem of meaning back into experimental psychology. Meaning is (as Garner argued persuasively) identified with the structure of the material. The structure of a text, just as the structure in which the representation of a word is embedded, is its meaning. A mental event or object is meaningful to the extent that it is part of a larger, more extensive, and usually more intricate organization. A nonsense syllable is "meaningless" only to the extent that it fails to provide obvious links or ties to groupings or other mental organizations. The notion of organization was used in the late 1960s and early 1970s extensively in the psychology of memory and even generated a volume on the topic in 1972.[49] *Organization* was then used widely to include the organizational (that is, categorical and grouping) approach but also any other usually nonassociative relations, such as linguistic and semantic aspects of words and

47. Mandler (1967, 1977).
48. Bower (1970, p. 18).
49. Tulving and Donaldson (1972).

texts. However, the movement for organizational theory ran soon out of steam, and what Bower called the "Mandler Manifesto"[50] was replaced by sophisticated associationist theories.

The Other Psychologies and the Consolidation of the "Revolution"

As significant changes started to take place in experimental psychology, a parallel but conceptually independent movement was stirring the "other" psychologies. In the latter part of the first half of the century, the fields were the psychologies concerned with individuals and their social context—as seen in the clinical, social, and professional psychologies, in the mental health movements in general, and (driven by circumstance) in military and personnel psychology. Those developments have been described extensively and persuasively by Ellen Herman.[51] She discusses the major movements in the way psychology was used for both military and democratic ends, the effects of the cold war, as well as the broader issues of race and gender that affected American society. It is significant that a similar social context gave rise to two quite different strands in psychology writ large. Little of the story that I have to tell emerges in Herman's account, any more than her accounts have appeared in the "cognitive" and experimental story.

The cognitive revolution itself tended to be long and convoluted, highlighted in a series of conferences. I discuss the ones on memory in chapter 11, but memory was not the only nor was it the first field of psychology to organize conferences on

50. Bower and Bryant (1991).
51. Herman (1995).

the new directions. Allen Newell and Herbert Simon[52] have suggested that 1956 was the "critical year" for the new psychologies, and certainly it was a year filled with relevant events, papers, and books.[53] One of the most direction-giving occasions was the Special Group on Information Theory of the Institute of Electrical and Electronics Engineers, which met at MIT in 1956.[54] At that meeting, Noam Chomsky, George Miller, and Allen Newell and Herbert Simon presented the initial papers of a trend that would be defining in the next decade. Another direction-giving meeting in 1956 was the Dartmouth Summer Seminar on artificial intelligence, whose participants included Herbert Gelernter, John McCarthy, Marvin Minsky, Trenchard More, Newell, Nat Rochester, Oliver Selfridge, Claude E. Shannon, Simon, and Ray Solomonoff. In 1958, there followed the RAND Summer Seminar, primarily oriented toward computer simulation, organized by Carl Hovland, George A. Miller and Simon. Lectures were given by the organizers, as well as Newell, Minsky and J. C. Shaw. Most important was a group of invitees, many of them from a younger generation, among whom were such important later leaders of the field as Robert P. Abelson, Richard C. Atkinson, William F. Battig, Daniel E. Berlyne, Jack Block, James S. Coleman, Ward Edwards, Bert F. Green, Lyle V. Jones, Edmund T. Klemmer, Gilbert Krulee, Nissim Levy, Irvin Pollack, Roger N. Shepard, and Donald W. Taylor. A similar pace setter, in that case for the emergence of artificial intelligence and its relation to cognitive processes, was the London Symposium on the Mechanisation of Thought Processes in

52. Newell and Simon (1972).

53. For example, Bruner, Goodenough, and Austin (1956); Miller (1956).

54. See Baars (1986, passim).

1958.[55] As has been shown, the 1950s surely were ready for the emergence of the new information-processing psychology—the new cognitive psychology. In other areas, the attention to cognitive factors developed at various times during the decades following the 1950s, as in emotion,[56] perception,[57] and personality theory.[58]

In the next chapter, I present two case studies of the changes that took place during the revolution. They illustrate the successive steps that were taken toward different ways of looking at a discipline. But these changes occurred relatively late. One might conjecture about what might have happened in the field of memory if behaviorism had not dominated American psychology for forty years. Among the possibilities is that mechanisms like schemas would have been adopted early on from Bartlett and Piaget, that Weston Bousfield's notions about clustering together with Katona's book on organization would have resulted in early attention being paid to organizational factors, that Kenneth Craik's thoughts about representation would have been attended to, and that questions about the structure of syntax and semantics would have been addressed. All of this happened eventually, but some decades later. What followed eventually in the last decade of the twentieth century was a period of consolidation and general quietude in the memory field.

Psychology, just as many other intellectual endeavors, conforms to Hegel's view of the spiral of thought, with topics recurring repeatedly in the history of a discipline, often at a more

55. Mechanisation (1959).
56. Schachter and Singer (1962).
57. Hochberg (1968).
58. Mischel (1968).

sophisticated or developed level. The advent of connectionism has already shown a return of a variety of associationism in modern clothing. In the early twenty-first century, we are in the midst of a preoccupation with neurophysiological reduction, a concern that psychology had previously displayed at a periodic cycle of some forty to fifty years. The notion of recurring cycles is alien to a recent attempt to see the future of the "cognitive revolution."[59] The mirror displayed in that book is cloudy, indeed, with a variety of different predictions. One of the more unlikely is the one presented by the keystone chapter of a book in which Jerome Bruner endorses a postmodern view of cognitive science,[60] which is the one position least likely—given its postulates—to foresee any future at all. But psychology has been one of the disciplines that has essentially been unchanged by postmodern attempts (in contrast, for example, to literature and anthropology). The most likely case is that psychology will—as it has in the past—muddle along, encountering other revolutions, whether cognitive or not.

59. Johnson and Erneling (1997).
60. Bruner (1997).

11 Two Case Histories from the New Psychology

The motive forces of the new psychology of the twentieth century were varied and part of the larger social fabric. However, the impact of the cognitive revolution has been important enough to have lasted half a century, fifty years that were marked both in society at large and in the corner called psychology by a preoccupation with cognition—that is, with knowledge and its processing. By the end of the twentieth century, this revolution had spawned the notion of the cognitive sciences, concerned with the way that organisms, and primarily human ones, take up information from the environment, transform and store it, and use it in action and communication and how our brain provides the material basis of cognitive activity. This chapter illustrates the history of the emergence and appeal of cognitive psychology with two extensive case histories. The first examines the way we handle serial order in information that is taken up from the environment and used to communicate within it, and the second looks at a part of the way memory research entered the new era. Both of these case studies show how researchers have tried to go beyond the constraints of associationism and demonstrate the rather slow pace of the revolution.

The Problem of Serial Order

Hermann Ebbinghaus's approach to serial order—the primary memory problem addressed in his monograph—had a lasting effect. It established an associationist analysis as the preferred way to look at the way humans impose serial orders on memorial contents. More precisely, Ebbinghaus and his descendants were concerned with the way we reflect the serial orders provided for us. As is shown in chapter 4, Ebbinghaus had expanded the classical notion that associations are established by immediate succession or simultaneous experience by introducing the concept of remote associations. Both concepts were used by him and his successors in explaining the reproduction of serial order. And whereas some Gestalt arguments were made about the inadequacy of mere association in establishing connected materials, it was not until Karl Lashley's paper at the Hixon symposium in 1948 that an organized critique of the associative position was launched and eventually listened to.[1]

The symposium was organized by Lloyd Jeffress of the University of Texas and held at the California Institute of Technology. The participants were Ward Halstead, Heinrich Klüver, Wolfgang Köhler, Karl Lashley, Rafael Lorento de Nó, Warren McCulloch, and John von Neumann, and they were joined by a number of discussants. In retrospect, the array of leaders of the psychological and neurophysiological community might have been sufficient to start a concerted movement against the regnant behaviorism. This would be particularly true of the physiologists who would have been acutely aware of the fact that Clark

1. My discussion of Lashley and the Hixon symposium is indebted to a detailed and insightful article by Darryl Bruce (1994).

L. Hull's dominant behaviorism had little basis in known brain mechanisms. On the other hand, it is significant that one could assemble such a distinguished and influential group without not even a nod in the direction of representing behaviorist thought. The symposium was not published until 1951, but like many of the developments I discussed in previous chapters, the events of the 1940s and earlier were precursors of the new psychology. Their full impact came later.

Lashley's paper had two main components: arguments against associative chaining and suggestions for the kind of theory that would replace it. As far as chaining was concerned, Lashley had previously demonstrated the inadequacy of the notion.[2] He addressed three problems: (1) how are individual elements of a list activated to produce temporal order, (2) what are the processes that put a restriction on the serial behavior within defined limits, and (3) what is the syntax of the act? The search was for "a generalized pattern or schema of integration which may be imposed upon a wide range and a wide variety of specific acts."[3]

Lashley's argument against associative chaining was based to a large extent on an analysis of language—specifically, that syntax does not involve a link between the adjoining words of a sentence. He extended his analysis to such skills as typing and piano playing, emphasizing some of the anticipatory motions involved in these action sequences. In the end, he was looking for an integrative organizational notion that would provide a schema of order to be imposed on the elements to be ordered. Most of Lashley's analyses were concerned with temporal

2. Lashley (1930, 1942).
3. Lashley (1951, p. 122).

ordering, though he also noted that the same problems were relevant to spatial orderings.[4]

Lashley's paper had little impact initially, and Darryl Bruce's analysis of its citation record shows that it was not frequently cited until the 1960s or 1970s, after which it was cited about thirty times per year, a rate still very much apparent in citations of thirty-seven and thirty-two in 2002 and 2003. As Bruce noted, the Lashley serial-order paper did not energize new trends but rather supported and shaped them. The same can be said of many other significant contributions of the time: they were all supporters, and the energy came from larger forces in contemporary history.

Much has happened in the intervening years, but it seems to have been inaccessible to many of Ebbinghaus's children, whose early upbringing may have prevented them from paying attention to revolutionary texts. Thus, one of the eminent investigators of memory was able to say in 1983: "How does a subject learn a serial list if not by forming associations from item to item? The question remains open.... The mechanisms underlying serial learning remain one of the enigmas waiting around for a fresh approach."[5] But as I show presently, fresh approaches had been around for quite some time. Even within the associationist tradition, Donald H. Kausler had added "if anything," when he talked about "the mystery of what, if anything, is the true functional stimulus, if anything."[6] Modes of thinking die

4. As we noted years later, spatial and temporal order are frequently confounded, though the underlying structures could be assessed independently, and one can "use temporal and spatial structures as independent and additive retrieval cues" (Mandler and Anderson, 1971, p. 128).

5. Underwood (1983, p. 196).

6. Kausler (1974, p. 267).

hard. It was generally assumed that serial order involved some kind of chaining and that paired associates were, so to say, little chains or links. That also assumes that paired associates, the learning of what goes with what, represent some kind of stimulus-response link or chain.[7]

What were the alternatives? If not chaining, then what? On the issue of paired associates, Solomon Asch and Sheldon Ebenholtz had shown that associative links, were, at least, doubtful.[8] In fact, item pairs are acquired as independent (novel) units that do not incorporate clues to directionality.[9] Linguists have known for a long time (and psychologists should have known since Lashley) that syntactic order is not and cannot be associatively acquired.[10] In 1970, F. Restle and E. R. Brown tackled the question of the structure of serial ordering, and Restle produced a theory of serial pattern learning—that is, of "the integration of a sequence of responses that are organized in a meaningful way."[11] This followed an earlier conclusion that "conventional theories of serial verbal learning are inadequate to account for serial learning in general since they do not deal with S's ability to generate abstract and flexible rules to guide his performance."[12]

Serial learning, then, is not a question of how people reproduce the serial order imposed by the environment in a

7. The stimulus-response terms were later abandoned, but the basic approach was maintained in such new labels as *context* and *target*.

8. Asch and Ebenholtz (1962).

9. Mandler, Rabinowitz, and Simon (1981).

10. See also Miller and Chomsky (1963).

11. Restle (1970, p. 481).

12. Restle and Brown (1970, p. 124).

mirrorlike fashion but rather how they may use the structural and organizational tools at their command to bring order and meaning into the sequence so that it can be reproduced in the required order. If we ever return to Ebbinghaus's problem, it is likely that we will find that the reproduction of serial order of words (or even nonsense syllables) involves the application of a variety of techniques and mental structures, which vary from occasion to occasion and from person to person. In other words, the very "Mnemotechnik" that Ebbinghaus wanted to avoid and that the American establishment also declared beyond the pale of scientific investigation provides the format for a better understanding of the problem of serial order, when a formal syntactic structure is not invoked. However, even in the absence of semantic structure, serial learning requires grouping and structuring operations. Temporal and spatial information may well be independently encoded,[13] and both temporal and spatial information seem to depend on the encoding of temporal-spatial patterns. Using knowledge about serial position is one type of useful information, using spatial contiguities is another, and preferential treatment of new items, primacy, and recency are additional tools that may be used in the acquisition of serial order. The acquisition of serial order requires an active organizing system that imposes structure on its inputs as well as on its products. People adopt a serial ordering, which reflects more the ordering they impose on the list of items than the one chosen by the experimenter.[14] The acquisition of serial order involves structuring and is an organizational structure like categorization and hierarchical structure.

13. Mandler and Anderson (1971).
14. Asch and Ebenholtz (1962).

The Cognitive Shift in Memory Studies[15]

The field was called *verbal learning* under the behaviorist aegis, continuing a belief that basic learning processes (no different from those operative for nonhuman animals) were being investigated. Since learning—the novel association of stimuli with responses—was the basic law of psychology, all behavioral phenomena, including so-called memory processes, had to be brought under the operation of that basic law.

Deviations from the behaviorist stimulus-response orthodoxy occurred early on in the field of verbal learning. A case history of the area is interesting because the field was populated not only by revolutionaries but also by large number of orthodox conservative researchers. I note in chapter 10 some of the excursions prior to 1950 that signaled the coming changes. In the 1950s, one of the early indicators was Weston Bousfield's work showing that in free recall categorically related words tend to cluster.[16] Then in the early 1950s, Charles N. Cofer convened an informal Group for the Study of Verbal Behavior (GSVB) that met at the fringes of conventions. The GSVB established the early deviations from the verbal-learning dogma by providing a forum for the discussion of such revolutionary topics as free recall (the occurrence of responses without discernible stimuli) and categorical clustering. We can track further developments in four conferences—at Minnesota in 1955, at Gould House in New York State in 1959 and 1961 (I refer to these as Gould 1 and Gould 2), and at the University of Kentucky at Lexington in 1966.

15. The following is a version of a more extended discussion to be found in Mandler (2002c).

16. Bousfield (1953).

• At the 1955 Minnesota conference, the following presented papers: Bousfield, Cofer, Davis H. Howes, James J. Jenkins, L. J. Postman, W. A. Russell, and S. Saporta.

• At Gould 1 (1959), all of the above with the exception of Howes and Saporta were present, together with James Deese, Albert E. Goss, G. Mandler, Arthur W. Melton, B. S. Musgrave, C. E. Noble, Charles E. Osgood, and B. J. Underwood.

• At Gould 2 (1961), the members of Gould 1 came, with the exception of Bousfield and Osgood (who had been invited but were unable to attend), and the following were added: Roger W. Brown, George A. Miller, Bennet B. Murdock, Jr., L. R. Peterson, Roger N. Shepard, A. W. Staats, and D. D. Wickens.

• At the Kentucky (1966) conference, attendees from the previous conferences were Cofer, Deese, Jenkins, Mandler, Osgood, Postman, and Underwood (who withdrew his paper), together with Solomon Asch, William F. Battig, T. G. Bever, L. E. Bourne, T. R. Dixon, D. E. Dulany, Jerry A. Fodor, M. Garrett, D. L. Horton, N. F. Johnson, F. H. Kanfer, H. H. Kendler, G. Keppel, P. M. Kjeldergaard, H. Maltzman, D. McNeill, H. Pollio, Endel Tulving, and R. K. Young. The list included people interested in language, some additional ones in the memory and verbal-learning area, as well as general behaviorists.

There was obvious continuity among the four conferences. Five (out of seven) speakers at the Minnesota conference were at Gould 1, four of them were at Gould 2, and Gould 2 was designed to be a continuation of Gould 1 with only two Gould 1 speakers unable to attend. More interesting are the additions that appear in Gould 2. With the exception of Staats, they were all significant contributors to the cognitive psychology of the next thirty years. Staats, a traditional behaviorist, tried to defend the status quo with a spirited defense of a physicalistic stimulus-response psychology, sprinkled with such pejorative comments about cognitive concepts as "improper method" with "mentalistic overtones."[17]

Seven members of the original Gould 1 group were at Kentucky. However, the object of the latter conference was to gather specialists in the area of verbal behavior and to address the relation of their work to general behavior theory (interpreted as stimulus-response theory). That goal was, as we shall see, anachronistic at best.

The early setting for the transformation was set in 1955 at the Minnesota conference, which is described in Jenkins and in Jenkins and Postman.[18] Apart from the novel interaction with a genuine linguist (Saporta), the conference contents heralded the changes that were about to happen. There was still some preoccupation with the nature and manipulation of associative responses, but these were put in terms of different contexts, norms, and instructions. The influence of the linguistic environment was mirrored in a new interest in understanding grammatical categories and the functions of syntax. And in Davis H. Howe's presentation, there were the first glimmers of the coming mathematical models. But the old traditions of learning lists of nonsense syllables seemed to be well on their way out.

Then in 1958 in discussions with Charles N. Cofer, the Office of Naval Research (ONR), which had supported many of the researchers in verbal behavior, offered to fund a conference of some of its grantees and other interested parties. Gould 1 met

17. Cofer and Musgrave (1963, pp. 272–273).
18. Jenkins (1955); Jenkins and Postman (1957).

in the fall of 1959. With a couple of notable exceptions (George A. Miller was invited but unable to attend), the attendees represented the range of interests and ages of the field. Commitments to the status quo ranged from Arthur W. Melton (the *eminence grise* of verbal behavior) to a trio of young Turks (Deese, Jenkins, and Mandler). Hard-line stimulus-response behaviorism was represented by Albert E. Goss. The conference proceedings were published in 1961, and a verbatim record of most of the discussions was recorded by Musgrave.[19]

The topics in Gould 1 were themselves a deviation from the seventy-five-year history of the field since Ebbinghaus initiated the experimental study of memory. Relatively little was said about the use of nonsense syllables, and much was said about language and meaning. It can be argued that the major new interests developed by this conference arose out of the repeated consideration of semantics and syntax. The latter, in particular, was initiated by discussions of Goss's view of sentence production. The behaviorist implication that sentences were sequences of stimulus-response chains mediated by verbal labels was strongly attacked and disputed. A summary of the syntactical problems was generally accepted: "The occurrence of a new word in a syntactic structure determines its position and form in most other syntactic structures in that language. This constraint cannot be explained in terms of the distribution of response probabilities or contingent probabilities between encoded units."[20] This was a direct rejection of associationist positions and heralded the importance of organizational processes in the next decade.

19. Cofer (1961); Musgrave (1959).
20. Cofer (1961, p. 78).

The report of the conference also included a general statement that usually was facetiously referred to as the "manifesto" and probably was authored by Deese, Jenkins, and Mandler. It arose out of assertions such as that the "speculative naming of mental states and entities" would not add to our knowledge (hence the manifesto was sometimes called the "anticognitive manifesto"). The statement questioned whether "syntactical problems can be adequately handled" by an associative orientation or whether "conceptual schemas which depend on verbal labels [can] explain the general problem of syntactic structure." Attempts to explain syntactic structures by currently available approaches were rejected. At the same time, it attacked the "glib invocation" of mental mechanisms and rejected "facile criticisms and the mere postulation of new processes."[21] The "manifesto" was an attempt to undermine associationist dogma, on the one hand, and to quiet the fears of the conservative establishment of theoretical excesses, on the other.

In his summary of the Gould 1 conference, Cofer noted the following novel emphases: the problem of response integration (acquisition of a response independent of the stimulus-response connection), the emphasis on one-trial learning, the recognition that nonsense syllables are "complex affair[s]," the notion that recall is a constructive and guessing process (a point only glossed by Cofer but of great emphasis in later years), and the attempt to assess meaning experimentally (not very successful). At the same time, long-held assumptions, such that frequency of experience determines associative probabilities or that responses are always acquired in the context of stimuli, were questioned and often put aside. Approaching the footsteps of other

21. Cofer (1961, p. 80).

developments in the coming revolution were a single passing reference to Noam Chomsky's *Syntactic Structures* and a mention of the impending and influential book by Miller, Eugene Galanter, and Karl H. Pribram.[22]

Gould 1 generated enough light (and some heat) for the Office of Naval Research to sponsor a follow-up conference. In Gould 2, the new orthodoxies had just about arrived. The conference was held in June 1961, and its report was published in 1963.[23] Apart from the character of the conference participants, the topics and the flavor of the discussion acknowledged the changed climate. Among the formal papers presented, there were an analysis of recognition by Bennet B. Murdock, Jr. that was essentially devoid of stimulus-response concepts, a discussion of the acquisition of syntax by Roger W. Brown (and Colin Fraser) that was both naturalistic and nonbehaviorist, a discussion of purpose by Russell, and an influential paper on immediate memory (not verbal learning) by Lloyd Peterson. The most modern of the presentations was Miller's discussion of Postman's paper on one-trial learning. Significantly, it ended with a presentation of Edward Feigenbaum and Herbert Simon's EPAM (elementary perceiver and memorizer) theory as an example of "human cognitive processes." EPAM was one of the earliest attempts to develop computer-oriented models of human memory, originally presented in 1959.[24]

In the summary of the conference, Wickens noted that the discussion had been divided into two opposing camps. One of these "clearly reads S-R," but he could not identify the other. It

22. Chomsky (1957); Miller, Galanter, and Pribram (1960).
23. Cofer and Musgrave (1963).
24. Feigenbaum (1959).

was not quite Gestalt or structuralist or functionalist, and Wickens ended up calling it "non-S-R, or should it be anti-S-R?"[25] He characterized the two groups as showing (1) a difference in generating research problems (with the S-R group looking for problems to which their theory can be applied, whereas the antis were indifferent to current psychological theory), (2) a difference in accepting innovations (with the S-R group applying "whenever possible the timeworn concepts of their system," whereas the antis were "receptive to...theoretical formulations which are new to psychology," and (3) a commitment in the S-R group to physiology, associationism, and Pavlovian conditioning, whereas the antis had no "residual...sentiment for this physicalistic way of thought."[26]

The goals of the Kentucky conference were broader than those of the other three—an integration under the aegis of stimulus-response principles. However, it was too late for such an effort; most of the papers were departures from stimulus-response orthodoxy. The proceedings of the conference were published in 1968.[27] These papers (and the often fiery disputations at the conference) showed that the result was a contentious confrontation between quasi-behaviorist associationism and an assertive attack by the new cognitive practitioners. Some fifteen years after the initial signs of change in American psychology, it was now possible to say such things as: "Is anybody really willing to assume that the general laws of habits, as developed in simple behavior in lower animals, apply to verbal behavior in man?"[28]

25. Quoted in Cofer and Musgrave (1963, p. 374).
26. Cofer and Musgrave (1963, pp. 375–376).
27. Dixon and Horton (1968).
28. Dixon and Horton (1968, p. 110).

Central to the attack were a rejection of associationism and the new distantiation of language from the other traditional verbal behavior concerns. The attack on associationism and S-R approaches in several papers centered on the claim that association was a descriptive term and that associations did not explain anything but were something to be explained. As Asch noted: "It may even be in order to entertain the possibility that it is not necessary, nor perhaps fruitful, to be an associationist in the study of associations."[29] The new approaches to language, fueled now by Chomsky's contributions, rejected associationism out of hand and required new logical structures for the study of language. And seven years after Gould 1, the rejection of the "glib invocation of 'schemas', 'structures' and 'organization'" had been replaced by principled discussions of these feared concepts.

Dixon and Horton noted in their summary that instead of an integration within some general behavior theory, the conference produced "significant objections concerning [the] restrictions and adequacy of [S-R theory]." They noted the "heated discussion" and concluded: "it appears that a revolution is certainly in the making."[30] One can argue that the (r)evolution had already taken place. On the other hand, the feeling of many of the cognitive participants that both behaviorism and associationism had been defeated was clearly in error. As George Humphrey suggested in 1951, the history of the psychology of thinking consists mainly of an unsuccessful revolt against the doctrine of associationism.[31]

29. Dixon and Horton (1968, p. 227).
30. Dixon and Horton (1968, pp. 573, 580).
31. Humphrey (1951).

The conferences were followed by the change of the Group for the Study of Verbal Behavior (GSVB) into the organizing group for a new *Journal of Verbal Learning and Verbal Behavior*,[32] but the name of the journal was not changed into the current *Journal of Memory and Language* until 1982.

These two case histories demonstrate the cumulative nature of the change. Behaviorism—as a generally accepted direction for mainstream psychology—was rejected, though the associationist doctrine was contested but not replaced. The changes that did take place were relatively slow and took place between the late 1940s and the mid-1960s. Not until the end of the century was the cognitive revolution seen as a *fait accompli* and did cognitive science become the new orthodoxy.

32. Cofer (1978).

12 Old Problems and New Directions at the End of the Century

A discussion dealing with current trends and directions—presumably as guideposts to the future—is fraught with danger and error: *caveat lector*. I take as a point of departure Hegel's *Science of Logic*, in which he implies that knowledge changes (advances?) not by destroying the past but rather by preserving what is known and improving it at a "higher" level (a process that sometimes is referred to as "Hegel's spiral").[1] We are now more than half a century away from the cognitive revolution and its energizing drive: is it time for a new change of direction? I start with some of the general trends that are discernible in the new century, with a stress on their psychological counterparts.

Reductionism and Finalism

One theme in the current cultural scene apparently impinges on scientific enterprises—reductionism and finalism. First, a cyclical

1. I was introduced to the notion that psychological knowledge may be an excellent example of a repetitious history when I learned many years ago from E. H. P. Klatskin that between the mid-nineteenth and mid-twentieth centuries advice to new mothers changed cyclically every twenty to twenty-five years between advocating schedule and demand feeding of infants.

phenomenon has once again aroused much interest—the claims of *reductionism*. I look at both the excessive claims of some reductionist arguments and the reasonable "reduction" implied in current neuropsychological research. In the world at large, some excesses are demonstrated in the tendency to ascribe human traits primarily, if not entirely, to our genetic makeup. In the cognitive sciences in general, this is paired with a belief that knowing that the brain is active may be adequate to explain behavior and thought. Society at large is fascinated with what the brain does and with the cerebral substrates of social and individual phenomena. The increasing interest in brain and behavior relationships and the rise of neuropsychology have contributed to a view that complex (mental) phenomena can be understood (reduced to) in their entirety as more basic (physiological) ones.

The reductionist argument cannot be left in isolation from other reductionist claims in the sciences. Reduction without conceptual remainders can be rejected for psychology, just as it has been rejected for chemistry and biology.[2] Reductionism must not be confused with materialism, nor is an antireductionist position an idealist position. The general (originally philosophical) materialist position does not require a reductionist inference. Its relevance to psychology was well stated by B. Pippard in terms of a "materialist objectivism" that incorporates most contemporary "materialist" positions. Pippard suggests that "the material world is a real thing, which in appropriate circumstances can generate the property of consciousness, but this consciousness is part of the material world and its perceptions of that world are incomplete and imperfect."[3] Put differently, the

2. Eldredge and Tattersall (1982); Mandler (1969, 1985b); Pippard (1985); Putnam (1980).

3. Pippard (1985, p. 8).

so-called mental events are products of material bodies, just as different "physical" manifestations are products of a particular organ (for instances, the structure and function of bodily organs).

But such a modern materialism does not imply a radical reductionist position. Explanations at the psychological level cannot be reduced, without remnant, to explanations of the same phenomena at the physiological or hormonal level. This is not to say that the investigation of the relation between psychology and neurophysiology is either unnecessary or fruitless. On the contrary, it has created a new and budding field, and observations and hypotheses have usefully gone in both directions. It seems to be the case that explanations in science in terms of more basic processes have occurred after the more complex observations and theories were well established. This has happened in biology, where gene theory was a necessary precursor of molecular explanations; in physics, where an understanding of atomic and molecular functions preceded nuclear physics in the modern sense; and in psychology in both vision and acoustics. At the present time, the emergence of neuropsychology as a productive and informative discipline followed the exploration of language and memory in psychology and linguistics.

The most consistent form of reductionism in psychology wants to eliminate all intervening concepts and experiences and go directly to physiology as the *complete and exhaustive* explanatory basis of human behavior. It was never clear how a complete reductionism would be possible in terms of current knowledge, how the experience of dread or beauty (or their "meaning") would be entirely covered by the understanding of the relevant brain processes, how neurology would explain mathematical reasoning, or how fear could be "reduced" to neurochemistry—any more than the understanding of social phenomena could be explained entirely in terms of the behavior of individual persons.[4] In its most extreme form, a psychologically naive science-fiction version of a radical reductionist program proposes that human conscious experience can be completely eliminated and that we can directly "experience" wavelengths instead of colors, thalamic impulses instead of emotions, and so on.[5] In the late nineteenth century, the basic attitude was that physiology will eventually be the explanatory basis for all of psychological phenomena. William James and Wilhelm Wundt both invoked neurophysiology as a necessary part of any psychological explanation, whether in James's words as codeterminants or in Wundt's as *Hülfkenntnis* (auxiliary knowledge).[6] At the end of the nineteenth and the beginning of the twentieth century, independent theoretical terms were widely introduced into psychology by such diverse movements as psychoanalysis, the Würzburg discovery of imageless thought, and the Gestalt school. These developments ameliorated the reductionist stance of the late nineteenth century, but even within these contexts there were attempts at (nonradical) reduction as in Sigmund Freud's search for the physiology of thought and Wolfgang Köhler's extension of field theory to brain functions. But the reductionist movement remained relatively quiescent in the early twentieth century and during the subsequent behaviorist period in the United States. The major reason was that Clark L. Hull's and Edmard C. Tolman's behaviorist theories

4. See also Putnam (1980).

5. Churchland (1984).

6. James (1890, p. 4); Wundt (1896, p. 29).

were not receptive to neurophysiological speculation, whereas B. F. Skinner eschewed theoretical terms and appealed to an undefined physiology as being explanatory of behavior. There was a brief revival of neuropsychology in the 1940s and 1950s with D. O. Hebb's conceptual nervous system,[7] Warren McCulloch and Walter Pitts's neural nets (the forerunners of current connectionism),[8] and an important paper by Jerome Lettvin, Humberto Maturana, McCulloch, and Pitts.[9] The new cognitive psychology arrived in the late 1950s and swamped reductionist neuropsychological thought. After cognitive psychology stopped being a novelty and settled into a routine course by the last quarter of the century, neuropsychology stirred again. The theoretical and experimental sophistication of the new psychology and of neuropsychology generated a new atmosphere that was devoid of the simplistic reductionist notions of earlier times. The new cognitive neuroscience focused on initial inquiries on how the brain might accomplish psychological phenomena. Just as British psychology had preempted cognitive advances during the 1930s and 1940s, so did British psychologists, such as Oliver L. Zangwill and Richard C. Oldfield, prefigure neuropsychology in the 1970s (more about cognition and physiology in chapter 13).

I have given the name of *finalism* to the notion that humanity is reaching ultimate solutions or positions in a variety of fields. On the scientific side, we are frequently presented with the notion that recent developments in physics, such as string theory,

7. Hebb (1949).

8. McCulloch and Pitts (1943, 1948); see also McCulloch's contribution to the Hixon symposium listed in chapter 11.

9. Lettvin, Maturana, McCulloch, and Pitts (1959).

will produce the final theory that will explain everything, and similarly the popular notion persists that the exploration of the human genome will give final answers to our genetic predispositions. In the political field, we have been told that liberal democracy is the final state of human political organization, and the trend toward fundamentalism in Christian, Islamic, Jewish, and other religious communities proclaims another ultimately "correct" condition, not to mention the predicted imminent arrival of the apocalypse. Economically, we are sometimes told that globalization will solve local economic problems. In psychology, the birth of cognitive science is sometimes interpreted as the submergence of an identifiable psychology in a better and general disciplinary solution. The form of finalism that has invaded the humanities and social sciences is represented by postmodernism (to be discussed later in some detail).

Varieties of Psychology

I next address some special trends in psychological research. One is psycholinguistics, which is of special interest as an intense interplay of theoretical and empirical matters that involves the neighboring field of linguistics. Another concerns the possibility of adding different and sometimes novel approaches of research to the experimental tradition.

Psychology and the Origin of Language

Though the study of language belongs historically to anthropologists and linguists, psychologists have consistently been involved in its investigation, and the psychology of language is an integral part of language studies. Psychologists have also taken part in speculations on the origins of language, specifically

wondering whether psychological processes partake in its generation or whether language arises *sui generis*.

In 1900, Wilhelm Wundt discussed the miracle theory (*Wundertheorie*) of the origin of language. He described it as a theory
that asserts "that the function of language is closely connected
with human nature, and that therefore to understand the
miracle of the creation of language implies the understanding
of the creation of humankind itself."[10] Given that premise,
Wundt notes that it is not surprising that the creation or origin
of language was seen as having emerged all at once just as human beings were supposed to have done. Language was seen in
these theories as a discontinuous event—a sudden emergence.
But even in the nineteenth century, other (and better) theoretical treatments were available, such as Wundt's own, in the volume on language of his *Völkerpsychologie*, where he notes that
"language presumably developed out of the simpler forms of expressive movements."[11] And in his introductory text, Wundt
comments on the power of the naturally occurring sign language of deaf and mute children, who, when raised without
any deliberate instruction, communicate by means of "a natural
development of gestural speech, which combines meaningful
expressive movements." A combination of miming and panto-
miming signs produced both pointing and painting gestures,
which "generate a type of sentence construction whereby
objects are described and events told."[12] Elsewhere, Wundt
spends a chapter on gestural language and its complexity, grammar, and likely place as a forerunner to verbal language. In the

10. Wundt (1900–1909).
11. Wundt (1900–1909, Vol. 1).
12. Wundt (1896).

contemporary literature, similar suggestions appear, as in the conclusion that "even a limited combination of vowels and consonants, reinforcing facial expressions and manual signs, must have offered [*Homo habilis*] practical advantages."[13] Talmy Givòn has discussed both ontogenetic and phylogenetic considerations of the development of grammar that puts primary emphasis on the necessary precursors of verbal grammar in the race and in the child.[14]

Various candidates have appeared in the twentieth century for the elucidation of the origin of language. Continuing from the nineteenth century in various forms were such theories as the imitation theory, which assumes that the names of creatures and objects are imitations of the sound they make, and the interjectional theory, which derived words from the natural exclamations. Most of these theories paid little attention to the problem of grammar, nor did the more modern continuity theories, which postulated a clear descent from the expressive and communicative behavior of other animals. By midcentury, the field was wide open for a new development, and an evolutionary theory put language directly into the genetic substratum that won the honors, even though as late as 1967 Eric Lenneberg had concluded that there is no need to assume "genes for language."[15]

A great variety of different approaches appeared, in part presumably in response to the theoretical failure of the nineteenth-century attempts, such as *Wundertheorie*, but the notion of the sudden discontinuous emergence of language surfaced again in

13. Andrews and Stringer (1993).
14. Givòn (1979).
15. Lenneberg (1967).

mid-twentieth century. Noam Chomsky coupled his insights into the structure and function of language with a theory of its origin that is again a miracle theory. It is based on a rationalist (rather than empiricist) approach to problems of knowledge and posits an innate language skill, similar to the innate ideas of earlier philosophers. Chomsky approaches the description that Wundt gave for a *Wundertheorie* when he notes that in the study of human language we approach something like "human essence."[16] His quasi-evolutionary hypothesis is an intellectual curiosity for evolutionary thought since he argues for a single move, a single step from no language to language, without the usual intermediate steps (adaptive by themselves) that characterize Darwinian thought. Macromutations produce a miracle theory, a *deus ex machina*, to explain the origins of language. In implying that human language has little or nothing in common with the communication systems of other animals or that it cannot be shown to develop from more primitive systems, Chomsky also ignores more sophisticated and as yet incomplete approaches to the emergence of language. In fact, he asks for evidence of a "single" evolutionary process, when it is more likely that a number of different processes may have contributed to the wonders of human language.[17] One can understand why the nineteenth century produced miracle theories, but it seems indefensible to do so a hundred years later with much better knowledge of evolutionary processes and the cognitive capacities of humans. But the cyclical nature of the arguments started to turn in the mid-1990s as a variety of nonmiracle approaches to language vied for attention.[18] Happily, they are of a higher

16. Chomsky (1956, 1972).

17. Bates, Thal, and Marchman (1991).

18. For example, Bates et al. (1991); Deacon (1997); Tomasello (1995).

quality than the successors to the *Wundertheorie* failures of the nineteenth century.

I conclude this brief excursion into linguistics to note that one of the products of the new cognitive psychology was the burgeoning of an experimental psycholinguistics. Language was a field ready made for an information-processing approach, and the last quarter of the twentieth century saw the inevitable marriage of psychology and linguistics.[19] An important consequence was the development of psychological models of word and sentence processing, initiated primarily by John Morton's logogen model, which dealt with the various representations of words in their different syntactic and semantic characteristics.[20]

Opportunities and Options: Beyond Physics Envy

We have seen how Wundt bifurcated psychology into its experimental and nonexperimental sections. This step had two consequences: one was the establishment of a dominance order in psychology, with the experimentalists becoming cocks of the roost; the other was an attempt—which reached its peak by the middle of the twentieth century—by the previously nonexperimental areas to establish their experimental credentials. Little thought was given to the possibility that Wundt's psychological dualism may have been at least partially right. The main reason was the intent that psychology as a whole was to become a science and sciences were—by definition—experimental. Wundt had not given any indication how the nonexperimental psychological topics could be scientific without being experimental. One of the results was a kind of social psychology (though cer-

19. See Clark and Clark (1977).
20. Morton (1969).

tainly not all of it) so decried by some of its critics.[21] The sometimes extreme attempts to experimentalize social topics resulted
in laboratory experiments that were sometimes rather poor cari-
catures of the social phenomena to be investigated. What was
missed was the opportunity to adopt scientific models that were
not experimental but certainly had perfectly sound scientific
credentials. I am thinking specifically about such fields of endeavor as paleontology and astronomy.

Astronomy, in particular, has some rather interesting parallels
with nonexperimental psychological phenomena. Astronomers
deal with objects—such as planets, stars, and galaxies—that are
each unique and also follow general laws. These objects exist in
aggregations that are characterized by the fact that the interactions among them determine in part the features and behaviors
of the individual objects. Astronomers tend to find new objects
that display characteristics not seen before, and they adjust their
theories to take account of these new findings. To bring some
structure into their endeavor, astronomers also survey the types
of objects (such as stars) that they encounter, and such surveys
establish typologies—categories of objects that have similar
defining characteristics. There are no experiments in the sense
of manipulating variables and observing their effects. The simi-
larities between this kind of endeavor and a possible psychology
of persons are obvious. An intensive use of such a model that
would soon repair the situation is unlikely. Astronomy is as
effective as it is because its theories (and observations) have
been accumulated, adjusted, repaired, and corrected over many
hundreds of years. Astronomy has also been—over the years—
interdisciplinary as it appropriated and used the insights of

21. For example, Deese (1985); Postman (1988).

mathematics, physics, chemistry, geology, and other fields. Such an accretion of knowledge cannot be replicated overnight or over years. All that might be possible is to take existing observations and existing theories (usually experimentally derived) and start, however tentatively, a kind of "psychoastronomical" endeavor.

There are, of course, significant strands of nonexperimental empirical and conceptual analyses in psychology and the other social sciences. Some of the developments in the now quiescent personality theories are similar to the astronomy examples given above but without their depth or extensive history.[22] The best surviving example is probably psychoanalytic theory. Unfortunately, it fails the crucial test of cumulative accretion of empirical knowledge and theoretical consistency. Instead, we have extensive internecine warfare with various "schools" claiming the mantle of succession to Freud or wanting to be seen as independent innovators. But there is no paradigmatic established corpus. Nor have its original interdisciplinary goals been pursued in the succession to Freud. The decline of personality research in general is related to the absence of an agreed mainstream direction and a generally uncoordinated approach. The anthropological approach of seeing individual societies and cultures as units of examination—and systematization—has been challenged by postmodernist atomization and often trivialization of "the human science."

The other model of scientific method—paleontology and more specifically paleobiology—uses both astronomical and historical methods. Paleobiologists observe unique objects and relate them to general laws, but they also are sensitive to the

22. See chapter 13 for contemporary advances in single-subject studies.

contingencies involved in linear historical development. Development in the individual human is also contingent, and developmental psychology has—at times—concerned itself with such "longitudinal" phenomena. What needs stressing more, however, is the way in which the unique individual is the cumulative product of historical process. Thus, we often fail to see in the adult (or the young child) the traces of processes and contingencies that occurred earlier in its history. The way in which the infant encounters and learns the world is not suddenly replaced by later functions or processes, but rather older individuals reveal the continuing influences and remnants of their evolutionary development.

A final point on the methods of psychology: Critics have attacked the tendency to describe the human being "in the aggregate" and to discover average behavior. If it is the case that human development is contingent, then it cannot be averaged. Contingencies are not normally distributed occasions of "noise." Under the influence of B. F. Skinner, operant conditioning has appreciated this argument and has usually looked at the behavior of individual organisms—but unfortunately often no further. And vast experiments, where many dozens of subjects are needed to achieve a "significant" result, have become less frequent today than they were in the 1950s. But the thought that we ought to understand the individual has not been a major theme in psychology. Modelers in particular (whether old-style mathematical or modern connectionist) usually simulate averages, when it is the very characteristic of a model that it should be able to be more precise and veridical.

Essentially, the question about doing psychology without experiments is about psychology and the everyday world. Just as astronomers are concerned with everyday stars but are supported by not very everyday theories, psychologists have begun to perceive how their theories may apply to the events of the real world. One outstanding recent example is in the application of Daniel Kahneman's and Amos Tversky's work on prediction and representativeness to "real" politics, as seen in the important contributions of Sam Popkin to American politics.[23] A search for the mechanisms and processes that eventuate in everyday human thought and action must, I believe, involve the rejection of facile explanations of complex human behavior that frequently are couched in appeals to innateness and to apparently inevitable evolutionary adaptations. Such approaches reveal a certain scientific laziness. We should not accept apparently inescapable (but often untestable) biological or genetic explanations until we have explored in depth other alternative explanations. Complex human actions and thoughts are unlikely candidates for unique, singular evolutionary events.

There is no value-free psychology: all of psychology is imbued with explicit values or is directed by implicit values that have their source in the social and historical context in which a particular psychological approach is situated. And in a wider sense, our psychology reflects abiding traditions of Western society. These Western traditions also may limit the generality of our knowledge. I have noted that not only are our theories and methods partially a product of our society but so is the behavior of our experimental subjects. The vast majority of our research is conducted by scientists and subjects (often university students) from Western, industrialist societies. During the past quarter

23. Popkin (1991).

century, a variety of studies and research groups have begun to study cultural differences in cognitive functions.[24] The studies of individuals, in particular, would benefit from a judicious sampling across human populations, and personality theory has been harmed by the absence of a reasonable sampling across non-Western as well as Western populations. Based on the cognitive consistencies that have been found across cultures, as well as on the failures to generalize such functions, further development of a systematic cross-cultural cognitive psychology, particularly in non-Western, nonindustrial societies, would be a likely future expansion. A healthy infusion of cultural anthropology might occur through the catholic appeal of cognitive science, but the occasions of such collaboration are still few.

Modern Psychology: A Cognitive Science but Not Postmodernist

I have indicated some of the new directions that psychology may explore. At the present time, modern psychology has—to a large extent—been absorbed by the new umbrella field of cognitive science. The field arose in part because of increasing curiosity and the desire for better bridges among the various cognitive sciences, in part because shrinking funding opportunities suggested more appeal when two or more intellectual directions are combined, in part because the artificial intelligence community had difficulty in finding an intellectual or academic home, and in part because of a genuine dream for a science of knowledge, human and otherwise.

24. See, for example, Altarriba (1993); Medin and Atran (2004); Scribner and Cole (1981).

The coinage of the term *cognitive science* is another example of a social background generating an event simultaneously in various places. As far as can be ascertained, pride of place of the first published occasion of the term (in 1975) goes to Daniel Bobrow and Alan Collins, with Donald Norman and David Rumelhart close behind.[25] These books generated much of the flavor and energy of the new field. But many others took part and may claim partial parenthood.

The major consolidation of cognitive science as a defined field took place in the last quarter of the century. The Cognitive Science Society was started following an inaugural conference in 1979 at the University of California, San Diego, and the first independent department of cognitive science was founded there by Donald Norman in 1986. Cognitive science includes such fields as anthropology, artificial intelligence, computer science, education, linguistics, neuroscience, and psychology. A quarter of a century after its various births, there still is no such thing as a core cognitive science. Depending where one looks, what departments one queries, and who one's friends are, the core of cognitive science will be asserted to be neurophysiology, psychology, artificial intelligence, linguistics, or some more vague concept like human/machine interaction or symbolic or connectionist modelling. The result may not have been a defined cognitive science, but it has been exciting and scientifically fruitful. It has created a community of interests and increased interdisciplinary communication. But as of now, there are still viable independent cognitive sciences such as neurophysiology,

25. Bobrow and Collins (1975); Norman and Rumelhart (1975). I am grateful to the many (aging) friends who took part in a search for the elusive parent in the summer of 2005.

linguistics, and psychology that flourish with or without the cognitive science label or affiliation. In the long run, it seems inevitable that at the core of the cognitive science establishment will be psychology (to tell us how the mind works) and neuroscience (to tell us how the brain does it). It is difficult to say at this point where it will lead.

In some psychological habitats, as in the humanities and other social sciences, the last quarter of a century has seen the emergence of the postmodernist trend in art and politics.[26] Postmodernism is probably another symptom of the finalism discussed earlier—that that we are arriving at the end point of various scientific endeavors. It probably is the flip side of that other finalist position that the millennium had arrived and that the final model that intervenes between the brain and behavior had been found in the computer analogy.[27]

Postmodernism in psychology stresses the social construction of knowledge, with language (and intuition) used as a way of establishing local, rather than general, "truths," and seeing psychological scientific statements as narratives rather than attempts to approach some undefined "reality."[28] The clarion call to the discipline came in the 1980s.[29] From an initial invitation to develop new criteria for the evaluation of psychological observations, the field was eventually promised "new and exciting vistas of theoretical, methodological, and practical

26. For a general statement, see Lyotard (1984).

27. Dennett (1991); Jackendoff (1987).

28. Scientists would probably be more likely to accept Kant's approach in which the phenomena that we perceive and describe are attempts to approximate some of the noumena of nature.

29. See Gergen (1985).

significance" that would lead to a "profound change in the profession."[30] However, during the intervening quarter of a century, little path-breaking work or insight seems to have emerged. Despite this lack of significant postmodern successes, some psychologists have seen in the postmodern critique an occasion of fearing for the future of the field.[31]

In a fairly balanced evaluation of the postmodern approach to psychology, Bruce Ryan has suggested that some psychological concepts (such as intelligence, aggressiveness, introversion, and so on) are most likely to be subject to some changes in the light of postmodern critiques, whereas neuroscience and physiology are essentially immune, and experimental psychology has been bypassed.[32] Postmodern critiques have not come to terms with the modernist achievements of psychological science in such fields as sensation and perception, attention, memory, psycholinguistics, and reinforcement schedules.

Several commentators friendly to postmodernism have agreed that an extreme postmodern subjectivity that rejects a physical reality outright is untenable, but in that physical reality they include physical objects but not behavioral events. It can be maintained that an experimental science that works with physical objects and includes behavioral manifestations is not likely to be the mere plaything of social and cultural story telling, though we must note that some aspects of psychological science base their generalizations on the behavior of Western college students. It is here that an attention to cultural variation would be useful to make our generalizations apply without doubt to a

30. Gergen (2001).
31. Smith (1994).
32. Ryan (1999).

cross-section of humanity. It does not abandon principles of scientific method to accept the possibility of cultural variations in thought and behavior—within a framework of general principles. In fact, such cultural variations are needed to be studied the more consistent the results and theories within one (Western) culture become.

Psychologists are clearly not willing to abandon general principles, but there is a trend apparent that sees phenomena as self-contained, with explanations, representations, and forms collected from a variety of sources. There are some symptoms that reflect a sociocultural response to the attitudes that have generated postmodernism. Jerry A. Fodor's multimodularity view of the human mind with each module doing "its own thing" is possibly a postmodern symptom, as are some aspects of the "deconstructive" tendencies of connectionism, as well as the general atomization of psychology into different and unconnected subfields. The psychophysics of vision and hearing, once the heartland of psychological science, have become highly successful and quasi-independent fields. All this might well be the result of successes as new fields separated out, as they did from philosophy in the preceding centuries. It might also be the case that in some fields the flight to postmodern atomization is a reincarnation of the battle between *Natur-* and *Geisteswissenschaft* of more than a century ago. If mental and social regularities are not, or cannot be, represented in laws that are simple or useful in the sense of the laws of the natural sciences, then some method other than that of the latter might be more useful.

Postmodern storytelling and sociologizing are the consequences of abandoning the search of regularities and general principles. Postmodernism has returned to an attention to anecdotes, long after Western society agreed that the plural of *anecdote* is not *data*. Dependence on anecdotal recitals reveals an essentially lazy intellectual attitude. Conversely, however, one might return to the social psychology of Wundt and consider a nonexperimental but rigorous science of mind and of society. I have indicated above some of these directions.

Modern science has had good run for a few centuries and is likely to develop its own postmodern style. In the areas where postmodernism has succeeded, it too is a transitional state. In short, the next set of changes should indeed be interesting in their novel ways of cutting up reality and synthesizing new ways of seeing mind and behavior. An attention to cross-cultural generalization of experimental methods, a distinction among the methods and interests of various subfields of psychology, and the abandonment of mind and consciousness as mythical objects may, in the coming decades and centuries, lead to a new modern psychology—safely ensconced in our umbrella field of cognitive science.

13 The Clouded Crystal Ball: Psychology Today and Tomorrow

Any attempt to review the most recent developments in psychology must keep in mind that in the final decades of the twentieth century psychologists' products were no less the reflection of their cultural background than were Wilhelm Wundt's contributions in the German environment, Plato's imagery of an aviary of memories, or the memory mirrors found in the photographic and phonographic devices of the nineteenth century. The ebb and flow of these metaphors has been described in instructive and fascinating detail by Douwe Draaisma.[1] He notes how metaphors are repeated over the ages, though no "single metaphor or theory repeats itself in an identical shape" (p. 232). As far as the current scene is concerned, Draaisma comments that neural networks are the metaphors most compatible with the surrounding technology. One should keep in mind the time-bound quality of our psychologies as we applaud their modernity. In my brief review of the most recent scene, I illustrate some aspects of theory and research that appear to be having lasting effects into the twenty-first century. My selection is personal and illustrative. Generally, I avoid

1. Draaisma (2000).

anything as recent as the last two decades—and it will be some time before a history of this period can be written from a more objective point of view.

The Revival of Conscious and Unconscious Processes

In chapter 5, we saw how the German psychologists struggled with the discovery that not all mental processes had their reflection or counterpoint in consciousness. Somehow, they still wanted to maintain the major functions of consciousness—for example, by referring to apparently nonobservable processes as *Bewusstseinslagen*—conscious dispositions. Throughout that period, the general thrust of German psychology was referred to as *Bewusstseinspsychologie*—the psychology of consciousness. At the same time, Sigmund Freud's invocation of the unconscious— the dynamic unconscious to which extensive mental processes and scenarios were assigned—may have prevented the use of the unconscious as an important part of the mental armamentarium of experimental psychology. In the United States, the early twentieth century saw the banishment of conscious processes as an important part of empirical psychology. Thus, for a variety of reasons, the first quarter of the century lacked any major discussions of either conscious of unconscious processes.

With the first signs of the new cognitive psychology, there came also a recognition that important mental functions were in fact unconscious ones. Freud's dynamic unconscious was seen as too reflective of the interplay of drives and wishes and never quite relevant to experimental questions of thought and memory. However, there had in fact been other reasonable and persuasive arguments for important unconscious functions.

Apart from variously interpretable mentions in antiquity, there had been occasional references, particularly in the area of perception, by philosophers such as Johann Friedrich Herbart, Gottfried Wilhelm Leibniz, and Immanuel Kant. There even was available a program for a conscious and unconscious interface in the work of the German physician Carl Gustar Carus,[2] which was apparently completely ignored. I quote from the introduction to his 1846 book:

The key to an understanding of the nature of mental life lies in the region of the unconscious.... We can learn from just a glance into our inner life that by far the greatest part of our mental life resides in the unconscious. While we are actually conscious of only a few representations, there still exist at the same time thousands of representations that are entirely withdrawn from consciousness. At any moment, they are not conscious, but they still exist and thus illustrate that the major part of our mental life falls into the darkness of the unconscious.... It is because the major part of our conscious thoughts repeatedly disappears into the unconscious and emerges only temporarily and partially into consciousness that the unconscious can be characterized as the basis of the conscious. But the relationship is even deeper and more extensive. All of our mental life, the entire world of our internal mental thought, differentiated from the external world, is based on the unconscious and is constructed out of it. As soon as we take a look at the construction of our entire self-conscious mental life, we become aware that it is based entirely on thoughts and representations that have been gone for a long time, which have long ago disappeared into the unconscious.... Something once known becomes an unconscious event, and yet that unconscious becomes the basis of our current consciousness.[3]

2. Carus (1846). For a translation of the 1851 edition, see Carus (1970).

3. Freely translated from Carus (1846, p. 1). I include this quote because it is such a modern description of unconscious and conscious relations and has been generally unknown to psychologists.

It was to take more than a hundred years before these insights became part of empirical psychology. In the meantime, others had made similar moves, such as Hermann von Helmholtz's 1867 invocation of the perceptual *unbewusster Schluss* (unconscious conclusions).[4] An extensive, though discursive and speculative, discussion of the unconscious in 1869 by Karl Robert Eduard von Hartmann, which was a popular success, had little effect on philosophers or budding psychologists.[5]

Following these fits and starts, by the second half of the twentieth century the importance of unconscious processes was fully accepted. In part, this was because the many theoretical concepts introduced by the new cognitive psychology (such as memory traces) were assigned to the unconscious, and in part it was because most brain functions (by then an intense focus of interest) were realized to be unavailable to direct conscious representations.

The major initial empirical demonstrations of unconscious processes and of demonstrable constraints on conscious processes emerged during the second half of the century. I mention some of the most vivid, though there were a number of others equally important.

Probably the single most influential article at the beginning of the "revolutionary" period was George A. Miller's paper on the limitations of human ability to process information. The arguments in the paper for the importance of information processing and the limitations of our conscious capacity for handling information was such an abrupt discontinuity from what psychologists considered their major areas of concern that it was

4. Helmholtz (1867).
5. Hartmann (1869).

properly cited and hailed far beyond its immediate application. Miller did not spell out the processing limitation as one of conscious processing, but after some fifty years it may reasonably be included in that category.[6]

Some thirty years later, a series of influential experiments by Anthony J. Marcel demonstrated conclusively how unconscious (unnoticed and unreported) presentations affect semantically related material. For example, priming the word *doctor* outside immediate consciousness could be shown to activate related words, such as *nurse*. This demonstration of implicit effects put an end to what until then had been a much debated set of phenomena—rejected by the neobehaviorist community.[7]

In the interplay of conscious and unconscious processes, another important step in making consciousness and its functions acceptable to the psychological community was the work of Roger N. Shepard and his collaborators on mental imagery and its effect on the experience of objects and their representations.[8]

One of the best diagnostic indications of a shift in emphases is the introduction and adoption of a new vocabulary. Two of the most visible new distinctions were the implicit/explicit and the declarative/procedural bifurcations. Implicit/explicit was apparently first introduced by Arthur S. Reber[9] and refers generally to unconscious versus conscious acquisition and use of cognitive content or processes—as, for example, in the implicit use of grammars or the explicit recovery of some historical knowledge. The related declarative/procedural distinction refers to

6. Miller (1956).

7. Marcel (1983a, 1983b).

8. Shepard and Cooper (1982); Shepard and Metzler (1971).

9. Reber (1967).

"knowing that" versus "knowing how." For example, one knows (usually consciously) *that* for playing cards a king has a higher value than a jack, but one knows (often unconsciously) *how* to shuffle the cards.[10]

The enthusiasm for complex unconscious processes and contents tended to displace a concern with conscious phenomena. This was particularly apposite in the context of the lingering effects of the behaviorist interlude when conscious contents had been written out of the scientific canon. Supported by many philosophers, many psychologists considered consciousness an unnecessary epiphenomenal occurrence that hid the more interesting unconscious effects. It was not until the last quarter of the twentieth century that voices arose that argued for a search for the functions of conscious phenomena—in conjunction with the underlying unconscious ones. The result was a number of proposals on the functions of consciousness, and somewhat belatedly philosophers started to consider the implications of a new *Bewusstseinspsychologie*. Important in this development was the new role played by attention.

During the behaviorist period, the term *attention* was frequently used as a synonym for awareness or consciousness.[11] With the new psychologies, it became a term worthy of extensive research in its own right. Central to its development was the British psychologist Donald E. Broadbent, particularly in his emphasis on selective attention and the role of attention in identification.[12] For the current state-of-the-art of attention re-

10. Cohen and Squire (1980).

11. Wundt had drawn attention to the confusion between attention and consciousness as early as 1907 (see chapter 5).

12. Broadbent (1958).

search, see Anne Treisman's work and Harold Pashler's analyses and summary.[13]

It is too early to identify the most likely survivors of this rush to consciousness, though it is likely that one of its functions is to provide a serial alternative to the parallel processing of the underlying processes. In any case, the field of consciousness is now alive and well and is the subject of continuing spirited contention.[14]

Modeling Psychology

With the growth of psychology as a discipline after World War II, there also came a differentiation within the discipline. Separate clinical psychology programs were developed within departments, and empirical psychology became more self-consciously scientific. One of the characteristics of the late twentieth century was the development of models, usually in the style of what are called *mathematical models*—using the apparatus of mathematical structures. While many of these models were important in pointing out and developing significant aspects of human cognitive functioning, there was relatively little cross-fertilization among them. The trend was illustrative of Michael Watkins's quip that models were like toothbrushes: everybody has one but would never use anybody else's.

The single most influential early model was Richard C. Atkinson and Richard M. Shiffrin's model of human memory in 1968, which provided a way of integrating short-term and long-term

13. Pashler (1998); Treisman (1980).
14. See Mandler (2002a) and Baars, Banks, and Newman (2003) for a compendium of the various proposals for the new consciousness.

memories using a flow-chart model that described many aspects of memory research.[15] Shiffrin and W. Schneider followed up with a more ambitious development in 1977.[16] Equally extensive were John Anderson's models, which produced prolific extensions to most fields of cognitive processes.[17] Anderson relied initially mostly on production rules and on an emphasis on declarative and procedural knowledge.

In a development that affected much of cognitive theory and modeling, in 1972 Allen Newell and Herbert Simon published their book on human problem solving that was to determine research in the area for the next thirty years. Very briefly, they postulated that the information-processing system consisted of a long-term memory with very large capacity, a short-term memory with limited capacity, and an external memory with potentially infinite capacity. Problem solving is goal-directed, using a problem space in which states are searched. Knowledge states are searched sequentially, one knowledge state at a time, until the required knowledge state is reached.[18] A subsequent development and a descendant of the Newell and Simon problem-solving model was the SOAR system.[19] SOAR postulates a problem space within which cognitive acts operate as search tasks. Memory is procedural only, and the primary mechanism for learning consists of chunking, which generates the contents of long-term memory and satisfies production rules.

15. Atkinson and Shiffrin (1968).

16. Shiffrin and Schneider (1977); Schneider and Shiffrin (1977).

17. Anderson (1976, 1983).

18. Newell and Simon (1972).

19. Laird, Newell, and Rosenbloom (1987); Newell (1973, 1990).

There were a number of other significant modeling contributions, such as the E. D. Neimark and W. K. Estes stimulus sampling model[20] and R. Duncan Luce's choice model,[21] but their use was generally restricted to specialized problems rather than to overarching models of cognitive processes.

Toward the end of the century, there emerged the most ambitious modeling of cognitive processes—*connectionism*, which was based on parallel distributed processes. Connectionism became one of the most popular and successful modeling enterprises of the late twentieth century. Whereas the approach had a number of important predecessors,[22] clearly this kind of modeling was part of the Zeitgeist of the last quarter of the century. The initially motivating statement of connectionism was proposed in the PDP (parallel distributed processes) approach of David Rumelhart, James McClelland, and associates, though the connectionist name was first used in 1981.[23] Connectionist models differ from most of their predecessors primarily in their neural network approach—by using quasi-neurons rather then symbolic rules as the basic units of their architecture. Connections among these neurons are assigned weights that determine the probability of interneuron interactions. The specific modeling is often achieved by training—for example, by backpropagation, in which an initially random array is changed by the presentation of numerous examples of the discrimination to be acquired in conjunction with corrective feedback. More

20. Neimark (1967).

21. Luce (1959).

22. Morton (1969); Hinton and Anderson (1981, see pp. 41–44 for a description of its ancestry); Rumelhart (1977).

23. Feldman (1981); Rumelhart and McClelland (1985).

recently, methods have been used that learn solution structures without such feedback. Successful modeling has been achieved in categorization, reading, face recognition, grammar, language acquisition, and other fairly complex cognitive tasks.

Connectionism can be seen as a distant and sophisticated cousin of associationism but a family member nonetheless. Despite its obvious successes, it has some of problems seen in earlier associationist models. For example, connectionist models have difficulty in handling meanings and competing meanings (illustrated in chapter 12).

Finally, a contribution that was not quite a modeling example but directly influenced the modeling of human choice behavior was Daniel Kahneman and Amos Tversky's prospect theory.[24] The theory deals primarily with human risk behavior and related matters of choice, and whereas it had little direct influence on the thought and memory field, it has colored many aspects of contemporary psychology.

Mind and Brain: The Passing (Contemporary) Scene

I have discussed the general propositions of a radical reductionism in the previous chapter. I now turn to some of the contemporary positions and problems. If one maintains that the mind is what the brain does, then the question of how the brain "does it" becomes of interest. At one extreme, we have the astounding suggestion that humans will be able to think and talk about their mental events in neurophysiological terms. A more attenuated position makes the classic reductionist claim that "eventually" we will be able to explain and understand

24. Kahneman and Tversky (1979).

mental events entirely in terms of their materialist, neural basis.[25] For the time being, one can assert that whatever its eventual possibility (or impossibility), we are indeed far removed from that state of knowledge. For example, in an extensive investigation of the neural basis of a small corner of behavior, saccadic movements, Jeffrey D. Schall has demonstrated the conceptual and technical complexity of such an endeavor. He concluded: "if the relationship between neural events and control of gaze is so difficult to elucidate, what hope have we of understanding the mechanisms of more elaborate cognitive processes?"[26] In general, there is no evidence that a radical reductionist program—that is, a complete reduction of psychological phenomena to their physical substrate without loss of meaning—can be accomplished in the near future, if at all.

The past half century has produced astounding advances in our understanding of brain structure and functions, and the uses of modern scanning techniques have produced some impressive findings that substantiate how complex mental processes and differentiations are echoed in specific brain functions (and vice versa), though speculative hypotheses outnumber hard evidence.[27] The great advances in neuropsychology have made the mind/brain connection central to current cognitive science, a development that was anticipated (as I indicate in chapter 12) by neuropsychological advances in British psychology.

In contrast to attempts to find specific mind and brain relations for mental operations that are consistent with both

25. Churchland (1986); Crick (1994).

26. Schall (2004).

27. For example, see Crick and Koch (1995) and Kinsbourne (1996) for two contrasting views of the neural basis of consciousness.

psychological and neurophysiological theories, an extensive cottage industry has engaged in demonstrating that any behavioral and mental event is indeed accompanied by changes in some brain activity. Assuming that modern science is indeed a materialist enterprise that asserts the material, and not spiritual, basis of mental life, such demonstrations are not surprising. What would indeed be surprising is a finding that some mental event has no material correlate. On the other hand, the specific enterprise of relating cognitive events with neurological ones—eventually dubbed as cognitive neuroscience—burgeoned in the last quarter of the twentieth century and received its defining impetus with Tim Shallice's book in 1988.[28]

Memory

A Case History of Cognitive/Neural Relations

I next discuss an example of a cognitive research enterprise that eventually turned into a neuroscience enterprise. The example—and I use one of my own projects here—is also an interesting demonstration of how the general tenor of the times generated parallel but independent developments of more or less identical empirical and theoretical findings.

The story concerns the nature of human recognition memory and starts around 1970 in our laboratory in San Diego and in that of Richard C. Atkinson at Stanford.[29] In 1971, the Atkinson group published a paper that suggested that recognition involved a rapid check for the prior occurrence of an event and

28. Shallice (1988).

29. I should add that as far as anybody can recollect, these two developments occurred in parallel with little if any awareness of the occurrence of similar experiments and thoughts five hundred miles away.

that, if it was unsuccessful, it was followed by a retrieval search of the original list of items.[30] In 1969, our group had similarly suggested a second (retrieval) process in recognition. In 1972, I published a chapter that showed that, contrary to previous thought, recognition was only an automatic "checking" processes—that recognition also involved organizational, conceptual search processes.[31] These two sets of events were quickly followed by several papers from Stanford showing a combination of decision and search processes in recognition performance.[32] Our own work on retrieval processes in recognition[33] produced *inter alia* a theoretical paper on the dual-process model in 1979 and a paper on recognition in 1980 to argue that the two processes—perceptual/activation (mapping into familiarity) and conceptual/organizational (mapping into recall or recollection)—occurred in parallel.[34] The dual-process theory has been extensively used in the memory field and was summarized in a 1991 chapter and in an extensive and scholarly review of the field in general by Andrew P. Yonelinas.[35]

So much for the behavioral basis, which laid the groundwork for neuropsychologists to start looking for the material basis for those two processes in recognition—recall/recollection and familiarity. Most of that work occurred in the 1990s and reached provisional conclusion in the early 2000s. In 2003, Charan Ranganath et al. concluded that functional magnetic resonance

30. Juola, Fischler, Wood, and Atkinson (1971).
31. Mandler (1972); Mandler, Pearlstone, and Koopmans (1969).
32. Atkinson and Juola (1973, 1974); Atkinson and Wescourt (1975).
33. Mandler and Boeck (1974).
34. Mandler (1979b, 1980).
35. Mandler (1991); Yonelinas (2002).

imaging studies provided evidence for differential cerebral activation patterns in the rhinal cortex for familiarity, whereas activity in the hippocampus and posterior parahippocampal cortex predicted recollection.[36] That same year, Michael D. Rugg and Yonelinas reviewed the literature and concluded that it is likely that "familiarity and recollection are supported by distinct neural mechanisms."[37] In an event-related-potential study in 2004, Audrey Duarte et al. demonstrated that "familiarity and recollection reflect the outcome of neurally distinct memory processes at both encoding and retrieval."[38] Lisa Cipolotti et al. have concluded that "the hippocampus is involved in recollective processes of verbal and topographical stimuli. It also plays an appreciable role in familiarity processes for these stimuli. However, recollection and familiarity of human faces appear not to depend on this region."[39]

In short, we have an example of the demonstration of distinctive behavioral processes showing the expected parallels in the neural substrate. Today the psychology and neuroscience interface is a two-way street with psychological phenomena motivating the search for their physiological basis and the latter leading to a confirmation of the psychological concepts.

Episodic and Semantic Memories

A distinction between two kinds of memories that has received a substantial following during recent years is that between epi-

36. Ranganath et al. (2004).

37. Rugg and Yonelinas (2003).

38. Duarte, Ranganath, Winward, Hayward, and Knight (2004).

39. Cipolotti, Bird, Good, Macmanus, Rudge, and Shallice (2006); see also Yovel and Paller (2004).

sodic and semantic memories introduced by Endel Tulving.[40] The distinction presents another case of parallel histories when the scientific culture is ready for a distinction that then occurs independently in more than one place or mind. As Tulving was composing his 1972 paper on semantic and episodic memory in Toronto, two young psychologists at Oxford University were coining and using the identical distinction between *lexicon* and *topicon*. Geoffrey Sampson circulated an unpublished paper in which he originally used the terms, and Guy Claxton employed them extensively in his Ph.D. thesis.[41] The only public use was in a presentation in April 1972.[42] Subsequently, there seem to have been one or two references in the literature, but the topicon/lexicon distinction died a quiet death, whereas the episodic/semantic distinction flourished.

At a general level, episodic memories involve "the recording and subsequent retrieval of memories of personal happenings and doings," whereas semantic memories deal with "knowledge of the world that is independent of a person's identity and past."[43] The distinction has great heuristic value and is phenomenally immediately appealing. It presents a ready and comprehensible way of dividing up different kinds of experiments as well as subjective experiences. On the other hand, it is questionable whether these two kinds of memories represent different systems with different rules or laws governing their operation. At the simplest level, episodic memories draw on semantic knowledge (a point that is not disputed). But semantic

40. Tulving (1972). See Tulving (1983) for an extensive presentation.
41. Claxton (1974); Sampson (1972).
42. Smith and Claxton (1972).
43. Tulving (1983, p. 9).

memories also have personal, episodic characteristics. It is unlikely that different people's knowledge of foods, bears, or history is unaffected by the personal conditions under which it is acquired. Nor can it be argued for long that episodic memories are any less conceptually organized than semantic ones or that they are primarily (or even uniquely) temporally organized. For example, our (semantic) knowledge of historical events is often mainly temporally organized, whereas my memory of how I played a game of chess or the pictures I saw at an exhibition may well be conceptually organized by opening gambits or genre.

In a general review of the increasingly popular use of the notion of episodic memory, Tulving has presented a highly instructive, though curiously defensive, presentation. The article presents a general defense, as well as excellent summary of the various criticisms that have been leveled at the concept.[44] In a more ambitious new definition, episodic memory is described as "a recently evolved, late-developing, and early-deteriorating past-oriented memory system, more vulnerable than other memory systems to neuronal dysfunction, and probably unique to humans," which also drops the strong distinction between episodic and semantic memory. Apart from the argument about the utility of the concept at a theoretical level, it remains an important heuristic tool in portioning memory research.

Levels of Processing

In 1972, Fergus I. M. Craik and Robert S. Lockhart offered an alternative to the multistore approach to memory.[45] They pro-

44. Tulving (2002).
45. Craik and Lockhart (1972); see also Conway (2002).

posed that likelihood of access or distinctiveness of a memory trace is dependent on the depth of the level of processing at the time of storage or encounter. Level or depth of processing is defined in terms of such factors as elaboration and distinctiveness. The latter can probably be usefully defined within organizational theory.[46] It also appears that the levels approach can be used in conjunction with, rather than opposition to, the multistore approach, thus enriching our knowledge of the processing of events to be remembered.

The Revival of the Schema

The notion of the schema was revived in the twentieth century. It was originally developed by Immanuel Kant, who gave the useful example of a schema of a dog being described as a mental pattern that "can delineate the figure of a four-footed animal in a general manner, without any limitation to any single determinate figure as experience, or any possible image that I can represent *in concreto*, actually presents."[47] In modern times, it was used by Henry Head[48] for motor schemas, used extensively by Jean Piaget to described developmental issues, and then invoked by Frederick C. Bartlett[49] in cognitive contexts. Extensive use of schemas can be found in the work of David Rumelhart, under whose aegis it eventually led to connectionist theories.[50]

46. Mandler (2002b).

47. Kant (1781).

48. Head (1920).

49. Bartlett (1932).

50. Rumelhart (1980); Rumelhart and McClelland (1985); Rumelhart and Ortony (1978); see also Mandler (1984).

Varieties of Memories and the Contributions of Clinical Studies

In addition to the various developments in memory research discussed above, there appeared a greater differentiation among various types of memories, such as recognition, recollection, working memory,[51] and especially prospective memory.[52]

In light of my previous discussion of the need for studies of individual cases and psychological objects, the last quarter of a century has seen a large number of sophisticated studies of individual clinical cases that shed important light on memory mechanisms, language disorders, and many other general issues. Whereas these investigators use individual patients and groups of such patients, they do have an advantage over other students of individual cases: they are more likely to be able to conduct experimental interventions. Important among these contributions in illuminating brain-behavior links and cognitive functions and pathologies are Elizabeth K. Warrington's studies of amnesia and other disorders,[53] studies of semantic systems,[54] and differentiations among memory stores.[55]

Learning Revisited

Learning was one of the main concerns of the behaviorist theories, some of which were called *learning theories*. It was soon after the start of the revolution that common knowledge

51. Baddeley and Hitch (1974).
52. Brandimonte, Einstein, and McDaniel (1996).
53. Warrington and Weiskrantz (1970).
54. Patterson et al. (2006); Warrington (1975).
55. Shallice and Warrington (1970).

accepted what had become clear in the waning years of the behaviorist period—namely, that the acquisition of action and knowledge was too complicated a topic to be handled by simple theories. The result was a flood of new beginnings toward an understanding of how new knowledge, new concepts, and new views of the world are acquired. This was most obvious in the field of cognitive development, where Piaget had made crucial and innovate beginnings. By the end of the century, the work of such people as Esther Thelen, Linda Smith, Susan Carey, J. Mandler, Susan A. Gelman, Renee Baillargeon, and many others had made it clear that such topics as motor learning,[56] perceptual learning, concept acquisition,[57] and the acquisition of number[58] in the young child all required different and theoretically rich approaches before we could understand how the human being developed the apparatus for acquiring knowledge and for dealing with the world. As far as the adult was concerned, rich theories of concept learning and categorization by, among others, Frank C. Keil, Douglas L. Medin, and Lawrence W. Barsalou produced new data and insights into concept acquisition,[59] while Keith J. Holyoak, Dedre Gentner, and associates explored inference and induction.[60] Paradoxically, the term *learning* had all but disappeared from the world of human psychology.

56. Thelen and Smith (1994).

57. Baillargeon and Wang (2002); Carey (1999); Gelman (2003); Mandler (2004).

58. Gelman and Gallistel (1978); and see Butterworth (1999) for general advances in mathematical thought.

59. Barsalou (1999); Keil (2005); Medin and Coley (1998).

60. Gentner, Holyoak, and Kokinov (2001); Holyoak and Thagard (1997).

Signal Detection Theory (SDT): A Major Measurement Advance

Signal detection theory (SDT) is a powerful measurement device that is based on statistical decision theory.[61] Originally applied to the detection of auditory signals in noise,[62] it soon became more widely used in fields ranging from radar to areas of psychology.[63] Eventually, it was used in many psychological experiments involving recognition, classification, and discrimination.[64]

In brief, SDT may be used in any situation or task that requires discrimination. Its use involves the parameters of d' (which indicates the sensitivity of a detector in a signal detection system) and β (which is a measure of the criterion used to choose between detecting a signal when present and not reporting it when absent). The theory deals with the underlying distributions of signals and of signals+noise and the discrimination between the two distributions. This basic approach can be applied to any situation in which persons make the judgment that a signal (or event) was present or absent and therefore that a "hit" (the correct identification) and a "false alarm" (the incorrect identification of a signal in its absence) can occur. These two identifications extend far beyond simple recognition experiments and have made it possible to apply transsituational measures to a variety of different psychological experiments. The measure is of more general applicability since it also applies to

61. Wald (1950).
62. Peterson, Birdsall, and Fox (1954).
63. Swets, Tanner, and Birdsall (1961).
64. Green and Swets (1966).

the forced-choice experiment when people simply choose between two exclusive alternatives.[65]

Envoi

One of the most salient aspects of these advances is that they are
occurring not just in the United States but also in Europe, Latin
America, Japan, China, and other countries with active psychological communities. It appears that psychology is developing a
catholic consensus, an international paradigm that did not exist
prior to the mid-twentieth century. It will be interesting to see
what a genuine paradigm shift in psychology will look like in
the decades to come. It has been an interesting ride for the past
couple of centuries, and in cognitive science, in the company of
related disciplines, it promises to be even more so.

65. See Green and Swets (1966).

References

Ach, N. (1905). *Über die Willenstätigkeit und das Denken*. Göttingen: Vandenhoeck und Ruprecht.

Altarriba, J. (Ed.). (1993). *Culture and cognition: A cross-cultural approach to cognitive psychology*. New York: North-Holland.

Anderson, J. R. (1976). *Language, memory, and thought*. Hillsdale, NJ: Erlbaum.

Anderson, J. R. (1983). *The architecture of cognition*. Cambridge, MA: Harvard University Press.

Andrews, P., & Stringer, C. (1993). The primates' progress. In S. J. Gould (Ed.), *The book of life* (pp. 219–251). New York: Ebury Hutchinson.

Asch, S. E., & Ebenholtz, S. M. (1962). The principle of associative symmetry. *Proceedings of the American Philosophical Society, 106,* 135–163.

Ash, M. G. (1995). *Gestalt psychology in German culture, 1890–1967: Holism and the quest for objectivity*. New York: Cambridge University Press.

Atkinson, R. C., & Juola, J. F. (1973). Factors influencing speed and accuracy of word recognition. In S. Kornblum (Ed.), *Attention and performance* (Vol. 4). New York: Academic Press.

Atkinson, R. C., & Juola, J. F. (1974). Search and decision processes in recognition memory. In D. H. Krantz, R. C. Atkinson, & R. D. Luce

(Eds.), *Contemporary developments in mathematical psychology*. San Francisco: Freeman.

Atkinson, R. C., & Shiffrin, R. M. (1968). Human memory: A proposed system and its control processes. In K. W. Spence & J. T. Spence (Eds.), *The psychology of learning and motivation* (pp. 742–775). New York: Academic Press.

Atkinson, R. C., & Wescourt, K. T. (1975). Some remarks on long-term memory. In P. M. A. Rabbitt & S. Dornic (Eds.), *Attention and performance* (Vol. 5, pp. 485–498). London: Academic Press.

Baars, B. J. (1986). *The cognitive revolution in psychology*. New York: Guilford Press.

Baars, B. J. (1988). *A cognitive theory of consciousness*. New York: Cambrdge University Press.

Baars, B. J., Banks, W. P., & Newman, J. B. (Eds.). (2003). *Essential sources in the scientific study of consciousness*. Cambridge, MA: MIT Press.

Baddeley, A. D., & Hitch, G. (1974). Working memory. In G. H. Bower (Ed.), *The psychology of learning and motivation* (pp. 199–242). New York: Academic Press.

Baillargeon, R., & Wang, S.-H. (2002). Event categorization in infancy. *Trends in Cognitive Sciences, 6*, 85–93.

Bain, A. (1855). *The senses and the intellect*. London: Parker.

Bain, A. (1868). *The senses and the intellect* (3rd ed.). London: Longmans, Green.

Barsalou, L. W. (1999). Perceptual symbol systems. *Behavioral and Brain Sciences, 22*, 577–660.

Bartlett, F. C. (1932). *Remembering*. Cambridge: Cambridge University Press.

Bates, E., Thal, D., & Marchman, V. (1991). Symbols and syntax: A Darwinian approach to language development. In N. Krasnegor, D. Rumbaugh, E. Schiefelbusch, & M. Studdert-Kennedy (Eds.), *Biological and behavioral determinants of language development* (pp. 29–65). Hillsdale, NJ: Erlbaum.

Berkeley, G. (1904) (original publication 1810). *A treatise concerning the principles of human knowledge.* Chicago: Open Court.

Binet, A. (1894). *Introduction à la psychologie experimentale.* Paris: Alcan.

Binet, A. (1903). *L'étude experimentale de l'intelligence.* Paris: Schleicher Frères.

Blumenthal, A. L. (1970). *Language and psychology: Historical aspects of psycholinguistics.* New York: Wiley.

Bobrow, D. G., & Collins, A. M. (1975). *Representation and understanding: Studies in cognitive science.* New York: Academic Press.

Boring, E. G. (1950). *A history of experimental psychology* (2nd ed.). New York: Appleton-Century-Crofts.

Bousfield, W. A. (1953). The occurrence of clustering in the recall of randomly arranged associates. *Journal of General Psychology, 49*, 229–240.

Bower, G. H. (1970). Organizational factors in memory. *Cognitive Psychology, 1*, 18–46.

Bower, G. H., & Bryant, D. J. (1991). On relating the organizational theory of memory to levels of processing. In W. Kessen, A. Ortony, & F. Craik (Eds.), *Memories, thoughts, and emotions: Essays in honor of George Mandler* (pp. 149–168). Hillsdale, NJ: Erlbaum.

Brandimonte, M., Einstein, G., & McDaniel, M. (Eds.). (1996). *Prospective memory: Theory and Applications.* Hillsdale, NJ: Erlbaum.

Brentano, F. C. (1874). *Psychologie vom empirischen Standpunkt (1 Bd.,* V1). Leipzig: Duncker & Humblot.

Broadbent, D. E. (1958). *Perception and communication.* London: Pergamon Press.

Brown, J. F. (1929). The methods of Kurt Lewin in the psychology of action and affection. *Psychological Review, 36*, 200–221.

Brown, T. (1820). *Lectures on the philosophy of the human mind.* Edinburgh: Black.

Brown, T. (1851). *Lectures on the philosophy of the human mind* (19th ed.). Edinburgh: Black.

Bruce, D. (1994). Lashley and the problem of serial order. *American Psychologist, 49,* 93–103.

Bruner, J. (1997). Will cognitive revolutions ever stop? In D. M. Johnson & C. E. Erneling (Eds.), *The future of the cognitive revolution.* New York: Oxford University Press.

Bruner, J. S., Goodenough, J. J., & Austin, G. A. (1956). *A study of thinking.* New York: Wiley.

Brunswik, E. (1952). *The conceptual framework of psychology.* Chicago: University of Chicago Press.

Brunswik, E. (1956). *Perception and the representative design of psychological experiments.* Berkeley: University of California Press.

Bühler, C. (1943). *From birth to maturity: An outline of the psychological development of the child.* London: Paul, Trench, Trubner.

Bühler, K. (1907). Tatsachen und Probleme zu einer Psychologie der Denkvorgänge. I. Über Gedanken. *Archiv für die Gesamte Psychologie, 9,* 297–365.

Bühler, K. (1908a). Tatsachen und Probleme zu einer Psychologie der Denkvorgänge. II. Über Gedankenerinnerungen. *Archiv für die Gesamte Psychologie, 12,* 24–92.

Bühler, K. (1908b). Tatsachen und Probleme zu einer Psychologie der Denkvorgänge. II. Über Gedankenzusammenhänge. *Archiv für die Gesamte Psychologie, 12,* 1–23.

Bühler, K. (1926). Die "Neue Psychologie" Koffkas. *Zeitschrift für Psychologie, 99,* 145–159.

Bühler, K. (1934). *Sprachtheorie: Die Darstellungsfunktion der Sprache.* Jena: Fischer.

Butterworth, B. (1999). *The mathematical brain*. London: Macmillan.

Carey, S. (1999). Sources of conceptual change. In E. K. Scholnick, K. Nelson, S. A. Gelman, & P. H. Miller (Eds.), *Conceptual development: Piaget's legacy* (pp. 293–326). Mahwah, NJ: Erlbaum.

Carus, C. G. (1846). *Psyche. Zur Entwicklungsgeschichte der Seele*. Leipzig: Kröner.

Carus, C. G. (1970). *Psyche. On the development of the soul: Part I* (Renata Welch, Trans.). Dallas, TX: Spring.

Chomsky, N. (1956). Three models for the description of language. *IRE Transactions on Information Theory, IT-2*(3), 113–124.

Chomsky, N. (1957). *Syntactic structures*. The Hague: Mouton.

Chomsky, N. (1959). Review of B. F. Skinner's "Verbal Behavior." *Language, 35*, 26–58.

Chomsky, N. (1972). *Language and mind* (2nd ed.). New York: Harcourt, Brace & World.

Churchland, P. M. (1984). *Matter and consciousness: A contemporary introduction to the philosophy of mind*. Cambridge, MA: MIT Press.

Churchland, P. S. (1986). *Neurophilosophy: Toward a unified science of the mind-brain*. Cambridge, MA: MIT Press.

Cipolotti, L., Bird, C., Good, T., Macmanus, D., Rudge, P., & Shallice, T. (2006). Recollection and familiarity in dense hippocampal amnesia: A case study. *Neuropsychologia, 44*(3), 489–506.

Claparède, E. (1917). La psychologie de l'intelligence. *Scientia, 22*, 353–368.

Claparède, E. (1934). *La genèse de l'hypotheses*. Geneva: Kundig.

Clark, H. H., & Clark, E. V. (1977). *Psychology and language: An introduction to psycholinguistics*. New York: Harcourt Brace Jovanovich.

Claxton, G. C. (1974). The role of memory and perception in verbal comprehension. Doctoral dissertation, University of Oxford, Oxford.

Cofer, C. N. (1961). *Verbal learning and verbal behavior.* New York: McGraw-Hill.

Cofer, C. N. (1978). Origins of the *Journal of Verbal Learning and Verbal Behavior. Journal of Verbal Learning and Verbal Behavior, 17*(1), 113–126.

Cofer, C. N., & Musgrave, B. S. (Eds.). (1963). *Verbal behavior and learning.* New York: McGraw-Hill.

Cohen, N. J., & Squire, L. R. (1980). Preserved learning and retention of pattern analyzing skill in amnesia: Dissociation of knowing how and knowing that. *Science, 210,* 207–209.

Collins, A. F. (2001). The psychology of memory. In G. C. Bunn, A. D. Lovie, & G. Richards (Eds.), *Psychology in Britain: Historical essays and personal reflections* (pp. 150–168). Leicester, UK: British Psychological Society.

Conway, M. A. (Ed.). (2002). *Levels of processing thirty years on.* Hove, UK: Psychology Press.

Craik, F. I. M., & Lockhart, R. S. (1972). Levels of processing: A framework for memory research. *Journal of Verbal Learning and Verbal Behavior, 11,* 671–684.

Craik, K. J. W. (1943). *The nature of explanation.* Cambridge: Cambridge University Press.

Craik, K. J. W. (1966). *The nature of psychology* (S. L. Sherwood, Ed.). Cambridge: Cambridge University Press.

Crick, F. (1994). *The astonishing hypothesis: The scientific search for the soul.* New York: Touchstone/Simon and Schuster.

Crick, F., & Koch, C. (1995). Are we aware of neural activity in primary visual cortex? *Nature, 375,* 121–123.

Cummins, R. (1975). Functional analysis. *Journal of Philosophy, 72,* 741–765.

Deacon, T. W. (1997). *The symbolic species: The co-evolution of language and the brain.* New York: Norton.

Deese, J. (1985). *American freedom and the social sciences*. New York: Columbia University Press.

de Groot, A. D. (1946). *Het Denken van den Schaker*. Amsterdam: Noord-Hollandsche Uitgevers Maatschappij.

de Groot, A. D. (1964). *Thought and choice in chess*. The Hague: Mouton.

Dennett, D. C. (1978). *Brain storms*. Montgomery, VT: Bradford Books.

Dennett, D. C. (1991). *Consciousness explained*. Boston: Little, Brown.

Descartes, R. (1642). *Meditationes de prima philosophia, in qua Dei existentia et animae immortalitas demonstratur*. Paris: Michaelem Soly.

Descartes, R. (1662). *De homine, figuris et latinitate donatus a Florentio Schuyl*. Lugduni Batavorum (Leiden): Petrum Leffen & Franciscum Moyardum.

Deutsch, K. W. (1951). Mechanism, teleology, and mind. *Philosophy and Phenomenological Research, 12*, 185–223.

Dilthey, W. (1959). *Einleitung in die Geisteswissenschaften*. Stuttgart: Teubner. (Originally published in 1883).

Dixon, T. (2003). *From passions to emotions*. Cambridge: Cambridge University Press.

Dixon, T. R., & Horton, D. L. (Eds.). (1968). *Verbal behavior and general behavior theory*. Englewood Cliffs, NJ: Prentice Hall.

Dollard, J., & Miller, N. E. (1950). *Personality and psychotherapy*. New York: McGraw-Hill.

Draaisma, D. (2000). *Metaphors of memory: A history of ideas about the mind* (Paul Vincent, Trans.). Cambridge: Cambridge University Press.

Duarte, A., Ranganath, C., Winward, L., Hayward, D., & Knight, R. T. (2004). Dissociable neural correlates for familiarity and recollection during the encoding and retrieval of pictures. *Cognitive Brain Research, 18*, 255–272.

Duncker, K. (1926). A qualitative study of productive thinking. *Pedagogical Seminary, 33,* 642–708.

Duncker, K. (1935). *Zur Psychologic des produktiven Denkens.* Berlin: Springer.

Duncker, K. (1945). On problem solving. *Psychological Monographs, 58*(5): ix, 113.

Ebbinghaus, H. (1885). *Ueber das Gedächtnis: Untersuchungen zur experimentellen Psychologie.* Leipzig: Duncker und Humblot.

Ebbinghaus, H. (1913). *Memory: A contribution to experimental psychology.* New York: Teacher's College, Columbia University.

Ehrenfels, C. v. (1890). Über "Gestaltqualitäten." *Vierteljahrsschrift für wissenschaftliche Philosophie, 14,* 249–292.

Eldredge, N., & Tattersall, I. (1982). *The myths of human evolution.* New York: Columbia University Press.

Esper, E. A. (1964). *A history of psychology.* Philadelphia: Saunders.

Feigenbaum, E. A. (1959). *An information processing theory of verbal learning.* (RAND Report P–1817). Santa Monica, CA: RAND Corporation.

Feldman, J. A. (1981). A connectionist model of visual memory. In G. E. Hinton & J. A. Anderson (Eds.), *Parallel models of associative memory* (pp. 49–81). Hillsdale, NJ: Erlbaum.

Fleck, L. (1935). *Entstehung und Entwicklung einer wissenschaftlichen Tatsache: Einführung in die Lehre vom Denkstil und Denkkollektiv.* Basel, Switzerland: Benno Schwabe.

Fleck, L. (1979). *Genesis and development of a scientific fact* (T. J. Trenn & R. K. Merton, Eds., and F. Bradley & T. J. Trenn, Trans.). Chicago: University of Chicago Press.

Frijda, N. H., & deGroot, A. D. (1981). *Otto Selz: His contribution to psychology.* The Hague: Mouton.

Gardner, H. (1985). *The mind's new science: A history of the cognitive revolution.* New York: Basic Books.

Garner, W. R. (1962). *Uncertainty and structure as psychological concepts.* New York: Wiley.

Gelman, R., & Gallistel, C. R. (1978). *The child's understanding of number.* Cambridge, MA: Harvard University Press.

Gelman, S. A. (2003). *The essential child: Origins of essentialism in everyday thought.* London: Oxford University Press.

Gentner, D., Holyoak, K. J., & Kokinov, B. N. (Eds.). (2001). *The analogical mind: Perspectives from cognitive science.* Cambridge, MA: MIT Press.

Gergen, K. J. (1985). The social constructionist movement in modern psychology. *American Psychologist, 40*(3), 266–275.

Gergen, K. J. (2001). Psychological science in a postmodern context. *American Psychologist, 56*(10), 803–813.

Givòn, T. (1979). *On understanding grammar.* San Diego: Academic Press.

Goldstein, K. (1939). *The organism: A holistic approach to biology.* New York: American Book Co.

Graumann, C. F. (Ed.). (1985). *Psychologie im Nationalsozialismus.* Berlin: Springer-Verlag.

Green, D. M., & Swets, J. A. (1966). *Signal detection theory and psychophysics.* New York: Wiley.

Greenwood, J. D. (1999). Understanding the "cognitive revolution" in psychology. *Journal of the History of the Behavioral Sciences, 35*(1), 1–22.

Hamilton, W. (Ed.). (1880). *The works of Thomas Reid* (8th ed., Vol. 2). Edinburgh: Maclachlan and Stewar. (Originally published in 1846).

Hammond, W. A. (Ed.). (1902). *Aristotle's psychology: A treatise on the principles of life (De anima and Parva naturalia).* London: Swan Sonnenschein.

Hartley, D. (1834). *Observation on man, his frame, his duty, and his expectations.* London: Tegg. (Originally published in 1749).

Hartmann, E. v. (1869). *Philosophie des Unbewussten.* Berlin: Duncker.

Head, H. (1920). *Studies in neurology.* London: Kegan Paul.

Hebb, D. O. (1949). *The organization of behavior.* New York: Wiley.

Heider, F. (1958). *The psychology of interpersonal relations.* New York: Wiley.

Helmholtz, H. v. (1867). *Handbuch der physiologischen Optik.* Leipzig: Voss.

Herbart, J. F. (1816). *Lehrbuch zur Psychologie.* Königsberg und Leipzig: Unzer.

Herbart, J. F. (1824–1825). *Psychologie als Wissenschaft* (Vols. 1–2). Königsberg.

Herman, E. (1995). *The romance of American psychology.* Berkeley: University of California Press.

Hessen, B. M. (1971). *The social and economic roots of Newton's* Principia. New York: Fertig. (Originally published in *Science at the crossroads.* London: Kniga, 1931).

Hinton, G. E., & Anderson, J. A. (1981). *Parallel models of associative memory.* Hillsdale, NJ: Erlbaum.

Hobbes, T. (1994) (original publication 1640). *The elements of law, natural and politic: part I, Human nature, part II, De corpore politico.* New York: Oxford University Press.

Hobbes, T. (1651). *Leviathan; or, The matter, form, and power of a commonwealth ecclesiastical and civil.* London: Crooke.

Hochberg, J. (1968). In the mind's eye. In R. N. Haber (Ed.), *Contemporary theory and research in visual perception.* New York: Holt.

Holyoak, K. J., & Thagard, P. (1997). The analogical mind. *American Psychologist, 52*(1), 35–44.

Hovland, C. I. (1952). A "communication analysis" of concept learning. *Psychological Review, 59,* 461–472.

Hughes, H. S. (1958). *Consciousness and society: The reorientation of European social thought 1890–1930.* New York: Knopf.

Hull, C. L., Hovland, C. I., Ross, R. T., Hall, M., Perkins, D. T., & Fitch, F. B. (1940). *Mathematico-deductive theory of rote learning: A study in scientific methodology.* New Haven, CT: Yale University Press.

Hume, D. (1739–1740). *A treatise of human nature: Being an attempt to introduce the experimental method of reasoning into moral subjects.* London: Noon.

Humphrey, G. (1948). *Directed thinking.* New York: Dodd Mead.

Humphrey, G. (1951). *Thinking: An introduction to its experimental psychology.* New York: Wiley.

Humphrey, N. (1992). *A history of the mind.* London: Chatto & Windus.

Jackendoff, R. (1987). *Consciousness and the computational mind.* Cambridge, MA: MIT Press.

Jacobson, E. (1911). On meaning and understanding. *American Journal of Psychology, 22,* 553–577.

Jaeger, S. (1993). Zur Widerständigkeit der Hochschullehrer zu Beginn der nationalsozialistischen Herrschaft. *Psychologie und Geschichte, 4*(3/4), 219–228.

James, W. (1890). *The principles of psychology.* New York: Holt.

Jenkins, J. J. (Ed.). (1955). *Associative processes in verbal behavior: A report of the Minnesota conference.* Minneapolis: Department of Psychology, University of Minnesota.

Jenkins, J. J., & Postman, L. J. (1957). The Minnesota conference on associative processes in verbal behavior. *American Psychologist, 12,* 499–500.

Johnson, D. M., & Erneling, C. E. (Eds.). (1997). *The future of the cognitive revolution.* New York: Oxford University Press.

Juola, J. F., Fischler, I., Wood, C. T., & Atkinson, R. C. (1971). Recognition time for information stored in long-term memory. *Perception and Psychophysics, 10,* 8–14.

Kahneman, D., & Tversky, A. (1979). Prospect theory: An analysis of decision under risk. *Econometrica, 47*, 263–291.

Kant, I. (1781). *Critik der reinen Vernunft*. Riga: Johann Friedrich Hartknoch.

Kant, I. (1929). *Critique of pure reason (Kritik der reinen Vernunft)*. London: Macmillan, 1929. (Originally published in 1781).

Katona, G. (1940). *Organizing and memorizing*. New York: Columbia University Press.

Kausler, D. H. (1974). *Psychology of verbal learning and memory*. New York: Academic Press.

Keil, F. C. (2005). Knowledge, categorization, and the bliss of ignorance. In L. Gershkoff-Stowe & D. H. Rakison (Eds.), *Building object categories in developmental time* (pp. 309–334). Mahwah, NJ: Erlbaum.

Kinsbourne, M. (1996). What qualifies a representation for a role in consciousness? In J. D. Cohen & J. W. Schooler (Eds.), *Scientific approaches to consciousness* (pp. 335–356). Hillsdale, NJ: Erlbaum.

Kitcher, P. (1993). *The advancement of science*. New York: Oxford University Press.

Klemm, O. (Ed.). (1934). *Bericht über den XIII. Kongress der Deutschen Gesellschaft für Psychologie (16–19 Oktober 1933)*. Jena: Fischer.

Klemm, O. (Ed.). (1935). *Psychologie des Gemeinschaftslebens—Bericht über den XIV. Kongress der Deutschen Gesellschaft für Psychologie (22–26 Mai 1934)*. Jena: Fischer.

Klemm, O. (Ed.). (1937). *Gefühl und Wille—Bericht über den XV. Kongress der Deutschen Gesellschaft für Psychologie (5–8 Juli 1936)*. Jena: Fischer.

Klemm, O. (Ed.). (1939). *Charakter und Erziehung—Bericht über den XVI. Kongress der Deutschen Gesellschaft für Psychologie (2–4 Juli 1938)*. Leipzig: Barth.

Koffka, K. (1912). *Zur Analyse der Vorstellungen und ihrer Gesetze*. Leipzig: Quelle and Meyer.

Koffka, K. (1925). Psychologie. In M. Dessoir (Ed.), *Lehrbuch der Philosophie. Band II. Die Philosophie in ihren Einzelgebieten.* Berlin: Ullstein.

Koffka, K. (1927). Bemerkungen zur Denk-Psychologie. *Psychologische Forschung, 9,* 163–183.

Koffka, K. (1935). *Principles of Gestalt psychology.* New York: Harcourt Brace.

Köhler, W. (1917). Intelligenzprüfungen an Anthropoiden. *Abhandlungen der Königlichen Preussischen Akademie der Wissenschaften, Phys.-Math. Kl. Nr. 1.*

Köhler, W. (1925). *The mentality of apes.* New York: Harcourt, Brace.

Köhler, W. (1929). *Gestalt psychology.* New York: Liveright.

Köhler, W. (1938). *The place of value in a world of fact.* New York: Liveright.

Köhler, W. (1941). On the nature of associations. *Proceedings of the American Philosophical Society, 84,* 489–502.

Köhler, W. (1959). Gestalt psychology today. *American Psychologist, 14,* 727–734.

Kuhn, T. S. (1970). *The structure of scientific revolutions.* Chicago: University of Chicago Press.

Külpe, O. (1893). *Grundriss der Psychologie.* Leipzig: Engelmann.

Külpe, O. (1912). Über die moderne Psychologie des Denkens. *Internationale Monatsschrift für Wissenschaft, Kunst und Technik* (June), 1070 ff.

Külpe, O. (1922). *Vorlesungen über Psychologie* (2nd ed.). Leipzig: Hirzel.

Laird, J. E., Newell, A., & Rosenbloom, P. E. (1987). Soar: An architecture for general intelligence. *Artificial Intelligence, 33,* 1–64.

Lashley, K. S. (1930). Basic neural mechanisms in behavior. *Psychological Review, 37,* 1–24.

Lashley, K. S. (1942). The problem of cerebral organization in vision. *Biological Symposia, 7,* 301–322.

Lashley, K. S. (1951). The problem of serial order in behavior. In L. A. Jeffress (Ed.), *Cerebral mechanisms in behavior: The Hixon symposium* (pp. 112–146). New York: Wiley.

Lenneberg, E. H. (1967). *Biological foundations of language.* New York: Wiley.

Lettvin, J. Y., Maturana, H. R., McCulloch, W. S., & Pitts, W. H. (1959). What the frog's eye tells the frog's brain. *Proceedings of the Institute of Radio Engineers, 47*, 1940–51.

Lewin, K. (1935). *A dynamic theory of personality.* New York: McGraw-Hill.

Locke, J. (1690). *An essay concerning human understanding* (Book 2). London: Thomas Basset. (Originally published in 1689).

Luce, R. D. (1959). *Individual choice behavior: A theoretical analysis.* New York: Wiley.

Lycan, W. G. (1987). *Consciousness.* Cambridge, MA: MIT Press.

Lyotard, J.-F. (1984). *The postmodern condition: A report on knowledge* (G. Bennington and B. Massumi, Trans.). Minneapolis: University of Minnesota Press.

Maier, N. R. F. (1930). Reasoning in humans. I. On direction. *Journal of Comparative Psychology, 10*, 115–143.

Makkreel, R. A., & Rodi, F. (1989). Introduction. In R. A. Makkreel & F. Rodi (Eds.), *Wilhelm Dilthey: Selected works.* Vol. I, *Introduction to the human sciences* (pp. 3–43). Princeton, NJ: Princeton University Press.

Mandler, G. (1967). Organization and memory. In K. W. Spence & J. T. Spence (Eds.), *The psychology of learning and motivation: Advances in research and theory* (pp. 328–372). New York: Academic Press.

Mandler, G. (1969). Acceptance of things past and present: A look at the mind and the brain. In R. B. McLeod (Ed.), *William James: Unfinished business* (pp. 13–16). Washington, DC: American Psychological Association.

Mandler, G. (1972). Organization and recognition. In E. Tulving & W. Donaldson (Eds.), *Organization and memory* (pp. 139–166). New York: Academic Press.

Mandler, G. (1977). Commentary on "Organization and memory." In G. H. Bower (Ed.), *Human memory: Basic processes* (pp. 297–308). New York: Academic Press.

Mandler, G. (1979a). A man for all seasons? Retrospective review of William James's *Principles of Psychology*. *Contemporary Psychology, 24,* 742–744.

Mandler, G. (1979b). Organization and repetition: Organizational principles with special reference to rote learning. In L.-G. Nilsson (Ed.), *Perspectives on memory research* (pp. 293–327). Hillsdale, NJ: Erlbaum.

Mandler, G. (1980). Recognizing: The judgment of previous occurrence. *Psychological Review, 87,* 252–271.

Mandler, G. (1985a). From association to structure. *Journal of Experimental Psychology, 11,* 464–468.

Mandler, G. (1985b). *Cognitive psychology: An essay in cognitive science.* Hillsdale, NJ: Erlbaum.

Mandler, G. (1986). Cognition in historical perspective. In B. J. Baars (Ed.), *The cognitive revolution in psychology* (pp. 253–269). New York: Guilford Press.

Mandler, G. (1991). Your face looks familiar but I can't remember your name: A review of dual process theory. In W. E. Hockley & S. Lewandowsky (Eds.), *Relating theory and data: Essays on human memory in honor of Bennet B. Murdock* (pp. 207–225). Hillsdale, NJ: Lawrence Erlbaum Associates.

Mandler, G. (1994). Hypermnesia, incubation, and mind-popping: On remembering without really trying. In C. Umiltà & M. Moscovitch (Eds.), *Attention and Performance XV: Concious and nonconscious information processing* (pp. 3–33). Cambridge, MA: MIT Press.

Mandler, G. (1996). The situation of psychology: Landmarks and choice-points. *American Journal of Psychology, 109,* 1–35.

Mandler, G. (2001). *Interesting times: An encounter with the twentieth century, 1924–.* Mahwah, NJ: Erlbaum.

Mandler, G. (2002a). *Consciousness recovered: Psychological functions and origins of conscious thought.* Amsterdam: Benjamins.

Mandler, G. (2002b). Organization: What levels of processing are levels of. *Memory, 10,* 333–338.

Mandler, G. (2002c). Origins of the cognitive (r)evolution. *Journal of the History of the Behavioral Sciences, 38,* 339–353.

Mandler, G. (2002d). Psychologists and the National Socialist access to power. *History of Psychology, 5,* 190–200.

Mandler, G. (2006). Mind: Ghosts, machines, and concepts. In K. Pawlik & G. d'Ydewalle (Eds.), *Psychological concepts: An international historical perspective.* Hove, UK: Psychology Press.

Mandler, G., & Anderson, R. E. (1971). Temporal and spatial cues in seriation. *Journal of Experimental Psychology, 90,* 128–135.

Mandler, G., & Boeck, W. (1974). Retrieval processes in recognition. *Memory and Cognition, 2,* 613–615.

Mandler, G., Pearlstone, Z., & Koopmans, H. J. (1969). Effects of organization and semantic similarity on recall and recognition. *Journal of Verbal Learning and Verbal Behavior, 8,* 410–423.

Mandler, G., Rabinowitz, J. C., & Simon, R. A. (1981). Coordinate organization: The holistic representation of word pairs. *American Journal of Psychology, 94,* 209–222.

Mandler, J. M. (1984). *Stories, scripts, and scenes: Aspects of schema theory.* Hillsdale, NJ: Erlbaum.

Mandler, J. M. (2004). *Foundations of mind: The origins of conceptual thought.* New York: Oxford University Press.

Mandler, J. M., & Mandler, G. (1964). *Thinking: From association to Gestalt*. New York: Wiley. Reprint edition: Westport, CT: Greenwood Press, 1982.

Mandler, J. M., & Mandler, G. (1968). The diaspora of experimental psychology: The Gestaltists and others. In D. Fleming & B. Bailyn (Eds.), *The intellectual migration: Europe and America, 1930–1960* (pp. 371–419). Cambridge, MA: Charles Warren Center, Harvard University.

Marbe, K. (1901). *Experimentell-psychologische Untersuchungen über das Urteil*. Leipzig: Engelmann.

Marcel, A. J. (1983a). Conscious and unconscious perception: An approach to the relations between phenomenal experience and perceptual processes. *Cognitive Psychology, 15*, 238–300.

Marcel, A. J. (1983b). Conscious and unconscious perception: Experiments on visual masking and word recognition. *Cognitive Psychology, 15*, 197–237.

Mayer, A., & Orth, J. (1901). Zur qualitativen Untersuchung der Association. *Zeitschrift für Psychologie, 26*, 1–13.

McCulloch, W., & Pitts, W. (1943). A logical calculus of the ideas immanent in nervous activity. *Bulletin of Mathematical Biophysics, 7*, 115–133.

McCulloch, W., & Pitts, W. (1948). The statistical organization of nervous activity. *Biometrics, 4*, 91–99.

McGeoch, J. A. (1942). *The psychology of human learning: An introduction*. New York: Longmans, Green.

Mechanisation of thought processes. (1959). (Vol. Symposium No. 10, National Physical Laboratory). London: Her Majesty's Stationery Office.

Medin, D., & Atran, S. (2004). The native mind: Biological categorization and reasoning in development and across cultures. *Psychological Review, 111*(4), 960–983.

Medin, D. L., & Coley, J. D. (1998). Concepts and categorization. In J. Hochberg (Ed.), *Perception and cognition at century's end: Handbook of perception and cognition* (pp. 403–439). San Diego: Academic Press.

Meinong, A. v. (1904). *Über Gegenstandstheorie, Untersuchungen zur Gegen-standstheorie und Psychologie.* Leipzig: Barth.

Melton, A. W. (1941). Review of Katona, *Organizing and memorizing.* *American Journal of Psychology, 54,* 455–457.

Messer, A. (1906). Experimentell-psychologische Untersuchungen über das Denken. *Archiv für die gesamte Psychologie, 8,* 1–224.

Michotte, A. (1954). *La perception de la causalité* (2nd ed.). Louvain: Université de Louvain.

Mill, J. (1878). *An analysis of the phenomena of the human mind* (2nd ed., Vol. 1). London: Longmans, Green, Reader, and Dyer. (Originally published in 1829).

Mill, J. S. (1874). *A system of logic* (8th ed.). New York: Harper. (Originally published in 1843).

Miller, G. A. (1956). The magical number seven, plus or minus two: Some limits on our capacity for processing information. *Psychological Review, 63,* 81–97.

Miller, G. A. (2003). The cognitive revolution: A historical perspective. *Trends in Cognitive Sciences, 7*(3), 141–144.

Miller, G. A., & Chomsky, N. (1963). Finitary models of language users. In R. D. Luce, R. Bush, & E. Galanter (Eds.), *Handbook of mathematical psychology.* New York: Wiley.

Miller, G. A., Galanter, E. H., & Pribram, K. (1960). *Plans and the structure of behavior.* New York: Holt.

Mischel, W. (1968). *Personality and assessment.* New York: Wiley.

Molesworth, M. (Ed.). (1839). *The English works of Thomas Hobbes: Leviathan (1651)* (Vol. 3). London: Bohn.

Molesworth, M. (Ed.). (1840). *The English works of Thomas Hobbes: Human nature (1650)* (Vol. 4). London: Bohn.

Moore, T. V. (1939). *Cognitive psychology.* New York: Lippincott.

Morton, J. (1969). Interaction of information in word recognition. *Psychological Review, 76*, 165–178.

Müller, G. E. (1911). Zur Analyse der Gedächtnistätigkeit und des Vorstellungsverlaufes, I. Teil. *Zeitschrift für Psychologie, Ergänzungsband 5*, xiv, 403.

Müller, G. E. (1913). Zur Analyse der Gedächtnistätigkeit und des Vorstellungsverlaufes, III. Teil. *Zeitschrift für Psychologie, Ergänzungsband 8*, 567.

Müller, G. E. (1917). Zur Analyse der Gedächtnistätigkeit und des Vorstellungsverlaufes, II. Teil. *Zeitschrift für Psychologie, Ergänzungsband 9*, viii, 682.

Müller, G. E. (1923). *Komplextheorie und Gestalttheorie: Ein Beitrag zur Wahrnehmungspsychologie.* Göttingen: Vandenhoeck & Ruprecht.

Müller, G. E., & Pilzecker, A. (1900). Experimentelle Beiträge zur Lehre vom Gedächtniss. *Zeitschrift für Psychologie, Ergänzungsband 1*, 1–300.

Müller, G. E., & Schumann, F. (1889). Über die psychologischen Grundlagen der Vergleichung gehobener Gewichte. *Archiv für die gesamte Physiologie, 45*, 37–112.

Müller, G. E., & Schumann, F. (1894). Experimentalle Beiträge zur Untersuchung des Gedächtnisses. *Zeitschrift für Psychologie, 6*, 81–190.

Murray, D. J. (1995). *Gestalt psychology and the cognitive revolution.* New York: Harvester Wheatsheaf.

Murray, D. J., & Bandomir, C. A. (2000). G. E. Müller (1911, 1913, 1917) on memory. *Psychologie et Histoire, 1*, 208–232.

Musgrave, B. S. (1959). *Memorandum: A few notes on the Conference on Verbal Learning.* Notes from the Verbal Learning Conference, Gould House, Dobbs Ferry, NY, Fall.

Myrdal, G. (1944). *An American dilemma.* New York: Harpers.

Nagel, T. (1986). *The view from nowhere.* New York: Oxford University Press.

Neimark, E. D. (1967). *Stimulus sampling theory: E. D. Neimark, W. K. Estes.* San Francisco: Holden-Day.

Neisser, U. (1967). *Cognitive psychology.* New York: Appleton-Century-Crofts.

Neumann, F. L. (Ed.). (1953). *The cultural migration: The European scholar in America.* Philadelphia: University of Pennsylvania Press.

Neumann, J. von (1958). *The computer and the brain.* New Haven, CT: Yale University Press.

Newell, A. (1973). Production systems: Models of control structure. In W. Chase (Ed.), *Visual information processing.* New York: Academic Press.

Newell, A. (1990). *Unified theories of cognition.* Cambridge, MA: Harvard University Press.

Newell, A., Shaw, J. C., & Simon, H. A. (1958). Elements of a theory of human problem solving. *Psychological Review, 65,* 151–166.

Newell, A., & Simon, H. (1972). *Human problem solving.* Englewood Cliffs, NJ: Prentice-Hall.

Norman, D. A., & Rumelhart, D. E. (1975). *Explorations in cognition.* San Francisco: Freeman.

Osgood, C. E. (1953). *Method and theory in experimental psychology.* New York: Oxford University Press.

Pashler, H. E. (1998). *The psychology of attention.* Cambridge, MA: MIT Press.

Patterson, K., Lambon Ralph, M. A., Jefferies, E., Woollams, A., Jones, R., Hodges, J. R., & Rogers, T. T. (2006). "Pre-semantic" cognition in semantic dementia: Six deficits in search of an explanation. *Journal of Cognitive Neuroscience, 18,* 169–183.

Peterson, W. W., Birdsall, T. G., & Fox, W. C. (1954). The theory of signal detectability. *Transactions of the Institute of Radio Engineers Professional Group on Information Theory, 4,* 171–212.

Piaget, J. (1926). *The language and thought of the child.* New York: Harcourt, Brace.

Piaget, J. (1953). *The origin of intelligence in the child.* London: Routledge and Kegan Paul.

Pippard, B. (1985). Discontinuities. *London Review of Books, 7,* 8–9.

Pollack, R. H., & Brenner, M. W. (1969). *The experimental psychology of Alfred Binet: Selected papers.* New York: Springer.

Popkin, S. L. (1991). *The reasoning voter: Communication and persuasion in presidential campaigns.* Chicago: University of Chicago Press.

Porter, T. M. (1986). *The rise of statistical thinking 1820–1900.* Princeton, NJ: Princeton University Press.

Postman, N. (1988). *Social science as moral theology: Conscientious objections.* New York: Knopf.

Premack, D., & Woodruff, G. (1978). Does the chimpanzee have a theory of mind? *Behavioral and Brain Sciences, 1*(4), 515–526.

Pringle-Pattison, A. S. (Ed.). (1924). *J. Locke: An essay concerning human understanding.* Oxford: Clarendon Press.

Prinz, W. (1985). Ganzheits- und Gestaltpsychologie und Nationalsozialismus. In P. Lundgreen (Ed.), *Wissenschaft im Dritten Reich* (pp. 55–81). Frankfurt: Suhrkamp.

Putnam, H. (1960). Minds and machines. In S. Hook (Ed.), *Dimensions of mind.* New York: Collier Books.

Putnam, H. (1980). Philosophy and our mental life. In N. Block (Ed.), *Readings in the philosophy of psychology* (Vol. 1). Cambridge, MA: Harvard University Press.

Ranganath, C., Yonelinas, A. P., Cohen, M. X., Dy, C. J., Tom, S. M., & D'Esposito, M. (2004). Dissociable correlates of recollection and familiarity within the medial temporal L=lobes. *Neuropsychologia, 42*(1), 2–13.

Reber, A. S. (1967). Implicit learning of artificial grammars. *Journal of Verbal Learning and Verbal Behavior, 6,* 855–863.

Restle, F. (1970). Theory of serial pattern learning: Structural trees. *Psychological Review, 77*, 481–495.

Restle, F., & Brown, E. R. (1970). Serial pattern learning. *Journal of Experimental Psychology, 83*, 120–125.

Rock, I., & Palmer, S. E. (1990). The legacy of Gestalt psychology. *Scientific American, 262*, 84–90.

Rugg, M. D., & Yonelinas, A. P. (2003). Human recognition memory: A cognitive neuroscience perspective. *Trends in Cognitive Sciences, 7*(7), 313–319.

Rumelhart, D. E. (1977). Toward an interactive model of reading. In S. Dornic (Ed.), *Attention and performance VI*. Hillsdale, NJ: Erlbaum.

Rumelhart, D. E. (1980). Schemata: The building blocks of cognition. In B. B. R. Spiro & W. Brewer (Ed.), *Theoretical issues in reading comprehension*. Hillsdale, NJ: Erlbaum.

Rumelhart, D. E., & McClelland, J. L. (1985). *Parallel distributed processing: Explorations on the microstructure of cognition*. Cambridge, MA: MIT Press.

Rumelhart, D. E., & Ortony, A. (1978). The representation of knowledge in memory. In R. C. Anderson, R. J. Spiro, & W. E. Montague (Eds.), *Schooling and the acquisition of knowledge*. Hillsdale, NJ: Erlbaum.

Ryan, B. A. (1999). Does postmodernism mean the end of science in the behavioral sciences, and does it matter anyway? *Theory & Psychology, 9*(4), 483–502.

Ryle, G. (1949). *The concept of mind*. London: Hutchinson's University Library.

Sampson, G. R. (1972). On the concept "semantic representation." Mimeo, Oxford University.

Schachter, S., & Singer, J. E. (1962). Cognitive, social and physiological determinants of emotional state. *Psychological Review, 69*, 379–399.

Schall, J. D. (2004). On building a bridge between brain and behavior. *Annual Review of Psychology, 55*, 23–50.

Schnabel, F. (1950). *Deutsche Geschichte im Neunzehnten Jahrhundert* (2nd ed.). Freiburg im Breisgau: Verlag Herder.

Schneider, W., & Shiffrin, R. M. (1977). Controlled and automatic human information processing. 1. Detection, search, and attention. *Psychological Review, 84*(1), 1–66.

Schwartz, B. (1986). *The battle for human nature.* New York: Norton.

Scribner, S., & Cole, M. (1981). *The psychology of literacy.* Cambridge, MA: Harvard University Press.

Searle, J. R. (1992). *The rediscovery of the mind.* Cambridge, MA: MIT Press.

Selz, O. (1913). *Über die Gesetze des geordneten Denkverlaufs. Eine experimentelle Untersuchung.* Stuttgart: Spemann.

Selz, O. (1922). *Zur Psychologic des produktiven Denkens und des Irrtums.* Bonn: Cohen.

Selz, O. (1924). *Die Gesetze der produktiven and reproduktiven Geistestätigkeit.* Bonn: Cohen.

Selz, O. (1926). Zur Psychologic der Gegenwart. Eine Anmerkung zu Koffkas Darstellung. *Zeitschrift für Psychologie, 99*, 160–196.

Selz, O. (1927). Die Umgestaltung der Grundanschauungen vom intellektuellen Geschehen. *Kantstudien, 32*, 273–280.

Shallice, T. (1988). *From neuropsychology to mental structure.* Cambridge: Cambridge University Press.

Shallice, T. & Warrington, E. K. (1970). Independent functioning of verbal memory stores: A neuropsychological study. *Quarterly Journal of Experimental Psychology, 22*(2), 261–273.

Shannon, C. E. (1948). A mathematical theory of communication. *Bell System Technical Journal, 27*, 379–423, 623–656.

Shannon, C., & Weaver, W. (1948). *The mathematical theory of communication*. Urbana: University of Illinois Press.

Sheehan, J. J. (1978). *German liberalism in the nineteenth century*. Chicago: University of Chicago Press.

Shepard, R. N., & Cooper, L. A. (1982). *Mental images and their transformations*. Cambridge, MA: MIT Press.

Shepard, R. N., & Metzler, J. (1971). Mental rotation of three-dimensional objects. *Science, 171*, 701–703.

Shiffrin, R. M., & Schneider, W. (1977). Controlled and automatic human information-processing. 2. Perceptual learning, automatic attending, and a general theory. *Psychological Review, 84*(2), 127–190.

Skinner, B. F. (1957). *Verbal behavior*. New York: Appleton-Century-Crofts.

Skinner, B. F. (1995). "The Behavior of Organisms" at fifty. In J. T. Todd & E. K. Morris (Eds.), *Modern perspectives on B. F. Skinner and contemporary behaviorism* (pp. 149–161). Westport, CT: Greenwood Press.

Smith, M. B. (1994). Selfhood at risk: Postmodern perils and the perils of postmodernism. *American Psychologist, 49*, 405–411.

Smith, P. T., & Claxton, G. L. (1972). Lexical and topical memory. Paper presented at the Experimental Psychology Society, Liverpool.

Smith, W. D. (1991). *Politics and the sciences of culture in Germany, 1840–1920*. New York: Oxford University Press.

Snygg, D., & Combs, A. W. (1949). *Individual behavior*. New York: Harper.

Sober, E. (1985). Panglossian functionalism and the philosophy of mind. *Synthese, 64*, 165–193.

Stern, F. (1961). *The politics of cultural despair: A study in the rise of the Germanic ideology*. Berkeley: University of California Press.

Surprenant, A. E., & Neath, I. (1997). T. V. Moore's (1939) *Cognitive Psychology*. *Psychonomic Bulletin and Review, 4*(3), 342–349.

Swets, J. A., Tanner, W. P., & Birdsall, T. G. (1961). Decision processes in perception. *Psychological Review, 68*(5), 301–340.

Taylor, F. W. (1911). *The principles of scientific management*. New York: Harper & Brothers.

Thagard, P. (1986). Parallel computation and the mind-body problem. *Cognitive Science, 10*, 301–318.

Thelen, E., & Smith, L. B. (1994). *A dynamic systems approach to the development of cognition and action*. Cambridge, MA: MIT Press.

Thorndike, E. L. (1932). *The fundamentals of learning*. New York: Teachers College.

Titchener, E. B. (1896). *An outline of psychology*. New York: Macmillan.

Titchener, E. B. (1898). The postulates of a structural psychology. *Philosophical Review, 7*, 449–465.

Titchener, E. B. (1909). *Lectures on the experimental psychology of the thought-processes*. New York: Macmillan.

Titchener, E. B. (1910). *A textbook of psychology*. New York: Macmillan.

Tocqueville, A. de (1889). *Democracy in America* (Henry Reeve, Trans.) (Vol. 2). London: Longmans Green.

Tomasello, M. (1995). Language is not an instinct. *Cognitive Development, 10*, 131–156.

Treisman, A. M., & Gelade, G. (1980). A feature-integration theory of attention. *Cognitive Psychology, 12*, 97–136.

Tuchman, B. W. (1966). *The proud tower: A portrait of the world before the war, 1890–1914*. New York: Macmillan.

Tulving, E. (1972). Episodic and semantic memory. In E. Tulving & W. Donaldson (Eds.), *Organization of memory* (pp. 381–403). New York: Academic Press.

Tulving, E. (1983). *Elements of episodic memory*. Oxford: Oxford University Press.

Tulving, E. (2002). Episodic memory: From mind to brain. *Annual Review of Psychology, 53*(1), 1–25.

Tulving, E., & Donaldson, W. (Eds.). (1972). *Organization of memory*. New York: Academic Press.

Turing, A. M. (1936). On computable numbers, with an application to the Entscheidungsproblem. *Proceedings of the London Mathematical Society, 42*, 230–265.

Turing, A. M. (1950). Computing machinery and intelligence. *Mind, 49*, 433–460.

Underwood, B. J. (1983). *Attributes of memory*. Glenview, IL: Scott, Foresman.

Van Gulick, R. (1980). Functionalism, information and content. *Nature and System, 2*, 139–162.

Wald, A. (1950). *Statistical decision function*. New York: Wiley.

Warrington, E. K. (1975). The selective impairment of semantic memory. *Quarterly Journal of Experimental Psychology, 27*, 635–657.

Warrington, E. K., & Weiskrantz, L. (1970). Amnesia: Consolidation or retrieval? *Nature, 228*, 628–630.

Watson, G. (1934). Psychology in Germany and Austria. *Psychological Bulletin, 31*(10), 755–776.

Watson, J. B. (1913). Psychology as the behaviorist views it. *Psychological Review, 20*, 158–177.

Watson, J. B. (1914). *Behavior: An introduction to comparative psychology*. New York: Holt.

Watson, J. B. (1919). *Psychology from the stand-point of a behaviorist*. Philadelphia: Lippincott.

Watt, H. J. (1904). Experimentelle Beiträge zu einer Theorie des Denkens. *Archiv für die gesamte Psychologie* (Vol. 4, pp. 1–154). Leipzig: Engelmann.

Watt, H. J. (1905–1906). Experimental contribution to a theory of thinking. *Journal of Anatomy and Physiology, 40,* 257–266.

Weinberg, S. (1995). Reductionism redux. *New York Review of Books, 62* (No. 15), 39–42

Wellek, A. (1968). The impact of the German immigration on the development of American psychology. *Journal of the History of the Behavioral Sciences, 4,* 207–229.

Werner, H., & Kaplan, B. (1963). *Symbol formation: An organismic-developmental approach to the psychology of language.* Hillsdale, NJ: Erlbaum.

Werner, H., & Wapner, S. (1952). Toward a general theory of perception. *Psychological Review, 59,* 324–338.

Wertheimer, M. (1912). Experimentelle Studien über das Sehen von Bewegung. *Zeitschrift für Psychologie und Physiologie der Sinnesorgane, 61,* 161–265.

Wertheimer, M. (1920). *Über Schlussprozesse im produktiven Denken.* Berlin-Leipzig: de Gruyter.

Wertheimer, M. (1921). Untersuchungen zur Lehre von der Gestalt. I. *Psychologische Forschung, 1,* 47–58.

Wertheimer, M. (1945). *Productive thinking.* New York: Harper.

Wiebe, R. H. (1967). *The search for order: 1877–1920.* New York: Hill and Wang.

Wiener, N. (1948). *Cybernetics: Or control and communication in the animal and the machine.* New York: Technology Press and Wiley.

Wundt, W. (1863). *Vorlesungen über die Menschen- und Thierseele.* Leipzig: Voss.

Wundt, W. (1874). *Grundzüge der physiologischen Psychologie.* Leipzig: Engelmann.

Wundt, W. (1896). *Grundriss der Psychologie.* Leipzig: Engelmann.

Wundt, W. (1897). *Outlines of psychology* (C. H. Judd, Trans.). Leipzig: Engelmann.

Wundt, W. (1900–1909). *Völkerpsychologie: Eine Untersuchung der Entwicklungsgesetze von Sprache, Mythus und Sitte.* Leipzig: Engelmann.

Wundt, W. (1904). *Principles of physiological psychology* (E. B. Titchener, Trans.) (5th ed.). New York: Macmillan.

Wundt, W. (1907). Über Ausfrageexperimente und über die Methoden zur Psychologie des Denkens. *Psychologische Studien, 3,* 301–360.

Wundt, W. (1912). *Elemente der Völkerpsychologie: Grundlinien einer psychologischen Entwicklungsgeschichte der Menschheit.* Leipzig: Kröner.

Wundt, W. (1916). *Elements of folk psychology: Outline of a psychological history of the development of mankind.* London: Allen & Unwin.

Wundt, W. (1920). *Erlebtes und Erkanntes.* Stuttgart: Kröner.

Yonelinas, A. P. (2002). The nature of recollection and familiarity: A review of thirty years of research. *Journal of Memory and Language, 46,* 441–517.

Yovel, G., & Paller, K. A. (2004). The neural basis of the butcher-in-the-bus phenomenon: When a face seems familiar but is not remembered. *NeuroImage, 21,* 789–800.

Name Index

Subject Index